Americans
in Conversation
with Tolstoy

ALSO BY PETER SEKIRIN

*The Dostoevsky Archive:
Firsthand Accounts of the Novelist from
Contemporaries' Memoirs and Rare Periodicals,
Most Translated into English for the First Time,
with a Detailed Lifetime Chronology and
Annotated Bibliography* (McFarland, 1997)

# Americans in Conversation with Tolstoy

*Selected Accounts, 1887–1923*

*Edited by*
PETER SEKIRIN

McFarland & Company, Inc., Publishers
*Jefferson, North Carolina, and London*

LIBRARY OF CONGRESS CATALOGUING-IN-PUBLICATION DATA

Americans in conversation with Tolstoy : selected accounts,
    1887–1923 / edited by Peter Sekirin.
        p.    cm.
    Includes bibliographical references and index.

    ISBN-13: 978-0-7864-2253-1
    ISBN-10: 0-7864-2253-X (softcover : 50# alkaline paper) ∞

    1. Tolstoy, Leo, graf, 1828–1910 — Appreciation — United States.
2. Tolstoy, Leo, graf, 1828–1910 — Interviews.   3. Authors,
Russian — 19rh century — Interviews.   I. Sekirin, Peter.
PG3409.7.U6A48    2006
891.73'3 — dc22
                                                            2006015605

British Library cataloguing data are available

©2006 Peter Sekirin. All rights reserved

*No part of this book may be reproduced or transmitted in any form
or by any means, electronic or mechanical, including photocopying
or recording, or by any information storage and retrieval system,
without permission in writing from the publisher.*

On the cover: Leo Tolstoy (Clipart.com)

Manufactured in the United States of America

*McFarland & Company, Inc., Publishers
  Box 611, Jefferson, North Carolina 28640
    www.mcfarlandpub.com*

This volume is dedicated to those who left their relatively unknown, rare memoirs of Tolstoy behind.

You Americans live in a light-house set upon a hill, this is the light and hope of the world, whose rays penetrated into its uttermost parts....

Pray that young Americans would see to that light, and keep it day and night. It is the flame that their fathers lit, and it has become the light of the world, as well as yours.

— Stephen Bonsul, "Tolstoy Prophesies..."
*New York Times*, 7 July, 1907

He is great among the greatest.

Tolstoy's world is a world bathed in the brilliance of the sun, a simple and bright world, in which all reflections are in the right measure and proportion; in which light and shade correspond to real phenomena and actualities; and the creative combinations develop in harmony with the organic laws of nature. Above his landscape, suffused with the light of day, is a sky specked with floating clouds.

Yes, this is a revelation of almost superhuman power of imagination, and of almost magic dominion over the seething movements of life. One may boldly assert that in the spontaneous force of creative fancy, in wealth of artistic material, there is no one in all contemporary literature who is the equal of Tolstoy.

— "Tolstoy as the World Figure," *Current Literature* (New York), 1908

Count Tolstoy is a firm believer in the maxim that work is a sacred duty. He always devoted four hours a day to manual labor of some kind, either ploughing in the field or making shoes.

— James Creelman. "A Visit to Tolstoy,"
*Harper's Weekly*, 1892.

This picture must always be treasured in the memory of those who ever were privileged to look upon it — the picture of Tolstoy in his home.

— Kellogg Durland, "Tolstoy at Home."
*Independent,* New York City, 1907.

# Contents

| | |
|---|---|
| *Introduction* | 1 |

THE ACCOUNTS OF CONVERSATIONS*

| | |
|---|---|
| 1. A Visit to Count Tolstoy *(George Kennan)* | 9 |
| 2. Count Tolstoy at Home *(Isabel Hapgood)* | 34 |
| 3. With Count Tolstoy *(Thomas Stevens)* | 36 |
| 4. A Visit to Tolstoy *(James Creelman)* | 51 |
| 5. How Count Tolstoy Writes *(Charles Johnston)* | 55 |
| 6. An Interview with Count Tolstoy *(Edward Steiner)* | 59 |
| 7. Home Life of Tolstoy *(John Holmes)* | 61 |
| 8. A Visit to Tolstoy *(John Coleman Kenworthy)* | 64 |
| 9. Russia of To-day (on Tolstoy) *(Sir Henry Norman)* | 71 |
| 10. Conversations with Ernest Crosby Embodying Personal Impressions of Count Leo Tolstoy *(Ernest Crosby)* | 75 |
| 11. Walks and Talks with Tolstoy *(Andrew Dickson White)* | 84 |
| 12. A Recent Interview with Tolstoy *(Th. Bentzon)* | 100 |
| 13. Tolstoy Today *(Edward Steiner)* | 106 |
| 14. My Last Memory of Tolstoy *(Alexandra Nicchia)* | 112 |

*Chronologically by date of publication

| | | |
|---|---|---|
| 15. | My Last Visit to Tolstoy *(Aymler Maude)* | 115 |
| 16. | Tolstoy in 1906 *(Louise Maude)* | 126 |
| 17. | Tolstoy Prophesies the Fall of America *(Stephen Bonsul)* | 132 |
| 18. | Tolstoy in the Twilight *(Henry George, Jr.)* | 139 |
| 19. | Tolstoy at Home *(Kellogg Durland)* | 145 |
| 20. | The Last Days of Leo Tolstoy *(Alexander Kaun)* | 151 |
| 21. | Talks with Tolstoy *(Richard Baeza and Alexander Goldenweiser)* | 163 |
| 22. | Three Evenings with Count Leo Tolstoy *(N. Everling)* | 174 |
| 23. | A Vacation with Tolstoy *(Theodore von Hafferberg)* | 179 |
| 24. | A Day in Tolstoy's Life *(Stefan Zweig)* | 193 |
| 25. | How Tolstoy Died *(General Lvov)* | 200 |
| 26. | What Tolstoy Means to America *(Virginia Wentz)* | 210 |

*Bibliography*     215
*Index*     217

# *Introduction*

Although Tolstoy was unable to visit America over the course of his lifetime, he nevertheless received more letters from the United States than from any other country. In fact, according to British journalist William Thomas Stead, Tolstoy actually received more than six times the number of letters from America than he did from England.

With millions of copies sold in both Russian and English, Tolstoy's novels, novellas, short stories, plays, essays, letters and diaries have enjoyed numerous editions. Strangely, memoirs about the great literary artist by his American visitors have not been published in English before in book form. They are scattered in numerous U.S. periodicals of 1895–1923, from *Harper's Weekly, Cosmopolitan, Atlantic Monthly* to *Dial, Living Age, Current Literature, Outlook* and *The New York Times*. The material from these years is now in the public domain.

As the first comprehensive collection of first-hand memoirs and reminiscences about Tolstoy by American friends and writers ever to be published, this volume attempts to bring both a sense of depth and detail about Tolstoy to English and American readers.

In the past, foreign publications similar to this one have been well received. A particular Russian collection of Tolstoy memoirs [*Tolstoy v vospominaniiakh sovremennikov*], for example, has sold over 300,000 copies over the course of its four editions, the earliest of which was published in 1955, the latest in 1985. However, because of Tolstoy's immense popularity and status as a literary genius, the sheer volume of primary source material has meant that many reminiscences were not included in the Russian publication. They are now scattered across numerous archival collections which contain essays, memoirs, and other rare publications originally printed between 1890 and 1925. Some of this rare and insightful material, when written by Americans, has been incorporated into this volume.

Tolstoy loved America and its people. It is perhaps not surprising that Americans came in droves to visit him. Journalists, writers, senators, pastors and university professors were among those fortunate enough to have visited Tolstoy before his death in 1910. While at his country estate in Yasnaya Polyana, Tolstoy and his visitors discussed everything from drinking tea and vegetarian food on the one hand, to literature and politics on the other. At times the topics of discussion were unusual and sometimes entirely unexpected.

However, members of America's upper class were not the only ones to have visited Tolstoy. In fact, many were tourists or business people hoping to meet a celebrity during their brief visit to Russia—something about which Tolstoy often mused. On 9 December 1888, he wrote in his diary, "When I woke from my sleep, I met two American women. They were sisters who had come to visit me. One sister had crossed the Atlantic Ocean while the other had crossed the Pacific. They had apparently seen everything they had wanted to see in Russia (including me), and were now preparing for their voyages home. Yet, despite their travels and all they had experienced, they did not seem to be any wiser."

American tourists and business people were often relentless in their desire to meet the great novelist. In fact, when Tolstoy was recovering from a serious illness in Yalta in 1902, he had to be propped up on a veranda so as to appease his American admirers. Unable to speak, Tolstoy sat quietly allowing the visitors to catch a glimpse of him as they passed; many even raised their hats and bowed in his direction.

Most of Tolstoy's visitors from the United States from the 1870s through the 1900s could be put into three major groups: (1) journalists and writers; (2) diplomats and public figures; (3) artists, professors, painters, musicians, architects, and others. Journalists and writers constitute the most prominent group: among the most distinguished, to name just a few, were George Kennan from *New York Herald*, *The Nation* and the *New York Times*; Isabel Hapgood and Aymler Maude, who were the first two English translators of Tolstoy's works; Thomas Stevens, the author of *Through Russia on a Mustang*; and James Creelman, who worked for *Illustrated American*, *Cosmopolitan*, and *Harper's Weekly* magazines.

The first American who documented his visit to Tolstoy was George Kennan (1845–1924), the author and traveler who shared the name and even the same birthday (February 16) of his great-nephew, George Frost Kennan (born 1904), the distinguished diplomat and historian who founded the Kennan Center for the Study of Russia in Washington, DC. As a result, few are aware that the elder George Kennan did not simply chronicle Russian life, but became an assiduous campaigner for democracy and human rights in the tsarist realm. When Kennan was growing up in Norwalk, Ohio, adventure for most Americans beckoned west, toward the Pacific. When Kennan learned in 1864 of plans to build an overland telegraph line from America to Europe across the Bering Strait and Siberia, he left for Alaska — then still Russian America. However, instead of Alaska, Kennan ended up in continental Russia. After his return from Russia, in 1878 Kennan landed a position as an Associated Press reporter in Washington, D.C., and worker for the *New York Herald* and the *New York Times*. A series of his articles subsequently appeared in his immensely influential book, *Siberia and the Exile System*, which was used by Tolstoy.

Kennan also wrote for prominent magazines such as *Century, The Outlook, The Nation,* and *Forum*. In 1891, his outspoken stand against the monarchy earned him banishment from his beloved Russia; when he returned to visit Moscow in 1901, he was ordered to leave the country. He met and spoke to Tolstoy on two occasions and wrote several articles dedicated to his memoirs about Tolstoy.

Thomas Stevens published his book *Through Russia on a Mustang* in 1891 in New York, one of the first books by an American journalist about Russia. His book is an incredibly articulate and fascinating account of a journalist from the American West traveling through the late 19th century Russia as he buys, describes and sells horses as his means of transport and companionship. He describes the major cities and the Russian people with a down-to-earth American eye of a keen observer, meeting the famous figures of the moment, like Tolstoy.

John Coleman Kenworthy visited Tolstoy in 1899–1900 and wrote *Tolstoy: His Life and Works* (1910), one of the first studies of Tolstoy which assesses his novels, renders several personal impressions and dwells on the novelist's relationships with the English and American writers.

A group of articles by journalist Edward Steiner on Tolstoy appeared in *The Outlook* (New York) in 1903; they were the result of several months' literary work in Russia. The time was spent in study of Steiner's book, *Tolstoy the Man*, in interviews with him and his family, and in gathering literary material from the Tolstoy circles in Moscow and elsewhere.

One of the first Tolstoy translators, Isabel Hapgood (1850–1928), was born in Boston, of colonial English-Scottish descent; she was a linguist from her earliest years, including Russian and Church Slavonic. Her love of Russian literature brought her to Tolstoy; eventually, she became Tolstoy's first American translator. They had several meetings together, during which the novelist shared his views on both British and American literature. While in Russia, she visited many other well-known personalities including Countess Tolstoy, Tsarina Alexandra, Patriarch Tikhon, and others; however, in 1917 she was caught in Moscow at the beginning of the Revolution, escaping only through the help of the American consul. When she died in 1928, at the age of 78, Isabel Hapgood left behind a valuable treasure-house of literature, both translations and original commentary of all kinds about Russia, including her extensive translations and memoirs of Tolstoy.

Louise Maude together with her husband Aymler Maude and Isabel Hapgood were the first Tolstoy translators into English. Tolstoy greatly admired their work and developed close friendships with the Maudes and Hapgood; they visited him repeatedly in his country estate, the last time in 1906.

Right after Tolstoy's short stories and novels were translated from Russian into English, one of the first Americans who visited Tolstoy was journalist James Creelman (1859–1915). Creelman was born in Montreal, Canada, and shortly moved to America. From 1876, he worked for *The New York Herald*, *Illustrated American* and *Cosmopolitan* magazine. As Creelman was hired by Joseph Pulitzer, he worked in 1901–1912 as a staff journalist of *New York World* and Associate Editor of the *New York Evening Mail* and specialized in feature interview profiles on individuals as diverse as Tolstoy, Edison, Roosevelt, Taft, Pope Leo XIII, Louis Kossuth and President Diaz of Mexico. Creelman's relationship with his employers Pulitzer and Hearst was, at times, stormy but each found him very valuable as a writer. His interviews with Tolstoy appeared in *Harper's Weekly* in 1892. These two interviews were eventually published to widespread acclaim in numerous American newspapers.

American writer Ernest Crosby visited Tolstoy at his country estate in Yasnaya Polyana and by 1901 had published several interviews with the novelist. These interviews led to a strong friendship between the two which lasted until Crosby's death in 1907. In fact, Tolstoy eventually wrote long commentaries about the nature of Crosby's work on William Shakespeare. After expanding on this material, Tolstoy eventually published it in an essay titled "About Shakespeare and Dramatic Art."

As the above mentioned journalists and translators contributed to

Tolstoy's popularity in the United States, several American diplomats and prominent public figures visited Tolstoy in his country estate.

Andrew Dickson White (1832–1918), American educator, diplomat and minister, visited Russia in 1892–94. New York Senator in 1864–67, the U.S. ambassador to Germany, and a close personal friend of Mr. Cornell, one of the founders and the first president of the Cornell University, White visited Tolstoy at his country estate in 1901. In his lengthy memoirs, White recounts Tolstoy's thoughts on such prolific writers as Ralph Waldo Emerson, Theodore Parker, and James Russell.

A traveler, politician and journalist who wrote *All the Russia: European Russia, Siberia and Central Asia,* Henry Norman (1860–1928) published in *Scribner's* magazine in 1900 his memoirs about his meetings with Tolstoy.

Another outstanding American journalist and diplomat, Stephen Bonsul, was fortunate enough to have received considerable praise from Tolstoy, who in a note to his daughter on 7 May, 1907, wrote: "If it is at all possible, you must come and visit me for I have a special visitor whom I think you should meet. He is an intelligent and rather clever American correspondent." Bonsul met with Tolstoy during his trip to Russia in 1906–1907; he wrote for the *New York Times* from 1901 to 1910 and was the author of two rather popular books, *Unfinished Business* and *Suitors and Suppliants: The Little Nations at Versailles.*

The next major book on Russia that appeared right after George Kennan's above-mentioned books on Siberia and the exile system was written by Kellogg Durland (1881–1911), an American journalist popular in the 1900s and 1910s. The book had the title *The Red Reign: The True Story of a Year in Russia* (New York, 1907) and included interviews with Tolstoy; it was the most widely known book on Russia and Russian conditions written by an American of that time. Durland spent all of the year 1906 and part of 1907 in the empire of the Czar, and it was at this time that he visited Count Tolstoy at his home, Yasnaya Polyana.

Among other prominent intellectuals who published their memoirs about Tolstoy in the United States were professor Alexander Kaun, pianist Alexander Goldenweiser, and journalist and social activist Henry George, Jr.

Alexander Kaun (1889–1944), a professor of Russian literature from the University of California, was born in Russia and emigrated to the United States in the 1900s; he taught in California in the 1920s and 1930s. Alexander Goldenweiser, a famous composer and pianist, published in 1921–22 two volumes of reminiscences, entitled *Near Tolstoy*. These reminiscences recorded conversations with Tolstoy during fifteen years of intimate companionship ending only with the great writer's death. Journalist Richard Baeza prepared and edited Goldenweiser's firsthand memoirs for publication. Theodore Haffenberg was a French and English tutor at the Tolstoy estate who taught Tolstoy's nephews between 1887 and 1890, and left his memoirs about his encounters with the great Russian novelist.

Stephen Zweig (1881–1942), Austrian-born writer and journalist, lived in the United States in the 1910s and 1940s; he published *Three Writers: Casanova, Stendahl, Tolstoy* in 1928. Zweig did not meet Tolstoy in person, but spoke to many people who personally knew Tolstoy in the 1900s. General Lvov was the Chief of Police of the Moscow District who wrote in 1910 a "strictly confidential" police report upon Leo Tolstoy's death. It was kept in the archives, and then was published in New York in 1923. Ivan Bunin, a Nobel Prize winner in literature, lived most of his life abroad, outside of Russia; however, he was a close personal friend of Tolstoy in the mid–1890s in Yalta. Bunin left extensive memoirs about Tolstoy and Chekhov during their stay in Yalta in the 1890s and early 1900s.

Henry George, Jr. (1862–1916) was one of the last Americans who visited Tolstoy. Tolstoy greatly admired the works of his father, Henry George (1839–1897), the American economist who founded the single tax movement. Born in Philadelphia, George moved to New York City in 1880, supported the Irish Land League and various economic and political reforms, and spent the remainder of his life writing and lecturing. In 1886 he ran for the mayor of New York, running ahead of the Republican candidate Theodore Roosevelt. His son, Henry George, Jr., was a Representative from New York in 1911–1915; from 1881 to 1897 he had been a journalist for the *Brooklyn Eagle*, and managing editor of the *Florida Citizen*. He published a biography of his father Henry George in 1900, and met with Tolstoy after several years of correspondence.

When he visited Yasnaya Polyana on 5 June, 1909, Henry George, Jr., was one of the last Americans to see Tolstoy alive. In an article titled "About My Future Meeting with Henry George Junior"—a piece that was eventually published in several leading Russian newspapers—Tolstoy wrote, "When I think about my future meeting with the son of one of the greatest men of the 19th century, I can clearly see the virtue in all that he has done." In response to Tolstoy's kind words, the November 14, 1909, edition of New York's *World* newspaper published Henry George, Jr.'s apt reply, "I was charmed by Tolstoy's hospitality."

Tolstoy spoke of his admiration for great American writers and thinkers, and predicted a great future for America. However, he thought Americans were too materialistic and generally failed to appreciate their own culture.

These and other comments are now scattered across numerous interview transcripts and memoirs, many of which were originally published in American periodicals between 1887 and 1923. Of all the memoirs and interviews that are now available, a little under 30 were selected for this publication on the basis of their credibility, reliability, and artistic or historical value.

Research has failed to produce substantial information about a few of those Americans whose memoirs and reminiscences on Tolstoy are included. The editor would be grateful if the readers of this book can provide any clues regarding biographical information on John Holmes, Alexandra Nicchia or Virginia Wentz.

Assessing the material was a difficult task, given that Tolstoy rarely conducted interviews in the traditional question-answer format. In fact, he rarely answered the questions put to him by his visitors at all. Instead, while engaging them in conversation he expressed his own views on issues that mattered most to him. Nevertheless, this volume will be an invaluable source of information for Tolstoy's biographers, as well as professors and students of literature, theatre, art, history, and culture. It will also be an engaging and enjoyable read for those who simply love Tolstoy for what he wrote.

The volume concludes with a 1908 article by Virginia Wentz, "What Tolstoy Means to America," which summarizes the attitude of Americans to Tolstoy during the last years of his life.

The memoirs and reminiscences are presented chronologically by date of first publication.

# 1

# A Visit to Count Tolstoy
## by George Kennan

George Kennan (1845-1924), the American author and traveler, shared the name and even the birthday (February 16) of his great-nephew, George Frost Kennan (born 1904), the distinguished diplomat and historian. As a result, few are aware that the elder and forgotten George Kennan did not simply chronicle Russian life, but became an assiduous campaigner for democracy and human rights in the tsarist realm. When Kennan was growing up in Norwalk, Ohio, adventure for most Americans beckoned west, toward the Pacific. When Kennan learned in 1864 of plans to build an overland telegraph line from America to Europe across the Bering Strait and Siberia, he left for Alaska — then still Russian America. However, instead of being sent to Alaska, Kennan ended up in Russia. After his return from Russia, in 1878 he landed a position as an Associated Press reporter in Washington, D.C., and also wrote for the *New York Herald* and the *New York Times*. A series of his articles subsequently appeared in his immensely influential book, *Siberia and the Exile System*, which was used by Tolstoy. Kennan wrote for prominent magazines such as *Century, The Outlook, The Nation*, and *Forum*. In 1891, his outspoken stand against the monarchy earned him banishment from his beloved Russia; when he returned in 1901, he was ordered to leave the country. He met and spoke to Tolstoy on two occasions. Kennan continued his career as a journalist and was a lecturer for over 30 years, while writing for popular magazines.

Kennan, George. "A Visit to Count Tolstoy." *The Century* (New York) vol. 34 (new series vol. 12) (1887): 252–265.

The visit to the Russian novelist Count Leo Tolstoy which forms the subject of the present paper was made in the latter part of the month of

June, 1886; but it had been planned nearly a year before that time at one of the convict mines in Eastern Siberia, and was the result of a promise which I made to a number of Count Tolstoy's friends and acquaintances who were then, and are still, in penal servitude in the vast lonely wilderness of the Trans-Baikal. My first knowledge of the fact that there were friends and acquaintances of the Russian novelist among the political convicts at the Nertchinsk mines came to me in the shape of a request that I would carry a copy of his "Ispoved," or "Confession," to one of his friends, a lady, who was serving out a sentence of twelve years' penal servitude at the mines of Kara. The book was under the ban of the ecclesiastical censor; its publication and circulation in Russia had been absolutely forbidden, and the copy which I was requested to deliver was in manuscript. How it had found its way in spite of censors, inquisitors, official package-openers, house-searchers, body-searchers, baggage-examiners, police officers, and gendarmes to the remote East Siberian village where I was asked to take charge of it I do not know; but there it was, a silent but convincing proof of the futility of repressive measures when directed against human thought. It showed that the Government had not been able to keep a forbidden book even out of the hands of its own political convicts, living under strict guard in a penal settlement of the Trans-Baikal, five thousand miles from the fertile brain in which the proscribed ideas had their origin.

I consented, of course, to take charge of the manuscript, and in less than three months I had made the acquaintance not only of the lady for whom it was destined, but of many other political exiles in Eastern Siberia who had either known the great Russian author personally or had at some time been in correspondence with him. All of these exiles were very desirous that upon my return to European Russia I should see Count Tolstoy and describe to him the working of the exile system and the life of the political convicts of the Trans-Baikal.

They seemed to have the impression that he was more or less in sympathy with their hopes, if not with their methods, and that the information which I could give him could strengthen that sympathy, and perhaps change his attitude toward the Government from one of passive resistance to one of active and uncompromising hostility. This belief in the possibility of enrolling Count Tolstoy among the active enemies of the Government was founded, so far as I could judge, mainly upon the fact known even to the exiles in Siberia that most of his later writings had been prohibited by the censor. The conclusion drawn from that fact was that the author had attacked the Government, or at least had openly expressed his disapproval of its political methods. The conclusion, however, was erroneous. If these exiled revolutionists had been able to get and read Tolstoy's later books and articles, they would have seen at once that the suppressed literature was obnoxious to the ecclesiastical rather than to the civil power, and that the very corner-stone of Tolstoy's religious and social philosophy is non-resistance to evil. Most of these revolutionists, however, had been many years in prison or in exile; they had no means of following closely the development of Tolstoy's ideas, and they were misled by a superficial resemblance between his views and theirs with regard to property and social organization, and by the attitude of hostility which the Government had taken toward his later writings. Believing, however, as they did, that he was wavering on the brink of open revolt, and that a little more provocation would cause him to throw the weight of his forceful personality and powerful influence against the despotism which they hated, they urged me to see him and tell him all that I knew about Russian administration in Siberia and about the treatment of the political exiles. They also turned over to me a ghastly narrative in manuscript of the "hunger strike" of four educated women in the Irkutsk prison — one of them was a well-known Russian publicist and political economist, V. Vorontsov — and made me promise that I would give the document to Tolstoy to read. I took the manuscript and gave the promise.

("A hunger strike," in the language of Russian prisons, means organized voluntary self-starvation, undertaken by the prisoners as a last desperate protest against intolerable treatment.)

These were the circumstances under which my visit to the great Russian novelist was planned.

Many months elapsed before I returned to the European Russia, and when at last I found myself once more in Moscow, I learned that Count Tolstoy had left the city, and was spending the summer on his estate near the village of Yasnaya Polyana [Clearfield], in the province of Tula. On the 16th of June I took the late evening train southward over the Moscow-Kursk railroad, and reached the town of Tula early the following morning. Count Tolstoy's estate is situated about ten miles from the town, on the old turnpike road from Moscow to Kursk. Selecting from a throng of droshky drivers at the railway station the one in whose face there was an attractive expression of shrewdness and good-humor, I called him to me and asked if he knew Count Tolstoy.

"I know our barin [landlord]," he exclaimed with a broad smile. "How is it possible not to know the Graf? Why, he is ours. He lives in Yasnaya Polyana, only fifteen versts from here."

"Is there an inn or a post station in Yasnaya Polyana where I can go?"

"No," replied the droshky driver. "But why go to an inn? You can stay with the Count — he is a plain, simple man. He would be glad if you stay with him."

We made an agreement with the driver for transportation to Yasnaya Polyana, and at 10 o'clock we rolled out of Tula upon the broad white turnpike which leads to Orel and Kursk.

It was a bright, sunny June morning; and as we reached the summit of a high hill behind the town, I looked out with delight over a vast cultivated landscape. Brown thatched houses hid themselves in clumps of olive foliage, and finally stretching away on the left to the distant horizon in one vast undulating expanse of growing wheat, far or near there was not a fence, nor a wall, nor even a hedge to break the stiff rectangle, the vast flowing outlines of the picture; nor could there anywhere be seen a single isolated house, barn, or granary. The high state of cultivation to which the land had been brought, and occasionally the green or golden dome of a village church, calling attention to a modest cluster of thatched cottages showed that the beautiful country was inhabited.

About ten versts from Tula, in a shallow valley beside a brook, we came suddenly upon one of those scenes which are so characteristic of Russian life. It was a group of "bogomoltsy" or pilgrims, who had been resting and eating their lunch of black rye-bread and tea beside the road under the shade of a clump of trees. They were nearly all women, past middle age; these God-worshippers had forsaken their homes, families and friends, had walked across half the empire, and were bound for the great Troitsa [Trinity] Monastery — the Canterbury of Russia — forty-five miles beyond Moscow. For weeks they had not changed their clothing, eaten a substantial meal, or slept in a bed, and for weeks to come they would trudge wearily along the highways of Russia in scorching heat and drenching rain, ready to do all, bear all, and suffer all, if at last they might press their faces to the cold stone floor of the Cathedral of the Trinity, drink out of the holy well of Saint Sergius, and pray before the massive silver shrine in which the relics of that holy man repose. During the months of May and June — and in fact throughout the summer — there are thousands of such parties of pilgrims on the march in all parts of the empire.

Some are bound for the catacombs of Saint Anthony, in Kiev; some for the ancient monastery of Saint Valaam on Lake Ladoga; some for the holy shrines of Novgorod the Great; some for the monastery of Solovetsk, on the bleak arctic coast of the White Sea; and a few for the holy places of far-away Jerusalem.

To a casual observer in the streets of Moscow these wandering "bogomoltsy" and "stranniki" [pilgrims and wanderers] seem at times to compose a quarter of the population of the city.

As we left behind us one by one the black-and-white barred posts which mark the long versts between stations on a Russian post road, the heat of the sun grew more and more oppressive, and the blinding reflection of its vertical rays from the white unshaded turnpike became more and more insupportable, until my head and eyes ached with the heat and the glare. I was just about to ask my driver if we were not almost there when he gathered up his reins, turned into what seemed to be an old wood-road leading away from the turnpike on the right in the direction of an enclosed forest, and said, "Na konets daekhali"—"At last we have arrived."

I looked eagerly around for the imposing baronial mansion which I had pictured to myself as the country home of the great author, who was at the same time a wealthy Russian noble; but, with the exception of a little cluster of thatched log-houses on the crest of a sloping ridge about a mile away, I could not see a sign of human habitation.

"Where is the Count's house?" I inquired.

"It is over there in the woods," replied the driver, pointing with his whip; "you can't see it until you get close to it. Here is the gate of the park," he added, as, skirting the edge of a mud-hole, we turned again to the right and passed between two high and evidently ancient brick columns, which were hollow on the inner side, as if to afford places of shelter for gatekeepers or sentinels. Nothing, except these columns and an artificial but long-neglected pond which glimmered between the trees on the left, indicated that we were in a park or upon the premises of a wealthy Russian landowner.

I should have supposed that we were taking "a short cut" through the woods to some peasant village. The road had not been graveled, and was muddy from recent rain; the grass under the forest trees was long, choked by weeds, and mingled with wild flowers; and there was not the slightest evidence anywhere of care, cultivation, or pride in the appearance of the grounds. About two hundred yards from the gateway the road turned suddenly to the right and stopped abruptly at one end of a plain, white, rectangular, two-story house of brick standing among the trees in such a position that it could not be seen from the road at a greater distance than thirty or forty yards. It would be hard to imagine a simpler, barer, less pretentious building. It did not remind of piazzas nor towers nor architectural ornaments of any kind; there were soft and hard rectangular outlines on the staring whiteness of its flat walls; and its front door, which looked so much like a side or back door that I did not dare to knock at it, was situated nearer the end than the center of the facade, and was reached by a flight of steps and a small square platform of gray, uncut paving-stones with grass growing in the chinks.

At the end of the house where the road stopped there was it croquet ground of bare, hard-trodden earth, and on a bench beside it, in the shade of a tree, sat a lady in a brimmed summer hat, reading. Not feeling sure that what I saw was the front of the house, and dreading the awkwardness of knocking at what might prove to be the kitchen or dining-room door, I crossed the sports ground, apologized to the lady for interrupting her reading, and inquired if the Count was at home.

She replied that she believed he was, and, asking me to follow her, she entered the house. I was seated in a small room, and then, turning to an open door of the wooden partition, she called in English, "Count, are you there?" A deep voice from the other side of the partition replied, "Yes."

"A gentleman wishes to see you," she said, and then, without waiting for a response, she returned to the croquet ground. There was the sound of a moving chair in the adjoining room, and in a moment Count Tolstoy appeared at the door.

I had heard not a little from his friends with regard to his eccentricities in his dress; I had been shown photographs of him in peasant garb, and I did not therefore expect to see such a man clothed in soft raiment; but I was hardly prepared for the unconventionality of his attire.

The day was warm and sultry one; he had just returned from work in the fields, and his apparel consisted of heavy calfskin shoes, loose, almost shapeless; trousers of the coarse homespun linen of the Russian peasants; and a white cotton undershirt without collar or neckerchief. He wore neither coat nor waistcoat. But even in this coarse peasant garb Count Tolstoy was a striking and impressive figure.

He stood for an instant on the threshold, as if surprised to see a stranger, but quickly advanced into the room with out-stretched hand, and when I had briefly introduced myself, he expressed simply but cordially the great pleasure and gratification which he said it gave him to receive a visit from a foreigner, and especially from an American. I explained to him that my call was the result partly of a promise which I had made to some of his friends and admirers in Siberia, and partly of a desire to make the personal acquaintance of an author whose books had given me so much pleasure.

"What books of mine have you read?" he asked quickly. I replied that

I had read all of his novels, including "War and Peace," "Anna Karenina," and "The Cossacks."

"Have you seen any of my later writings?" he inquired.

"No," I said; "they have all, or nearly all, appeared since I went to Siberia."

"All!" he responded, "then you don't know me at all. We will get acquainted."

At this moment my ragged droshky driver, whose existence I had wholly forgotten, entered the door. Count Tolstoy at once rose, greeted him cordially as an old acquaintance, shook his hand warmly as he had shaken mine, and asked him with great interest a number of questions about his domestic affairs and the news of the day in Tula. It was perhaps a trifling incident but I was not at that time as well acquainted as now I am with Count Tolstoy's ideas regarding social questions, and to see a wealthy Russian noble, and the greatest of living novelists, shaking hands upon terms of perfect equality with a poor, ragged, and not civilized droshky driver whom I had picked in the streets of Tula. It was the first of the series of surprises which made my visit to Count Tolstoy memorable. When the droshky driver, after inquiring affectionately with regard to the health of the Countess and of all the children, had taken his departure, Count excused himself for a moment and returned to the apartment out of which he had come, leaving me alone.

The room where I sat was small and seemed to serve a double purpose of a reading-room and a hall. Two of its walls were of white plaster; the third consisted of a large oven covered with glazed tiles; the fourth was pierced by a door which led apparently into Count Tolstoy's library or work-room.

The floor was bare; the furniture was old-fashioned in form, with two or three plain chairs, a deep sofa, or settle, upholstered with worn green morocco, and a small cheap table without a cover. There was a marble bust in a niche behind the settle, and the only pictures which the room contained were a small engraved portrait of Dickens and another of Schopenhauer. It would be impossible to imagine anything plainer or simpler than the room and its contents. More evidences of wealth and luxury might be found in many a peasant's cabin in Eastern Siberia.

Before I had had time to do more than glance hastily about me, Count Tolstoy reappeared in the act of belting around his waist, with a wide black strap, a coarse gray blouse, or tunic, of homespun linen, which he had put on in the adjoining room. Then seating himself beside me, he began to question me about the journey to Siberia from which I had just returned, and I — mindful of my promise to the exiles — began to tell him what I knew about Russian administration and the treatment of political convicts. It soon became evident that he was not to be surprised, or shocked, or aroused by any such information as I had to give him. He listened attentively, but without any manifestation of emotion, to my descriptions of exile life, and drew from the storehouse of his own experience as many cases of administrative injustice and oppression that were new to me as I could give that were new to him. He was evidently familiar with the whole subject, and had with regard to it well-settled views which were not to be shaken by a few additional facts not differing essentially from those that he had previously considered. I finally asked him whether he did not think that resistance to such oppression was justifiable.

"That depends," he replied, "upon what you mean by resistance; if you mean persuasion, argument, protest, I answer yes; if you mean violence — no. I do not believe that violent resistance to evil is ever justifiable under any circumstances."

He then set forth clearly, eloquently, and with more feeling than he had yet shown, the views with regard to man's duty as a member of society which are contained in his book entitled "My Religion," and which are further explained and illustrated in a number of his recently published tracts for the people: He laid particular stress upon the doctrine of non-resistance to evil, which, he said, is in accordance both with the teachings of Christ and the results of human experience. He declared that violence, as a means of redressing wrongs, is not only futile, but an aggravation of the original evil, since it is the nature of violence to multiply and reproduce itself in all directions.

"The revolutionists," he said, "whom you have seen in Siberia, undertook to resist evil by violence, and what has been the result? Bitterness, and misery, and hatred, and bloodshed! The evils against which they took up arms still exist, and to them has been added a mass of previously nonexistent human suffering. It is not in that way that the kingdom of God is to be realized on earth."

I cannot now repeat from memory all the arguments and illustrations with which Count Tolstoy enforced his views and fortified his position; but I still remember the eloquence and earnestness with which they were presented, and the deep impression made upon me by the personality of the speaker. The ideas themselves were not new to me; I had repeatedly heard them discussed in literary circles in St. Petersburg, Moscow, Tver, and Kazan; but they never appealed to me with any real force until they came from the lips of a strong, sensitive, and earnest man who believed in them with passionate fervor.

For a long time I did not suggest any difficulties or raise any objections; but at last I made an effort to escape from the enthrallment of Count Tolstoy's strong personal influence by proposing to him questions which would necessitate the application of his general principles to specific cases. It is one thing to ask a man in a general way whether he would use violence to resist evil; and quite another thing to ask him specifically whether he would knock down a burglar who was about to cut the throat of his mother. Many men would say "yes" to the first question who would hesitate at the second. Count Tolstoy, however, was consistent. I related to him many cases of cruelty, brutality, and oppression which had come to my knowledge in Siberia, and at the end of every recital I said to him, "Count Tolstoy, if you had been there and had witnessed that transaction, would you not have interfered with violence?" He invariably answered, "No." I asked him the direct question whether he would kill a highwayman who was about to murder an innocent traveler, provided there were no other way to save the traveler's life. He replied, "If I should see a bear about to kill a peasant in the forest, I would sink an axe in the bear's head; but I would not kill a man who was about to do the same thing."

There finally came into my mind a case which, although really not worse than many that I had already presented to him, would, I thought, appeal with force to a brave, sensitive, chivalrous man.

"Count Tolstoy," I said, "three or four years ago there was arrested in one of the provinces of European Russia a young, sensitive, cultivated woman named Olga Liubatovich. I will not relate her whole history; it is enough to say that, inspired by ideas which, even if mistaken, were at least unselfish and heroic, she, with hundreds of other young people of both sexes, undertook to overturn the existing system of government. She was arrested, and thrown into prison, and then exiled to Siberia.

She was allowed to have her own dress and her own underclothing; but at Krasnoyarsk the local governor directed that she should put on the dress of a common convict. She refused to do so upon the ground that administrative exiles had the right to wear their own clothing, and that if convict dress had been obligatory, she would have been required to put it on before she left Moscow.

The local governor insisted upon obedience to his order, and Miss Liubatovich persisted in refusal. I do not know the reason for her obstinacy, but as convicts are not always supplied with new clothing, and are sometimes compelled to put on garments which have already been worn by others and which are foul and full of vermin, it is not difficult to suggest a number of good reasons for objecting to such a change.

The chief of police and the officer of the convoy were finally directed to use force. In their presence, and that of half a dozen other men, three or four soldiers seized the poor girl and attempted to take off her clothes.

She resisted, and there followed a horrible scene of violence and unavailing self-defense. Her lips were cut in the contest and her face covered with blood; but she continued to resist as long as she had strength. In spite of her cries, appeals, and struggles, she was finally overpowered, stripped naked under the eyes of six or eight men, and forcibly re-clothed the coarse convict dress. "Now," I said, "suppose that all this had occurred in your presence; suppose that this bleeding, defenseless, half-naked girl had appealed to you for protection and had thrown herself into your arms; suppose that it had been your daughter — would you still have refused to interfere by an act of violence?"

He was silent.

His eyes filled with tears as his imagination pictured to him the horror of such a situation, but for a moment he made no reply. Finally he said, "Do you know absolutely that that thing was done?"

"No," I said, "because I did not see it done; but after her solitary confinement she was exiled to Siberia. I have it from two eye-witnesses, one of them a lady in whose statements I put implicit trust, and the other an officer of the exile administration. They saw it and they told me."

Again he was silent. Finally, ignoring my direct question as to what he personally would have done in such a case, Count Tolstoy said, "Even under such circumstances violence would not be justifiable. Let us analyze that situation carefully. I will grant, for the sake of argument, that the local governor was an ignorant man, a cruel man, a brutal man. You suddenly appear and set yourself up as a judge in the case; you assume that he is not doing his duty, — that he is committing an act of unjustifiable violence, — and then, with strange inconsistency, you proceed to aggravate and complicate the evil by yourself committing another act of unjustifiable violence. One wrong added to another wrong does not make a right; it merely extends the area of wrong. Furthermore, your resistance, in order to be effective — in order to accomplish anything, — must be directed against the soldiers who are committing the assault. But those soldiers are not free agents; they are subject to military discipline and are acting under orders which they dare not disobey. To prevent the execution of the orders you must kill or maim two or three of the soldiers, that is, kill or wound the only parties to the transaction who are certainly innocent, who are manifestly acting without malice and without evil intention. Is that just? Is it rational? But go a step further: suppose that you do kill or wound two or three of the soldiers; you may or may not thus succeed in preventing the completion of the act against which your violence is a protest; but one thing you certainly will do, and that is, extend the area of enmity, injustice, and misery. Every one of the soldiers whom you kill or maim has a family, and upon every such family you bring grief and suffering which would not have come to it but for your act. In the hearts of perhaps a score of people you rouse the anti-Christian and anti-social emotions of hatred and revenge, and thus you plant the seeds of further violence and strife. At the time when you interposed there was only one center of evil and suffering. By your violent interference you have created half a dozen such centers. It does not seem to me, Mr. Kennan, that that is the way to bring about the reign of peace and goodwill on earth."

My curiosity as to the extent to which Count Tolstoy would go in the application of his general principles to specific cases was entirely satisfied. The answer to this reasoning, from the point of view of sociology, is obvious, but it was not my purpose to object, or argue, more than might be necessary to bring out Count Tolstoy's views in their full strength.

Further conversation was prevented by summons to lunch, which was served in a large, cheerful, sunny room in the second story. This part of the house, so far as plainness and simplicity are concerned, was perfectly in harmony with the part that I had already seen.

The floor was bare; the furniture was homely and old-fashioned; the windows were hung with simple white muslin curtains without lace or unnecessary drapery; and the whitewashed walls were relieved only by a few oil portraits in faded gilt frames, which evidently represented ancestors and dated from the last century,

At lunch we met, for the first time, Count Tolstoy's large family, which consisted of the Countess, a stately, dark-eyed, dark-haired lady, who must in her youth have been extremely beautiful; the eldest son, who had recently been graduated from one of the Russian universities; the oldest daughter, a girl perhaps twenty years of age; two bright-faced nieces, and three or four younger children. There were also present a young man in a highly ornamented peasant costume, worn evidently from caprice or in imitation of the Count, and two ladies of middle age whose relations to the family I could not determine, but who were probably nothing more than friends and converts to the Tolstoy philosophy.

The lunch passed quickly with bright, spontaneous conversation, in which all joined without the least appearance of formality or restraint, and in the course of which Count Tolstoy himself manifested more gayety than I had yet given him credit for. When we had risen from the table he produced and proceeded to sell at auction to the highest bidder a richly embroidered towel, the work of a peasant woman, which, he said, had been brought to him as a present, but which he was unwilling to accept because the giver was very poor and really in need of the money that the towel represented. Amid general laughter Count Tolstoy's son and I, who were the principal bidders, ran the lance up by successive offers of five kopecks more to two rubles and a half, when the auctioneer, with non-professional candor, declared that that was too much; that the American traveler in the course of the bidding had offered two rubles, which was about what the towel was worth, and that consequently it was his duty to award it to him. Young Tolstoy, with mock indignation, protested against the unfairness of that sort of an auction, but his motion for a new trial was overruled on the novel ground that the towel belonged to the auctioneer, who therefore had an unquestionable right to knock it down to any bidder whom he chose. His son laughingly acquiesced in the ruling, and the merry group which had gathered about the auctioneer dispersed.

I had not yet had a favorable opportunity to show Count Tolstoy the manuscript with the narrative of the "hunger strike" in the Irkutsk prison, which I had promised the political exiles in the Trans-Baikal that I would give to him. Upon our return to the little reception-room on the first floor, I raised again the question of the treatment of the political convicts in Siberia, and, as an illustration of some of my statements, I handed him the manuscript. It was a detailed history of the voluntary self-starvation of four political convicts, all educated women, in the prison at Irkutsk. This hunger strike, which took place in December for sixteen days, brought all of the women very near to death. It was undertaken as the last possible protest against what they regarded as intolerable cruelty. The narrative was written by Madame Rossinskaya, one of the "hunger strikers," and was delivered from the prison by an administrative exile who occupied a cell near hers. [...]

I shall in a subsequent paper give a translation of this narrative, and I need only say here that it is a detailed account of perhaps the most desperate "hunger strike" recorded in the annals of Russian prisons.

Count Tolstoy read three or four pages of the manuscript with a gradually clouding face, and then returned it to me. His manner and his subsequent conversation conveyed to my mind the impression that he was already overburdened with a consciousness of human misery, and that he shrank from the contemplation of more suffering which he was powerless to relieve.

"I have no doubt," he said, "that the courage and fortitude of these people are heroic, but their methods are irrational, and I sympathize with them. They resorted to violence, knowing that they were liable to violence in return. Those unfortunate people in Siberia; people whose hearts are full of bitterness and hatred, and who, at the same time, are absolutely powerless even to return evil for evil.

"If," he added after a moment's pause, "they had only changed their views a little,— if they had adopted the course which seems to me the only right one to pursue in dealing with evil — what might not such people have done for Russia! Mine is the true revolutionary method. If the people of the empire refuse, as I believe they should refuse, to render military service — if they decline to pay taxes to support that instrument of violence, an army,— the present system of government cannot stand. The proper way to resist evil is to absolutely refuse to do evil either for one's self or for others."

"But," I said, surprised by this advocacy of a revolutionary method which seemed to me utterly impracticable and visionary, "the Government forces its people to render military service and pay taxes — they must serve and pay or go to prison."

"Then let them go to prison," he rejoined. "The Government cannot put the whole population in prison; and if it could, it would still be without material for an army and without money for its support."

"But," I objected, "you cannot get the whole people to act simultaneously in this way. If you were let alone, you could perhaps convert a few hundred thousand peasants to your views; but do you think that you would be let alone? As soon as your teaching began to be dangerous to the stability of the state it would be suppressed. Suppose, for the sake of argument, that you succeeded in converting a quarter of the population; the Government would draw soldiers enough from the other three quarters to put that one quarter in prison or in Siberia, and there would be an end of your propaganda and your revolution.

"It seems to me that the first thing to be done is to obtain freedom of action — peaceably if possible, forcibly if necessary. You cannot persuade, nor teach, nor show people how they ought to live, if some other man holds you by the throat and chokes you every time you open your mouth or raise your hand. How are you ever going to get your propaganda under way?"

"But do you not see," replied the Count, "that if you claim and exercise the right to resist by an act of violence what you regard as evil, every other man will insist upon his right to resist in the same way what he regards as evil, and the world will continue to be filled with violence? It is your duty to show that there is a better way."

"But," I objected, "you cannot show anything if somebody smites you on the mouth every time you open it to speak the truth." "You can at least refrain from striking back," replied the Count; "you can show by your peaceable behavior that you are not governed by the barbarous law of retaliation, and your adversary will not continue to strike a man who neither resists nor tries to defend himself. It is by those who have suffered, not by those who have inflicted suffering, that the world has been advanced."

I said it seemed to me that the advancement of the world had been promoted not a little by the protests — and often the violent and bloody protests — of its inhabitants against wrong and outrage, and that all history goes to show that a people which tamely submits to oppression never acquires either liberty or happiness.

"The whole history of the world," replied the Count, "is a history of violence, and you can of course cite violence in support of violence; but do you not see that there is in human society an endless variety of opinions as to what constitutes wrong and oppression, and that if you once concede the right of any man to resort to violence to resist what he regards as wrong, he being the judge, you authorize every other man to enforce his opinions in the same way, and you have a universal reign of violence?"

"If, on the other hand," I said, "oppression is advantageous to the oppressor, and if he finds that he can oppress with impunity and that nobody resists, when is he likely to stop oppressing? It seems to me that the peaceable submission to injustice which you advocate would simply divide society into two classes: tyrants, who find tyranny profitable, and who therefore will continue it indefinitely; and slaves, who regard resistance as wrong, and who will therefore submit indefinitely."

Count Tolstoy, however, continued to maintain that the only way to abolish oppression and violence is to refuse absolutely to do violence regardless of provocation. He said that the policy of passive resistance to evil which he advocated as a revolutionary method is in complete harmony with the character of the Russian peasant, and he referred to the wide and rapid spread of religious dissent in the empire as showing the chance of success which such a policy would have in spite of repressive measures.

After some further conversation Count Tolstoy proposed that we should take a walk, and I assented. A short distance from the house we met Miss Tolstoy, the Count's eldest daughter, dressed as a peasant girl, on her way home from the fields where she had been raking hay with the village girls of Yasnaya Polyana.

The peasant dress of bright scarlet, cut low in the neck all around, the braided hair, and the strings of large colored glass beads which hung in festoons over her breast, changed her appearance so completely that I did not recognize her until her father called her by name. It appeared that she shared his views with regard to manual work. Count himself had spent the morning in spreading manure over the land of a poor widow who lived near his estate, and would have devoted the afternoon to the same occupation but for my visit.

"I believe," he said, "that it is every man's duty to labor for those who need assistance, and to work at least a part of every day with his hands. It is better to actually labor for the poor in their particular employment, than it is to work in your own higher and possibly more remunerative intellectual field and then give the poor the results of your labor.

"If, on the other hand, you work exclusively in your own higher intellectual field and give the poor the results of your labor, as you would give to a beggar, you encourage idleness and dependence; you establish a social class distinction between yourself and the recipient of your alms; you break down his self-respect, and you inspire him with a longing to escape the hard conditions of his own daily physical toil and to share your life, which he thinks is easier than his; to wear your clothes, which seem to him better than his, and to gain admission to your social class, which he regards as higher than his. That is not the way to help the poor or to promote the brotherhood of man!"

"If I admit," I said, "that it is man's highest duty to do good to others, and that he owes a secondary duty to himself and to his family, I cannot dispute the soundness of your reasoning. If I accept your idea, I leave myself no ground to stand on in an argument; but, waiving that point, there is something in your scheme that strikes me most forcibly — it is its utter impracticability.

"You say," rejoined Count Tolstoy, "that if you admit my premises you leave yourself no ground to stand on in argument — but why should you not admit it? You must admit my premises, If every one would do good to every other man instead of evil, the condition of things would be better than it is now, would it not?

"Somebody must take a step in that direction and ask, is it possible to live so? What if modern organization of society and the existing traits of human character do make such step difficult — that has no impact on my personal duty. The question is not what is easy, but what is right. There is nothing sacred or necessarily immutable about the present organization of society and the existing traits of human character. They are the results of man's activity, and by man's activity they can be changed. I believe that they ought to be changed, and I am doing what I can to change them."

Count Tolstoy then related with great fullness of detail the history of his change of attitude toward the teaching of Christ.

His frequent references to the New Testament and the precepts of Christ as furnishing the only rule for the right government of human conduct, might lead one to regard Count Tolstoy as a devout and orthodox Christian, but judged by a doctrinal standard, he is very far from being so. He rejects the whole doctrine of the Christian scheme of redemption, including original sin, atonement, the true personality of God, and the divinity of Christ, and has very little faith in the immortality of the soul. His religion is a religion of this world, and it is based almost wholly upon terrestrial considerations.

If he refers frequently to the teachings of law, and accepts Christ's precepts as the rules which should govern human conduct it is not because he believes that Christ was God, but because he regards those precepts as an embodiment of the highest and noblest philosophy of life, and as a revelation, in a certain sense, of the Divine will and character. He insists, however, that Christ's precepts shall be understood — and that they were intended to be understood literally and in their most obvious sense. He will not recognize nor tolerate any softening or modification of a hard commandment by subtle and plausible interpretation. If Christ said, "Resist not evil," he meant resist not evil. He did not mean resist not evil if you can help it, nor resist not evil unless it is unbearable; he meant resist not at all. How unflinchingly Count Tolstoy faces the logical results of his system of belief I have tried to show.

We wandered aimlessly about his estate, talking and arguing, nearly the whole afternoon; I do not remember where we went; I cannot remember anything that I saw; I was conscious only of the stream of ideas, arguments, and illustrations which flowed unceasingly from his mind into mine, and the emotions which were roused by it, and by the strong, earnest, lovable personality of the man himself.

Late in the afternoon we were compelled by a summer shower to take refuge in the house, and Count Tolstoy invited me into his workroom. It was very small, not much larger than an ordinary bedroom, and the cell of a hermit could hardly have been less luxurious. It contained no furniture except a narrow iron bedstead, a single plain wooden chair, and a small table of stained pine covered with worn green morocco. There was a portrait over the table of a well-known Russian dissenter named Surtaev, and around the walls were book-shelves filled with books, mostly in paper covers, but I could see nothing else to distinguish Count Tolstoy's library from a room in the house of any well-to-do peasant.

"I receive many letters," said the Count, opening a drawer in the table, "from people in America who have read my 'Confession' and 'Religion'—here is one,"—and he put into my hands a letter from some man living in a village in the backwoods of Pennsylvania, informing the Count that he—the writer—and many of his fellow-villagers had long practiced the principles advocated in "My Religion"; that they "confessed the truth as it is in Jesus," and that they had recently organized a church.

"Now," said the Count, "what do you think of that letter? You see he doesn't understand; he thinks that he cannot have religion without a church. I wrote him that he didn't need a church in order to live rightly."

At this moment there entered the room a young man shabbily dressed in the garb of a common peasant, who brought to Count Tolstoy the day's mail from the neighboring village.

I took the man to be a servant employed about the stables, and did not rise from my seat: I was greatly surprised therefore when Count Tolstoy introduced him to me as Mr. F., one of his friends and co-workers. He proved to be an educated gentleman, a graduate of one of the Russian universities, and the most consistent and thorough-going of Count Tolstoy's disciples. He carried the latter's principles in fact to the utmost limit of logical application. He had no property, no home, not even a settled place of abode. He worked constantly for others, and refused absolutely to receive any compensation except food, clothing, and shelter.

Even these necessities of life he accepted not as payment for his labor, but merely as things which every man is bound to give every other man if they are needed. He toiled wherever he thought his work would be most useful; when he needed clothes, he asked some peasant woman to make them for him; when he was hungry, he went to the nearest house for food; and when night came, he slept under any roof where he happened to be. In short, he devoted his life to society at large, and society at large supported him.

He paid no taxes, refused to take out a passport, ignored the Government in every way, and was liable to arrest at any moment as a vagrant. If he had been arrested, he would have persisted in his refusal to pay taxes which might be used to support an army, and would have gone quietly, if not contentedly, to prison. Could there be a more perfect illustration of altruistic principles that came to their logical conclusion?

Among the letters and packages brought from the post-office by this young man was a copy of the English translation, published in New York, of Count Tolstoy's book entitled "My Religion." It was the first time he had seen it in its English dress, and he expressed a curiosity to know whether or not the translation, which had been made through the French, was a good one. He brought out the original manuscript, which bore evident traces of much handling and copying, and we compared three or four pages of it with the translation. The author seemed to be satisfied, and said, "The ideas are apparently all there."

The conversation then turned upon foreign editions of his books, and he said that he had recently received from the American publishers of one of his novels an offer of a royalty, upon condition that he should allow that firm to call theirs the authorized edition of his works. He had written them, he said, that he did not recognize nor believe in contracts or agreements, and that he did not desire to have anything to do with the foreign sale of his novels. He spoke slightingly, almost contemptuously, of his works of fiction, and seemed to regard them as monuments of misdirected energy. He had great difficulty, he said, in getting his religious ideas before the Russian people on account of the attitude of hostility taken toward them by Pobedonostsev, the Procurator of the Holy Synod, and by the ecclesiastical censor.

I told him that I had seen many lithographed and ksero-graphed copies of his later writings in circulation in St. Petersburg and Moscow.

"Yes," he replied, "the Government will not allow me to print them, but it cannot suppress them altogether. Sometimes it proscribes my ideas in one form and allows them to be printed in another. It refused me permission to publish in the form of an argument the ideas contained in 'Ivan Durak' [Ivan the Fool]. I recast them in the form of a short story for the common people, and the censor passed them without objection. I was forbidden to print my 'Ispoved' [Confession], but the ecclesiastical authorities finally printed it themselves in their own 'Orthodox Review,' with an elaborate refutation of my heresies by a prelate of the church. I am told," he added with a smile, "that in the public libraries the only leaves of 'The Orthodox Review' that are cut are those on which my 'Confession' is found."

Our conversation was interrupted at this point by the announcement of dinner. Tolstoy of course made no change in his dress; I was unable to make any change in mine even had I felt disposed to do so, and the ladies alone showed a disposition to respect the established conventionalities of life in the proper apparel. The dinner was simple, informal, and in every way enjoyable. The conversation, as at lunch, was bright and unconstrained, and Count Tolstoy himself in particular seemed to participate with keen rest in the laughter, raillery, and badinage of the younger people. His relations with his children, whenever I saw them together, were everything that such relations should be — cordial, sympathetic, and affectionate.

After dinner the family again separated. The young man who had brought the mail from the post-office, and one of the two ladies whom I supposed to be visiting disciples of Tolstoy joined us for dinner.

Then I asked him about the picture of the American antislavery agitator which hung near the window in the room where we were sitting. He said he had sent to the United States for the biography of Garrison by Oliver Johnson, and had read it with great interest; but he thought the author had not given prominence enough to Garrison's views with regard to non-resistance, and had shown a disposition to treat them in a deprecatory way, as if they were something to be apologized for.

In his (Count Tolstoy's) opinion, the fact that Garrison was, at one time at least, a non-resistant, did him more honor perhaps than any other fact in his history.

The Count also spoke with warm respect and admiration of Theodore Parker, whose "Discourse of Matters Pertaining to Religion" he regarded as the most remarkable effort of the American mind in that field. In the course of further conversation he said he thought it deeply to be regretted that America had in two particulars proved false to her traditions.

"In what particulars?" I inquired.

"In the persecution of the Chinese and the Mormons," he replied. "You are crushing the Mormons by oppressive legislation, and you have forbidden Chinese immigration."

"But," I said, "have you ever heard what we have to say for ourselves upon these questions?"

"Perhaps not," he answered. "Tell me."

I then proceeded to give him the most extreme anti-Chinese views that have ever prevailed upon the Pacific coast, and to draw as dark a picture as I could of the economic condition of a once prosperous and happy State "ruined by Chinese cheap labor."

"Well," he said when I had finished, "is that all?"

"All!" I exclaimed. "Isn't that enough? Suppose the Chinese should come to California at the rate of a hundred thousand a year; they would simply crush our civilization on the Pacific coast."

"Well," rejoined the Count coolly, "So, what of it? The Chinese have as much right there as you have."

"But would you not allow a people to protect itself against that sort of alien invasion?" I asked.

"Why alien?" said the Count. "Why do you make a distinction between foreigners and countrymen? To me all men are brothers, no matter whether they are Russians or Mexicans, Americans or Chinese."

"But suppose," I said, "that your Chinese brethren come across the sea in sufficient numbers to reduce you to slavery; you would probably object to that."

"Why should I?" rejoined the Count with quiet imperturbability. "Slavery is working for others — all I want is to work for others."

I abandoned the discussion. To argue with a man who would not resist enslavement by a Chinese was as unprofitable as to discuss surgery with a man who would not admit the desirability of relieving suffering and saving life. I allowed the Mormon question to go by default. In fact, I did not see upon what ground I could defend anything against an antagonist who would neither give me standing room nor allow me to use any of the weapons in my armory. Later in the evening something was said which brought up the subject of civil government, and that in turn led to a discussion of punishment in general and capital punishment in particular. Count Tolstoy, as might have been expected, was opposed to both, and in the course of the conversation he said that shortly after the assassination of Alexander II and the trial and sentence of the assassins, he wrote a letter to the present Tsar, making an appeal on behalf of the condemned regicides, setting forth the wrong fullness of taking human life, even by due judicial process, and imploring the Tsar not to begin his reign with murder. He sent this letter by a friend to Pobedonostsev, the Procurator of the Holy Synod, who had been the tutor of Alexander III, and was supposed to have great influence over him, and besought Pobedonostsev to lay the letter before the Tsar with a favorable recommendation. He received from Pobedonostsev in reply what he described to me as "a terrible letter" [uzhasnoe pismo], in which the writer said that he approved of the death sentence pronounced upon the murderers of Alexander II, that he did not sympathize with appeals for mercy based upon such considerations as those which Count Tolstoy urged, and that he must therefore decline to bring the letter to the Tsar's attention. He closed by saying, "Your religion is a religion of weakness and sentimentality, but there is a religion of authority and power" [vlast].

I could see by Count Tolstoy's manner while relating this incident that he had been deeply disappointed by the result of his intercession, though why he should have expected any other result it is hard to understand. The circumstance furnishes an illustration of what seems to me a weakness — or, if that word be too harsh, a peculiarity — which distinguishes Russian character as a whole, and which is to me one of the most noticeable features of the character and the philosophy of Count Tolstoy. I cannot think of any better word to describe that peculiarity than childishness, although that word has also a depreciatory significance which renders it objectionable, and which I should like in this case to reject. I mean that the Russian, as a rule, has a childish faith in the practicability and the speedy realization of plans, hopes, and schemes which an American, under precisely similar circumstances, would regard as visionary and chaotic, and would therefore throw aside as having no bearing on his present conduct. When this national trait is united, as it is in the Russian character, with a boundless capacity for self-sacrifice, it brings about results which, to the American mind, are simply bewildering and astonishing. This characteristic is no less apparent in the reasoning and the activity of the Nihilists than in the doctrines and the eccentric practices of Count Tolstoy. It was as childish for the Nihilists to suppose that they could attain their objects by assassinating the Tsar as it was for Count Tolstoy to suppose that he could save them from punishment for that act by urging such considerations as the barbarity and sinfulness of the death penalty upon a government which had already shot or hanged fifteen or twenty men for political offenses of far less gravity. Both the Nihilists and Count Tolstoy answered affirmatively the question, "Is the object to be attained desirable?" and then both proceeded at once to act, regardless of the equally important question, "Is the proposed method practicable?" The Russian seems to throw himself with a sort of noble, generous, but childish enthusiasm into the most thorny path of self-denial and self-sacrifice, if he can only see, or think that he sees, the shining walls of his ideal golden city at the end of it. He takes no account of difficulties, heeds not the suggestions of prudence, cares not for the natural laws which limit his powers, but presses on, with a sublime confidence that he can reach the ideal city because he can see it so plainly, and because it is such a desirable city to reach. From Count Tolstoy, striving to bring about the millennium by working for others and sacrificing himself, down to the poor pilgrims by the roadside, striving to better their characters and atone for their sins by laborious pilgrimages to holy shrines, there is manifested this same national characteristic — the disposition to seek desirable ends by inadequate and impracticable methods.

I had had no favorable opportunity during the day to ascertain Count Tolstoy's views with regard to modern science, but late in the afternoon such an opportunity presented itself in the course of a discussion of heredity as a factor in social problems. I said it seemed to me that in considering the possibility of eradicating evil by altruistic conduct and non-resistance he did not give the facts of heredity enough weight. He replied that he did not believe in inherited total depravity, and that as for Darwinism he regarded it as a "great deception" [bolsloi obman].

I do not pretend to be well informed upon the subject of development; but I told Tolstoy that a Russian scientist Danilevsky has written a book which will completely demolish the Darwinian theory. It was evident from his remarks that Count Tolstoy had no adequate conception of the relative strength of the mass of evidence which now supports the theory of development and I did not therefore pursue the subject. Although Count Tolstoy did not discontinue his shoe-making, the conversation soon became general, was directed to subjects of local interest.

At six o'clock it became necessary for me to return to the railway station, and I said good-bye, with sincere regret, to a man whom I had known only one day, but for whom I had already come to feel an almost affectionate respect. His theories of life and conduct seemed to me nobly, generously, and heroically wrong, but for the man himself I had, and could have, only the warmest respect and esteem.

It has of course been impossible, with limits of such as this, to give even the substance of a conversation which lasted many hours, and which ranged over the whole field of human conduct. I am conscious that in what I have written, from memory and fragmentary notes, I have failed to do even partial justice to Count Tolstoy's arguments, to his eloquence, and to the deep, earnest sincerity which pervaded them, and which impressed me more than all else. I hope, however, that I have at least reported fairly and understandingly.

Count Tolstoy is perhaps at the present time the most generally talked of and widely read author in Russia. His books and pamphlets circulate by tens of thousands among the educated classes, and by millions among the peasants; his theories of life are attacked and sometimes warmly defended by the Russian periodical press, and his religious ideas are discussed in the luxurious homes of the wealthy nobles and in the cottages of peasants, and from the capital of the empire.

The fifth collection of his works, in twelve volumes, has just been published in St. Petersburg. There had been sold nearly three million copies of his works for the common people. His teachings and his example will have an influence upon the course of events in Russia, but it is impossible as yet to predict their full impact. Thus far the results are unimportant, and the verdict of educated society is adverse to the philosopher and to his philosophy. I am not at all sure, however, that the results would long continue to be unimportant if the Government should allow Count Tolstoy's propaganda to get fairly under way: There is no doubt that his teachings are, to a certain extent, in harmony with the character of the Russian peasant; and that he spoke the simple truth when he said to me, "The muzhik is not naturally aggressive nor combative; but he is capable of passive resistance to an almost unlimited extent." Both of these facts are illustrated by the history of Russian dissent, and particularly by the springing up in various parts of the empire of such sects as the "Non-Tax-Payers," the "Hiders," and the "Followers of Surtaev." All of these sects hold views closely analogous to those of Count Tolstoy, and they hold them with a tenacity which neither prison nor exile can conquer. Siberia is full of people who have been banished for religious heresies which they could not be persuaded nor forced to relinquish, and the number of dissenters in the empire is now about fourteen million. If Count Tolstoy were allowed to sow the seeds of his doctrines broadcast in this fertile soil, it might possibly change to a very considerable extent the course of Russian history; but, as I have before said, he will not be permitted to do so. Nearly all of his later writings have been prohibited by the censor, in whole or in part, and if, notwithstanding these repressive measures, his religious heresy should gain adherents enough to make it dangerous, or even troublesome, to the state, it would be stamped out with imprisonment and exile, as scores of such dangerous heresies have been stamped out before.

The question most frequently put to me in St. Petersburg and Moscow after my return from Yasnaya Polyana was, "Did Count Tolstoy impress you as sincere and in earnest?" There seemed to be a prevalent belief that he was merely amusing himself with shoemaking, field-labor, and tract-writing, and that there was behind it all no real sincerity of conviction. In support of this belief it was urged that Count Tolstoy's practice did not in all respects accord with his preaching; that he pretended to regard his works of fiction as useless, if not pernicious, and yet superintended the publication of a fifth edition of them; and that he opposed private property and preached against money-getting, and yet continued to hold his estate and to take the proceeds from the sales of his books.

In reply to these attacks upon Count Tolstoy's sincerity it may be said that if there is any discrepancy between his preaching and his practice it arises from the fact that he is acting under restraint. It is an open secret in Russia that all of Count Tolstoy's family do not share his religious belief, and that in the attempt to put his ideas into practice he is obliged to choose between two lines of conduct, each of which involves evil and suffering, not only to himself, but to others.

Under such circumstances he has chosen what seems to him the least wrong alternative, and has made his practice conform to his preaching just so far as he can without bringing upon himself and upon others a greater evil than that growing out of his admitted inconsistency. It is therefore ungenerous, if not unjust, to attack him upon this ground, since he is precluded by the very nature of the case from making any defense.

In an authorized interview recently published in a Russian journal, Count Tolstoy refers to this subject as follows, in language whose graphic idiomatic simplicity and vigor can only be suggested in a translation:

"People say to me, 'Well, Lev Nikolaevich, as far as preaching goes, you preach; but how about your practice?' The question is a perfectly natural one; it is always put to me, and it always shuts my mouth. 'You,' it is said, 'but how do you live?' I can only say that I do not preach as passionately as I desire to do so; I might preach through my actions, but my actions are bad. That which I say is not preaching; it is only my attempt to find out the meaning and the significance of life: People often say to me, 'If you think that there is no reasonable life outside the teachings of Christ, and if you love a reasonable life, why do you not fulfill the Christian precepts?' I am guilty and blameworthy and contemptible because I do not fulfill them; but at the same time I say,— not in justification, but in explanation, of my inconsistency,— compare my previous life with the life I am now living, and you will see that I am trying to fulfill.

"I have not, it is true, fulfilled one eighty-thousandth part, and I am to blame for it; but it is not because I do not wish to fulfill all, but because I am unable. Teach me how to extricate myself from the meshes of temptation in which I am entangled,— help me,— and I will fulfill all I wish and hope to do it even without help.

"Condemn me if you choose,— I do that myself,— but condemn me, and not the path which I am following, and which I point out to those who ask me where, in my opinion, the path is.

"If I know the road home, and if I go along it drunk, and staggering from side to side, does that prove that the road is not the right one? If it is not the right one, show me another. If I stagger and wander, come to my help, and support and guide me in the right path.

"Do not yourselves confuse and mislead me and then rejoice over it and cry, 'Look at him. He says he is going home, and he is floundering into the swamp!' You are not evil spirits from the swamp; you are also human beings, and you also are going home: You know that I am alone,— you know that I cannot wish or intend to go into the swamp, then help me! My heart is breaking with despair because we have all lost the road; and while I struggle with all my strength to find it and keep in it, you, instead of pitying me when I go astray, cry triumphantly, 'See! He is in the swamp with us!'"

Never, it seems to me, was there written a simpler, franker, more sincere confession of inconsistency than this, and never was there a more eloquent and touching appeal for sympathy, encouragement, and support.

# 2

# Count Tolstoy at Home
*by Isabel Hapgood*

Isabel Hapgood, born in Boston in 1850, of colonial English-Scottish descent, studied languages from her earliest years, including Russian and Church Slavonic. Her love of Russian literature (she translated Tolstoy, Turgenev, and others) led her to investigate Russian culture on her first visit to Russia in 1887, and later. She visited many well-known personalities including Count and Countess Tolstoy, Tsarina Alexandra, Patriarch Tikhon, and others. In 1917 she was caught in Moscow at the beginning of the Revolution, escaping only through the help of the American consul. When she died in 1928, at the age of 78, Isabel Hapgood left behind a valuable treasure-house of literature, both translations and original commentary of all kinds about Russia, including her extensive translations of Tolstoy.

Hapgood, Isabel. "Count Tolstoy at Home." *The Atlantic Monthly*. Boston, 1891 (8) v. 15: 71–76.

During our acquaintance in winter, in Moscow, with the family of Count Lev Nikolaevich Tolstoy, the famous novelist and the countess had said to us,

"You must come and visit us at Yasnaya Polyana next summer. You should see Russian country life, you will see it with us. Our house is not elegant, but you will find it plain, clean and comfortable."

Such an invitation was not to be resisted. When summer came, the family wrote to say that they would meet us at the nearest railway station. [...]

Throughout the drive my "izvozchik" (cart driver) delighted me with his discourse. It began like this.

I asked, "Did he know Count Tolstoy?"

"Did he know Count Tolstoy? Everybody knew him. He was the first gentleman in the empire. There was not another such man in all the land."

"Could he read? Had he read the count's tales?"

"Yes. He read every one of count's books that he could lay his hands on." [...]

But the gem of the discourse dropped from his lips when I asked him what, in his opinion, would be the result if Count Tolstoy could reconstruct the world on his plan.

"Why, naturally," he replied, "if all men were equal, I should not be driving you, for example. I should have my own horse, and cow, and property, and I should do no work."

I must say that on reflection, I was not surprised that he should have reached this rather astonishing conclusion. I had no doubt that all of his kind — it is not a stupid kind by any means — think the same. I tried to tell him about America, where we all are equal in theory (I omitted "theory") and yet where some of us still "drive other people," figuratively speaking. But he only laughed and shook his head.

At last, we reached the stone gateposts which mark the entrance to the park of Yasnaya Polyana (Rus. "Clearfield") and he drove us up the formerly splendid and still beautiful avenue of huge white birch trees. The avenue terminated near the house in hedges of lilacs and acacias.

Most of the family were away in the fields, or bathing in the river.

The Count, who had been mowing, appeared at dinner in a grayish blouse and trousers and a soft white linen cap. He looked even more weather-beaten in complexion than in Moscow last winter, if that were possible. After dinner, on the first evening, the Countess invited us to go in the field and see her husband at work. [...] We hunted him across several meadows and finally came upon him in a sloping orchard lot seated under the trees. He was talking to the peasants.

"Look at the oldest of these men," he said to us in English. "He had lost the first joint of all the fingers on one hand from frost." We watched the party for a while. The Count made a good progress.

# 3

# With Count Tolstoy
## *by Thomas Stevens*

Thomas Stevens published his book *Through Russia on a Mustang* in 1891 in New York. His book is an incredibly articulate and fascinating account of a journalist from the American West traveling through late 19th century Russia, meeting the figures of the moment, like Tolstoy, while buying, describing and selling horses as his means of transport and companionship. He described the major cities and the Russian people with a down-to-earth American eye of a keen observer.

Stevens, Thomas. "With Count Tolstoy," in his *Through Russia on a Mustang*. New York, 1891: 92–102.

On Friday, July 4, our road from Tula led through Yasnaya Polyana, the ancestral estate of Count Leo N. Tolstoy, the novelist. We had ridden out to Tula that morning, and striking the great Moscow-Kharkov highway, turned our horses' heads toward the south. For some distance our road cut a swath through a magnificent forest. A stone pillar, surmounted by the imperial arms of Russia, told us that it was government property. We turned to the left, and a short distance from the road we came to a pair of circular pillars at the end of an avenue.

It was the entrance to the Tolstoy estate. Both pillars and avenue seemed sadly neglected, to one accustomed to the neatness of England and America. The former were in decay, and the latter was overgrown with weed and vagabond tree shoots. We seemed to be entering the domain of fallen grandeur rather than the abode of Russia's greatest and best known novelist.

On the plastered wall of a tumble-down little lodge, near the pillars, was chalked, in Russian, "Come to the house." We rode up the avenue to the house. It is a white two-story structure of stone and wood — a roomy, though unpretentious abode. The only striking feature about it was a very broad veranda, with rude carvings of horses and birds on the railings. It was six o'clock in the evening, and on the portico sat the Countess and several young ladies. The Countess was doing the honors behind the samovar, and the party were regaling themselves with tea and strawberries. The author sent in his card. Our horses were taken to the stables, and in five minutes we were of the interesting party about the samovar. Beside the Countess were the eldest daughter, the Countess's sister, two nieces from St. Petersburg, and two or three others.

"The Count has been mowing hay this afternoon," said the Countess, "and has not yet come in. I have sent him your card. He will be here in a minute."

Every person at the table could speak English, some of the young ladies so fluently that it was difficult to believe they had not been born and brought up in an English-speaking community.

Presently there appeared on the steps of the portico a thin, sun-browned man of medium height, clad in a coarse linen suit. His bushy eyebrows thatched a pair of kindly yet shrewd blue eyes, and his gray beard and long gray hair looked like a peasant's. A cheap homemade cap, of the same material as his suit, adorned the head to which the world is indebted for "War and Peace," "Anna Karenina," and other masterpieces of the Russian realistic school. Rude boots, as ungainly as the wooden shoes of Germany, attested mutely to the eminent novelist's skill — or lack of it — as a cobbler. Both cap and boots were the Count's own handiwork. The linen trousers were loose and the shirt looser. The latter was worn, moujik fashion, outside the trousers, and was gathered about the waist with a belt of russet leather.

"I am very happy to see you," said Count Tolstoy, cheerily. "I hope you will stay some days. We have had American visitors occasionally; you are, I see, from New York."

"We are riding from Moscow to the Crimea," I said, "and, of course, couldn't think of passing without calling to pay our respects."

The Count looked thin and worn from a recent illness, but said he was now in good health. He was taking a season of "koumiss cure." At Samara, on the Volga, is an establishment for the manufacture of koumiss, to which the invalids of Russia resort. Count Tolstoy did not care to spend the summer at Samara, so he had set up a little koumiss establishment of his own.

"Come and see it," he said, "and take my koumiss. I have been mowing hay. I must now drink koumiss. I drink it six times a day, and take nothing else but a little soup or tea."

At the end of another short avenue, we came to a round wattle hut with a conical roof. It was a nomad "aoul," or tent, of the steppes, improvised out of the best material at hand instead of the felt matting of the tribes in their own homes. Three young colts were tethered to a rope outside, and three big, fine brood-mares, their dams, were grazing in the orchard.

A family of Bashkirs occupied the aoul — husband, wife, and two small children. They had been obtained from the koumiss establishments of Samara and brought to Vasnaya Polyana. The three mares each gave about a gallon of milk a day, the Count explained, and the foals were allowed to run with them at night. They were milked several times a day, and gave a pint at each milking.

Inside the aoul the Bashkir woman was plying a dasher in a horsehide churn of milk. A big jar of koumiss stood on a table, the Count poured some into a wooden bowl.

"See how you like it," he said.

It tasted very much like buttermilk, and betrayed to the palate no suggestion of alcohol.

"I thought it had to be fermented," I said.

"It is fermented," returned the Count, "and if a man were to drink enough of it he would feel it go to the head."

"And so you have been mowing hay. You do not, then, like Mr. Gladstone, confine yourself to one form of manual exertion?"

Tolstoy is an admirer of Mr. Gladstone, but freely criticized the motive of that statesman in chopping down trees as compared with his own ideas of why everybody should work. He had nothing to say against Mr. Gladstone felling trees, but thought it would be better were he to ply his ax for less selfish reasons than to exercise his body and maintain his health. Mr. Gladstone should wield his ax, if he prefers to chop down trees rather than to dig potatoes or mow hay, not merely for the same reason that an athlete goes to the gymnasium, but to earn his living.

"Every man," said the novelist, "ought to do enough work each day to pay for the food he eats and the clothes he wears. Unless he does that he is sponging his living off the labor of other people, and is doing an injustice to his fellow-men. Some days I mow, others I sow grain, plow, dig in the garden, pick berries or apples, or, like Mr. Gladstone, fell a tree. I live very simply. I make my own boots, and if my women would let me, would also make all my own clothes. I do not have to work very long hours to pay for what I consume, and so I find plenty of time to write and study. I am only sixty-two years old, and intend to write a great deal. My only concern is that life may prove too short to enable me to finish all I wish to do."

"What particular literary work have you in contemplation?"

"My future works will be on educational rather than on purely social matters."

"Will you advocate a new system of education, or only suggest improvements in the present methods?"

"The present system is all wrong," replied the Count. "The foundation of the system which I shall advocate will be the purity and perfection of the parents. In the shadow of paternal perfection the boys will attain perfection, and the purity and goodness of the mothers will be transmitted to the girls. This will be the foundation of a better system of rearing and educating children than the world has yet seen. The present system is full of evils. People have become so used to evils that they are no longer capable of distinguishing the evil from the good. Or, if they recognize an evil, they have been used to it so long that they have lost the sense of proportion, and it seems to them less real and grievous than it is. I hope to expose the evils of the present system and to point out the way to a better order of things all round."

I asked the Count when he expected to bring out his first work on education. He could not say, he replied. Possibly it would not appear during his lifetime. All would depend on circumstances. Tolstoy thinks it would be a good thing if every author would pigeon-hole his manuscripts and publish nothing during his life.

"Then," said he, "there would be less printed paper in the world, and people would find time for reading what was really good."

No author, he argued, ought to receive any compensation for his work, either in money or fame. His reward should be the satisfaction of having done, or having tried to do, something for the improvement of his fellows. He has never willingly seen any of his work go to the publishers, but has always yielded to the importunities and wishes of his friends. His "Kreutzer Sonata," he said, was an unfinished work, and was not intended by him to be published in its present form. But his friends took it, and against his better judgment it was given to the world. He was then preparing the epilogue to it that shortly afterward appeared. He was also writing a treatise on intemperance, setting forth his ideas regarding tobacco, alcohol, opium, hashish, rich food, romantic love, and various other indulgences that come under the ban of his creed.

We talked of Siberia, and of the methods of the Russian government. Tolstoy said, "The government is altogether bad. It is a monument of superstition and injustice." As for himself, he went on in the even tenor of his way, doing whatever his conscience approved of, regardless of laws and governments. They usually let him alone, but collisions sometimes occur. The previous winter his eldest daughter had opened a school for the children on the estate. The village pope (priest) sent a memorial to the government asserting that the instruction given in the school was not orthodox. The Governor of Tula, Tolstoy's personal friend, was obliged to come down to Yasnaya Polyana and order the school closed.

The winter was then about over, and the children had to go to work in the fields anyhow, so not much harm was done. His daughter intended to open the school again, however, the following winter, and to reopen it as often as the authorities might close it up.

So, unless they tore it down, stationed a policeman at the door, or exiled the daughter, the school would be carried on.

"The government sins most against the people in the matter of education. None of the concessions it makes are of any value. They are only makeshifts. Schools are in every village, but nothing is taught but nonsensical catechism and the 'three Rs.' Yet, with the government restrictions dragging on the heels of the people, a great improvement had taken place since the emancipation of the serfs. It is now possible for every peasant to learn to read and write. All the people need, to make themselves heard, is a free rein to learn what they choose," continued Tolstoy.

The Count called to him a bright little peasant girl, in a blaze of red clothes.

"Look here," he said, "how intelligent these children are. The moujik children are always brighter than ours, brighter than the children of the rich and noble, up to a certain age. My daughter proved that last winter, and it is a fact well known to all of us. But after ten or twelve years they begin to get dull and fall behind. It's the hard life and the drudgery of toiling in the fields."

We talked of Africa and its people, the Count having heard of my adventures there the year before. He listened with intense interest as I told him that among the uncivilized Africans, as well as the moujiks of Russia, the children were brighter than the grown people.

I intended to send the Count a copy of "Looking Backward" that I had in Moscow. He had already read it. He didn't know whether the government permitted it to circulate in Russia, but he had received a copy through a friend. The story was very well told, he said, but that was all he could say for it.

"To be of value, the book should have shown how the results which are portrayed were to be arrived at. Without that 'Looking Backward' was nothing but a fairy tale. Then, men should live a life as happy and perfect as that which Mr. Bellamy describes, of their own free will and spontaneous goodness, and not require government regulation for all their actions."

Of the governments of the present day Tolstoy thinks the United States government a long way ahead. It is almost a mistake, he said, to call it a "government" at all in the general acceptation of the term. Certainly, it was not to be thought of as a "republic" in the sense that France is a republic. The French government is a "republican form of government" — the people of the United States have a "natural government" — they govern themselves. A people who are simply living under a "republican form of government," because they think it better than any other, may possibly change their minds in time of some great public excitement and think that a king or an emperor would be better after all, but no such change is possible where the government is really and truly a government of the people — "natural government."

We stayed all night, and the next morning the Count and the writer took a long stroll about the estate. On our return three pilgrims were standing outside the house waiting for alms. On the roads of Russia one meets every hour of the summer day little bands of ragged, sunburned men or women, toiling wearily along or sitting down resting by the way. These are people making pilgrimages to Moscow or Kiev, as good Muslims make pilgrimages to Mecca or Medina.

The three specimens who appeared at Tolstoy's were uncouth members of the species; their faces were a dirty yellow, their hair and beards were all over their faces and shoulders, and their garments were a mass of rags and dirt. We came up to them, and the Count stood looking at them for a minute with a smile of admiration. Then, with a sweep of the hand, such as an artist might make toward some long-worshiped masterpiece of art, "I like very much these people," he said.

He ordered a servant to give each of them a coin, and then questioned them. One of the men, he explained, was very well off and owned a large farm near Kiev. The life the pilgrims lead was his ideal of a perfectly happy, peaceful existence. The only lamentable thing about them was their superstition. They were not influenced by correct motives. They believed that there was virtue in visiting the icons at Moscow or Kiev;

whereas the real virtue of their condition was that, in imitation of the Savior, they were not afraid to start out on their long pilgrimages without so much as a single kopeck in their purses. This man, who owned a farm, had actually started out without a piece of money. The Count said he could, with the greatest pleasure, sever all the ties that bound him to his present mode of life and become a pilgrim.

"It is less of a tumble than most people think," he continued, "to descend from wealth to the bottom of the scale. In Switzerland, a boy who was running in the dark fell into a hole. He clutched frantically at the edge with his hands and managed to hang on. For a long time he shouted for help, and bruised and lacerated his hands struggling to keep from falling to the bottom, which he supposed was a terrible distance below. At length a man came and told him to let go. He did as he was bid, and to his astonishment found that the firm, safe bottom of the hole was but a few inches below his feet. It is the same with a rich man. He struggles frantically to keep himself up, thinking the bottom means death or worse. Finally, he is compelled to let go, and, like the Swiss boy, is agreeably surprised to find the change a very small one."

The Count told a story of a young man of good family, whom he had known in the Cadet Corps in St. Petersburg, who once turned up at his house as a pilgrim, as road-worn a specimen as any of the three before us. He had been a pilgrim for a year. After staying with Tolstoy awhile, and tasting the sweets of a comfortable life, he one morning suddenly disappeared, without a kopeck in his pocket, and again became a pilgrim.

In a sense, the Count thinks all travelers are pilgrims; and while the person who travels for pleasure or on business is not to be compared for righteousness to the pilgrim who sets out without purse or scrip, yet all travelers are worthier than stay-at-home people. Their virtues consist in their contempt for a life of ease. With delicate flattery he complimented the writer on being "almost a real pilgrim."

It was hot, sultry weather at Yasnaya Polyana, and rain and thunder and mud among the untrimmed vegetation about the house made a somewhat gloomy framework for the setting of Tolstoy at home. There were snatches of sunshine, however, in the morning prior to our departure, when the avenues and neglected grounds seemed a trifle more cheerful. From the Russian point of view, the Count's estate, probably, was in very good trim.

We sat on the portico talking until eleven o'clock on the day of our arrival, and we wandered about the estate and chatted next morning. Many subjects were touched upon. The Count likes to talk and to draw out the ideas of his visitors and compare them with his own.

I found him predisposed in favor of America, and the fact that I had just come from New York, and represented an American newspaper, was an open sesame to his sympathies and good will.

It requires but a few minutes' social intercourse with him to discover that, like the rest of us, he has his weak points. The Count does not altogether disdain notoriety, though he may not be conscious of it. He seemed to me to possess a fair share of "author's vanity." In spite of the humiliation of the spirit and suppression of human exaltation, which is the chief foundation of his creed, Tolstoy likes Americans, because of the English-speaking world, we were the first to translate, read, and appreciate his productions. The taste for Russian literature was acquired in the United States before it spread to England.

There have been visitors to Yasnaya Polyana who have carried away the uncharitable conviction that the peculiarities of the Count's daily life are theatrical; that he acts an eccentric part. Sometimes, during our conversations, I, too, thought him knowingly affected, but eventually decided that all his peculiarities come from sincere convictions and honest eccentricity of character.

At times, when talking, Tolstoy leaves the visitor momentarily in doubt whether he is not imposing on your credulity and trying to fathom your understanding; but the final impression is that he is sincere. There is a curious mixture in him of a deep knowledge of the world and the innocence and confidence of a child. Nobody would try to practice a deception on him as a man of the world, because he would feel in advance that Tolstoy would be sure to see through it. But by appealing to the benevolent side of his character, it required little penetration to see that the applicant would have him at a great disadvantage.

The young man who acted as a butler at the house, and whom I questioned about his master's habits, told me that the moujiks often imposed on his benevolence and shamefully abused his charity. From all the country round the peasants came to Tolstoy with their woes and grievances, much as the freed negroes of the South used to appeal to the St. Clairs among the former slave owners, after the war. A short time before our visit a moujik come to Tolstoy with a very long face and asserted that his horse had died and that he was unable to cultivate his land. The Count gave him a horse out of his own stables to plow his ground and get in his crops. The moujik, who was a worthless fellow, took the horse away, sold it, and spent the money on vodka. Only recently, too, the overseer of the estate had caught a moujik in the act of cutting down and carting off trees from the Count's forest. He brought the thief to Tolstoy and proposed to take him before the court.

"Let him go, poor fellow," said the author of "Christ's Christianity." "The trees are as much his as mine. I neither planted them nor cut them down."

Neither the timber thief nor the man who swindled him out of the horse was punished. The wonder is that Yasnaya Polyana does not become a nest of worthless vagabonds and that the Tolstoy's estate is not stripped as bare as a desert. The latter possibility would disturb the Count's equanimity little. He would, in fact, utter no word of protest at the spoliation of his property, and only the stand taken by the Countess and the children prevents the family possessions from melting entirely away.

The estate consists of two thousand acres of arable land and forest. Part of it is the old family estate, given to the Count's grandfather, General Tolstoy, by Catherine II, as a reward for military services. The remainder has been acquired chiefly from the literary earnings of the Count. All economic affairs, he leaves entirely in the hands of his wife. He seems scarcely a member of his own family. By residing in a good house and retaining land and property more than sufficient for his bare support, Tolstoy lives in perpetual violation of his own conscience. This state of affairs he submits to for the sake of his family, who are only partially in sympathy with his creed.

He believes not only that he has no right to the estate, but that it would be an act of pride and presumption to take upon him even the right to divide it up and give it away. "How can one have the presumption to give away what doesn't belong to him?"

In the matter of land-ownership, Tolstoy's declared himself a great admirer of the theories of Henry George. He declared George the greatest American citizen of the present time. He believed, however, in a system of communal, rather than a national, ownership of the land. The ideal state of society would be, to him, the simple, rural communes, in which every family would have the right to till soil enough for its own support. There would be no taxes and no government. The count believed that all forms of government are humbugs, and that the whole machinery of law and lawyers, courts and judges, is a barbarity, and an excuse for setting one man above another, and enabling the privileged to rob the many.

Russian governments he regards as the root of nearly all evils.

Tax collectors he considers highwaymen, who are able to rob people without bloodshed, simply because the tax-payers know that it would be useless to resist the powerful organization of which they are members. He was looking forward to a day when men would see through the fiction of government and would no longer consent to be robbed of money, nor to be instructed in the art of murdering one another in war.

He admires America because we have only a handful of soldiers, and the bitterness of his soul went out to the armed camps of which Berlin and Paris are the centers. In his younger days the Count was an officer and saw service in the Crimean war; but since his conversion the earth contains for him no more monstrous thing than a body of men drilling and practicing every day to perfect themselves in the art of killing the largest number of their brothers in the shortest possible time.

The accumulation of vast possessions by individuals the Count regards as one of the great evils that people have become so accustomed to seeing that they deem the wrong far less than it really is. He believed, however, that the mission of the large American millionaires would be to hasten the climax, when the eyes of the people will be opened by the display of tremendous contrasts. The moral consciousness of the people needs a rude awakening, he thought, and only the development of abnormal contrasts in wealth and poverty is likely to bring the people to consider seriously the equal rights of all. Just as the undue development of the military will one day result in general disarmament, so, he believes, will the vast accumulations of the few and the poverty of the many open the people's eyes to the fact that banks and government treasuries are robber's caves, in which is hoarded the money that has been taken from the people.

The Count, however, didn't think the equalization of property will be brought about by violence, but by a general moral awakening. Millionaires will become convinced that they have no right to the property that they now regard as their own, and will give it up; just as he would be willing to move off the family estate at Yasnaya Polyana.

America, he thought, will one day set the example. England will follow; then Russia. The thinkers of Russia, he said, are already seriously studying the problem of doing away with the private ownership of land.

One could not talk with Tolstoy for any length of time without the subject of religion coming to the fore. Only foolish people, he said, trouble their heads about whether there is or is not a personal God; or whether Christ was or was not more than human.

People are mistaken in doing well here in the hope of future reward. This is the essence of selfishness. It prostitutes the best in humanity to the level of commerce. There is no merit in making a bargain by which you are to receive a ruble some time in the future in return for giving a poorer brother a kopeck or a crust of bread today. This is not charity, but usury pure and simple. In Russia the best Christians are those who never go to church. Priests, ministers, and churches the Count holds in scant esteem. The priests he considered as part and parcel of the governmental machinery for grinding the faces of the poor and living without work. To swing a censer and chant senseless masses is, in his opinion, stage-acting. The time wasted on this buffoonery, if devoted to planting and digging potatoes would suffice them to earn their bread, and then there would be no need of preying on the ignorant and the superstitious.

Preachers should talk less about the future state and devote themselves, firstly, to earning their own livelihood by growing grain and vegetables, and, secondly, to bringing about the kingdom of heaven on earth. The Count had no patience with sectarianism, nor with preachers who are sticklers for certain forms of administering baptism or the sacrament. The spirit of hostility that brings ministers of the gospel on to the debating platform, he said, is not the spirit of Christ, but of Satan. Preachers and religious teachers should devote their energies to the work of compromising and the bridging of differences rather than disputing.

The world has more need of living examples than of weekly sermons. If all the preachers in the world would quit their fine houses, refuse their salaries, and take to sowing and reaping, and preaching everyday sermons of Christ-like lives, they would do more good in a week than they do now in a lifetime. According to the Count, a minister of the gospel who accepts a salary and lives off it, is a robber. The only difference between him and a footpad is that, whereas the latter knocks you down and rifles your pockets, the minister gets at the pockets of honest people by a more ingenious, if less violent, process. In both cases the results are the same: both minister and footpad eat food that they never produced and which, consequently, cannot possibly be theirs by right. Such is the Count's creed.

I found Tolstoy a vegetarian, and convinced that the ideal physical life is that of the Brahmins of India. He believed in reducing one's wants to a minimum, and in producing, so far as possible, with one's own hands the wherewithal both to feed and clothe the body. A state of society in which the condition of one would never be such as to excite envy in another is the secret of true social happiness. In Russia, the pilgrims who roam the country over, depending for their support from day to day on the alms of the people, approach this ideal, and Tolstoy would, so I inferred from his remarks, become a pilgrim himself were it not for the restraints of family ties and considerations.

When he took me into his little koumiss establishment to give me a drink of the beverage, he said with enthusiasm, that with an acre of grass land and a couple of milch mares, a man would possess ample property for his support. The mares would live off the grass and the man could milk them and live off koumiss.

Temperance finds in the great novelist an enthusiastic supporter. He neither drinks intoxicating beverages nor smokes, and he includes in the term many other indulgences that the ordinary advocates of temperance consider apart from their creed.

In his creed romantic love is also intemperance.

The tender passion that has from all time been the theme of the poet and the novelist, Tolstoy deems a species of moral depravity, on a par with gluttony, the smoking of opium, or indulgence in strong drink. A person finding himself, or herself, in love, particularly before marriage, should fight against it as against the opium habit or any other pernicious thing.

Theater-going, dancing, romantic literature of all kinds, anything, in short, that excites the imagination to thoughts of love, is intemperance. Cupid is the devil in his most artful guise.

In speaking of the relations of the sexes, Tolstoy talked with the same freedom from restraint as if he talked of digging potatoes or mowing hay.

The Countess and her sister from St. Petersburg sat at the other end of the table on one occasion, when the Count was particularly inquisitive about the natives of East Africa. To an ordinary mortal the situation would have been embarrassing in the extreme. The ladies, however, were busy chatting together, and their ears, of course, were closed to anything the Count or I might have said.

Tolstoy was deeply interested in the social life of the Masai and requested that a copy of "Scouting for Stanley in East Africa" might be sent him.

His interest in the relations of the sexes seemed to me to be abnormal, almost morbid. Men and women, he insists, should love one another only as friends or as brothers and sisters. Matrimony brought about by romantic love is an unholy and unnatural alliance, that in nine cases out of ten resulted in unhappiness for both parties to the contract.

The keynote of the Count's peculiar creed is "no violence." If cuffed on one cheek, he would turn the other. No matter what another person may be doing, the utmost force that is permitted to be used against him is passive resistance or persuasion.

"If a man robs you, who are you that sets yourself up to judge him whether he is in the right or the wrong? One man has no right to judge another, nor to assume the office of executioner by using violence against him. If a man knocks you down, who knows but you have deserved it?

"One person has no right to use violence against another under any circumstances whatever, not even to oppose violence. There must be no self-defense beyond passive resistance. To subdue the passions and gain the upper hand of our human pride is man's first duty to himself and to his fellows. After that, all the rest will come easy enough."

After listening to such talk the Count's advice to keep away from the churches sounded oddly.

An American minister from New York once visited Tolstoy at Yasnaya Polyana. Did I know him? I did not; and although Tolstoy spoke with every mark of respect for his visitor as a man, he let it be very plainly understood that the less the rising generation had to do with the modern expounders of the gospels the better for their comprehension of the true religion as he conceives it.

Previous to his conversion the Count had been an atheist. About ten years before there was a census of Russia. It is the custom of the government to impress the students of the universities to assist in taking a census. Tolstoy's eldest son was then a student in Moscow, and the father accompanied the son in going his rounds to number the people.

The task took them into some of the Moscow slums. The scenes of squalid poverty and wretchedness that the Count was then brought in contact with was the turning point in his career. For fifty years he had lived a life of selfish ease and pleasure. He had been through the whole mill of gay, fashionable existence. As a youth, he had been dissipated; as a man, well-to-do and successful. The world had been to him a pleasure-ground, and the future a subject of philosophical speculation.

He went home a changed man. It seemed as if all his life had been utterly wasted. The selfishness of a life that had been largely devoted to pleasure and self-seeking now seemed to him an enormity of error and wrong. How should he expiate the great crime of fifty years of wrong-doing?

He sought consolation in the existing forms of religion. He said he found them worse than honest atheism. He turned to the Scriptures and independent research and harkened to the teachings of Surtaev, a free-thinking peasant of Novgorod, who had been persecuted by the priests for independent action in the matter of baptizing his children. He drew inspiration from the child-like simplicity of the peasantry on his estate. He brought to bear on his observations and researches the mind of a cultured man and the intellect of a genius. The result has been the teachings that the world now recognizes as the Tolstoyan creed. After he had become convinced that salvation lay in living a Christian life in a truly unselfish sense, the Count was for getting rid of his property forthwith by distributing it among the peasantry. His plan was to descend at once to the level of the poorest of those about him, and earn his living with the plow and the hoe. That this was not done was due entirely to the Countess and friends of the family.

Such, then, was the apostle of this new religion, or, as he would say, of the Christian religion rightly interpreted, at home. Practical people in America would find in many of his ideas the vagaries of an ill-balanced but brilliant intellect.

Genius-like, he was not always logical and consistent. In discussing the merits of Bellamy's "Looking Backward," he condemned the author's judgment in presuming that such a state of society as he describes would be possible with human beings, possessed with the weaknesses and frailties of our kind. Only angels, he said, could exist under such conditions. Yet in the case of these same human beings, with the same weaknesses and frailties that would be the stumbling block in Bellamy's new social world, he advocated "no government, no police, no prisons, no army, no church, no judiciary, no punishment for wrong doing."

The Count's ideas of what is best were still in a state of development. A couple of years before my visit Mr. Stead, of the "Review of Reviews," paid him a visit. At that time he told Stead that he regretted every moment that "he did not feel he was dying." He longed to have done with this world and to fathom the mystery of the next. Tolstoy told me his only fear was not to live long enough to finish all the work he wanted to do.

The wife of Tolstoy is a buxom lady, who looked about forty. She has a broad, matronly figure; a kind, motherly face, and was the daughter of a St. Petersburg physician. She is the mother of thirteen children, of whom nine were living. The eldest daughter and the two youngest children were at home. The others were traveling or away visiting, and the eldest son was officiating as Secretary on a Commission at the Prison Congress, which was then sitting in St. Petersburg. He had just written a letter to his mother, expressing disgust at the round of speeches and dinners that appeared to him to be the only probable outcome of the Congress.

The Countess acted as her husband's amanuensis and copyist. She copied and corrected all of his manuscripts. She seemed to be a most excellent woman. The family life appeared to be altogether charming. Both wife and children fairly idolize the Count. The nieces also think their uncle the embodiment of wisdom and goodness, and the only point on which they openly take issue with him is, naturally enough, on the subject of romantic love as denounced in the "Kreutzer Sonata."

These young people do not always fathom the Count, but they never doubt the wisdom of his actions or the goodness of his motives. Everything he does is right. If you venture to criticize anything the Count has said or done, in their hearing, they defend him stoutly.

We stayed to lunch at twelve, then rode away. In the house of strict temperance, where the master lives on curds and kumiss, cutlets and a bottle of wine were set out for the visitors. We ate the cutlets but left the wine untouched.

"I thank you very much for coming," said the Count, as he shook hands and advised us to be careful of our horses.

"I wish you a pleasant journey to the Crimea," said the Countess, "and a safe return to America."

Russia is a country where fantastic religious ideas seem to find a congenial soil. The dwarfing of the people's intellects in matters political, is productive of curious expansions in other directions. Between Moscow and Tula I stumbled upon a truly queer religious idea. None but a logical mind could, however, have conceived it. It is intended chiefly to comfort and console people of a doubting and skeptical turn of mind. People who are so unfortunately constituted that they don't know whether or not to believe in the existence of a personal God, and are forever casting about for light on the subject, are instructed by the new religion to "pray to the power that is responsible for their existence." By adopting this broad ground, all fears of missing the mark, so to speak, are done away with, and none need be afraid of going astray through ignorance or misconception.

# 4

# A Visit to Tolstoy
## by James Creelman

James Creelman (12 Nov. 1859–12 Feb. 1915), a journalist, was born in Montreal, Canada. Beginning in 1876, he worked for *The New York Herald* and interviewed such people as Pope Leo XIII, Louis Kossuth, and Leo Tolstoy. In 1893, Creelman left the *Herald* and worked briefly for *Illustrated American* and *Cosmopolitan* magazines, attempting unsuccessfully to establish a London edition for the latter publication.

Creelman was hired in 1894 by Joseph Pulitzer's *New York World*. He specialized in feature interview-profiles of individuals as diverse as Edison, Roosevelt, Taft and President Diaz of Mexico. Later he was the Associate Editor of the *New York Evening Mail*. Creelman's relationship with his employers Pulitzer and Hearst was, at times, stormy but each found him very valuable as a writer.

Creelman, James. "A Visit to Tolstoy." *Harper's Weekly*. 36 (1892): 380.

I am pleasantly reminded of a great personality and a red-letter date in my life when I look upon the picture of the Count Leo Tolstoy in his work-room. The portrait from which his engraving has been made is one of several which Repin, the most distinguished of modern Russian painters, has executed in recent years of his illustrious countryman. But it stands apart from all the others in that it is not only a portrait, but a living, glowing presentment of Tolstoy, as he lives today, and as I have personally seen him in the seclusion of his chamber, simple almost as a monastic cell, through which the mystic lights and shadows play fitfully around the central figure of the giant of the Russian letters.

Yasnaya Polyana, where Repin painted this picture, is a rural retreat to which Tolstoy retired when he closed up his house in Moscow and quit the busy world. Formerly it had been his occasional resting place which he often sought when he wearied of the turmoil of the great city. Now it has become his permanent residence, and he intends to remain there until he dies.

Yasnaya Polyana is a little village set on a plain at the edge of a dense forest. It consists of a few thatched huts fronting on a single rude street. There are about three hundred persons in all the community. It is one of those little republics from which the great mother Russia is made up, and which are governed by the Mir, or a village council. It has no politics, and the Tsar is a distant and vague personality.

[...] The simple two-storied white wooden building in which Count Tolstoy lives is a kind of a manor house for a semi-civilized little community. A veranda runs around the lower story, and a few hundred feet away stands a horse stable which shelters a few horses. The farm attached to the dwelling is neither elaborate nor a valuable possession.

The visitor, on entering the house, finds himself in a rude, bare, uncarpeted apartment, on whose walls hang a few trophies of the chase indicating the count's skill as a hunter. There are skins of various animals, and beside them is Tolstoy's rifle. The walls are stained by time and usage, and from pegs are suspended half a dozen overcoats and caps, beneath which is a row of great boots of felt and leather.

The visitor is welcome to the temporary use of any of these articles. From here a small door leads to an uncarpeted chamber where the walls are lined with the book-laden shelves, whose tenants are brown dusty volumes, showing signs of frequent use. This library is selected with a catholic taste and contains the works of every philosopher from Plato to Henry George. At the end of the room there is a little iron bed, and wash-stand, and it was here that I slept during my visit. By the window there is a table on which is always set a bottle of ink and a pen. None other than an intense literary worker could live in such a place.

Beyond this bed-chamber is the count's work-room, with a collection of shoes in all stages of making and unmaking accompanied by scraps of paper scribbled with notes littering the floor.

This is the place where he works and talks for hours, and almost every object in sight is some implement of honest sturdy toil. The count seldom spends less than four hours a day in his room, invariably sitting in the attitude shown in the picture — with one leg drawn under him.

Upon rising in the morning he goes out for a long walk, having first taken a drink of tea from the samovar upstairs which is always filled with fragrant liquid. When Tolstoy walks, he does so with the stride which for its length and rapidity is something wonderful, and this fact was forcibly impressed upon me during the tramp I had with him across the fields. He usually walks a distance of three to four miles. On his return he has breakfast always consisting of a vegetable diet, for he regards the slaughter of dumb creatures as a senseless and cruel thing. I asked him once if he did not consider the practice of felling trees in which he himself occasionally indulges as a destruction of life, but he replied that plants represented the least sensitive form of animation, and further that there was some use in felling trees but none in killing animals. Tolstoy neither drinks spirits not uses tobacco, but for his guests he always provides both meat and wine.

Passing upstairs from the outer room already described, the visitor finds himself in the dining room, or general hall. There is absolutely no furniture in this chamber except a long table which is always spread, a few chairs, a piano and a writing-table. Some portraits of the illustrious ancestors of the Tolstoy family are on the walls. The floor is uncarpeted, and there is nothing to soften or relieve the savage scantiness of the surroundings. In this apartment, the count receives upon an equal footing prince and pauper, politician, poet, painter and exile. No distinctions of any kind are made, and the greatest noble in Russia will find himself sitting at the same board with one of the count's farm laborers. Countess Tolstoy does all her knitting here — a pursuit which occupies much of her time in conjunction of preparation of clothing for the poor, in which charitable task she is assisted by her daughter. The little boys in the family make their playground in the room, which is also the ante-chamber to the sleeping apartments of the countess and other members of the household. Everything about this establishment is simple and plain to the last degree. Life is truly real and earnest here, and when I asked the count if he thought it well for his family to live so completely apart from the intercourse with the centers of civilization, he replied,

"I do not believe in moving about much. Better to stay in one spot, for roving is a mistake. A man may study and learn from his fellow-men, and live a life of truth and love anywhere; the humbler his surroundings, the better."

Russia has been blessed in the possession of the Tolstoy family — a fact that has come home to her with peculiar force very recently in the presence of the famine disaster. When the cry of distress arose, a responsive echo of sympathy sounded from the quiet home of the Yasnaya Polyana, and not only the great recluse himself, but his self-sacrificing wife, daughter and sons set forth without an instant's hesitation to labor amid the suffering peasants in the sweet cause of charity.

From what I personally witnessed during my visit to the Tolstoys, I can form some idea of their work in the famine centers. During a walk through the village, which I was privileged to enjoy with the great writer's daughter, I had an excellent opportunity of observing the relations maintained by his family with the villagers. Everywhere we went, whether along the highway, or in the interiors of the humble houses, were evident the signs of love and veneration. Not a moujik we met but would raise his hat with an intense respect, and mumble a simple benediction on my companion; and when we entered a cottage where anybody was sick, she would tenderly inquire of the patient, either offer assistance on the spot, or arrange for its speedy arrival, and on every instance was called a good angel. The deeds of this noble family long after they have passed away will smell sweet, remaining a precious memory to every Russian heart.

# 5

# How Count Tolstoy Writes
## by Charles Johnston

Charles Johnston (1867–?), an Irish journalist and writer, was president of the Irish Literary Society. He visited many countries, among them India, the United States, and Russia, where he met with Tolstoy.

Johnston, Charles. "How Count Tolstoy Writes." *The Arena*. (Boston) vol. 21 (1899): 269–272.

How does Count Tolstoy work? "The Russian Weekly" gives an answer full of interesting detail, as it sheds a rather amusing side-light on the famous novelist's massive and earnest, if somewhat eccentric character, and at the same time lets us in some degree into the secret of a man who is certainly one of the greatest living writers, perhaps the greatest; a leader certainly of the strongest school of novelists in the world. Stories of Count Tolstoy too often show him in a cold light, dictatorial, full of fault-finding, and bitter zeal; it is a real pleasure to come upon something personal, which has quite another tone, showing in him a child-like eagerness, a certain self-distrust, and a fine enthusiasm for his work.

In his technical method, says the Russian writer, whose words I translate, Count Tolstoy is like one of the great painters of old. After forming the plan of his work, and gathering a great number of studies, he begins with a charcoal sketch, so to speak, and writes rapidly, not thinking of details. What he writes in this way he gives to Countess Sophia Andreevna to copy out, or to one of his daughters, or to one of his intimate friends, to whom this task may give pleasure. Lev Nikolaevich, Count Tolstoy, generally writes on quarto paper, of rather poor quality, in a big, rope-like handwriting, writing about twenty pages a day, accounting to some four or five thousand words. He has no special habits with regard to pens and paper. And when a firm in Moscow conceived the idea of giving to the world a "Tolstoyan pen," it was discovered that on the subject of pens Count Tolstoy had no opinion. He works mostly in the morning, and considers this the best time of the day for work.

When the clean copy of his manuscript makes its appearance on the writing table, Count Tolstoy begins at once to work it all over again. But it still remains very much of a charcoal sketch. The manuscript is quickly dotted over with corrections, alterations, interlinear additions; at both sides, above and below, appear new words and phrases, with inversions of sentences from one page to another. The whole is copied out again, and once more subjected to exactly the same process. On the third time exactly the same thing happens. Some chapters Count Tolstoy has written more than ten times. [...]

When he has once armed himself for writing, with reminiscences or observations, or with new views on the subject he is treating, Count Tolstoy works steadily and persistently at every chapter, only making short breaks for rest; and when he is in difficulties, taking refuge in a game of solitaire, until he sees his way clear. The intent search after the inner being of every hero he represents, forms at this stage Count Tolstoy's chief task, and his favorite expression on this subject is: "Gold is found by persistent sifting and washing."

It is only an occasional scene that Count Tolstoy succeeds in perfecting at first blush, under a vivid impression. In this way was written the race scene in "Anna Karenina," under the impression of a very graphic and exciting description by Prince N.

After this repeated copying and correcting, certain details come out ever clearer and clearer, while others are gradually obscured and dimmed.

After reaching a certain clearness by persistent work, Count Tolstoy reads his new production to a circle of his intimate friends, in order to profit by their impressions, while the work is still imprinted. After finishing "The Powers of Darkness," he read the play to the peasants, but received few guiding impressions from this reading. At the most affecting places in the drama, which Lev Nikolaevich himself cannot read without tears, some of his peasant listeners began to laugh, and chilled the writer completely.

The severest critic of Count Tolstoy's new work is generally Countess Sophia Andreyevna, who, with characteristic directness, expresses her opinion. Without the slightest softening Count Tolstoy sometimes agrees with her, and sometimes sticks firmly to his own opinion.

The moment word goes abroad that Count Tolstoy has finished a new work, admirers of his talent, of both sexes, begin to flutter over the horizon, with requests that he should hand over his work to them to supervise, in consequence of special knowledge. He generally accedes to these requests, in order to profit by the criticism of the specialist.

But his labor on the new work by no means ends here. There is still the proof correction, which generally calls forth in Count Tolstoy a flood of extraordinary activity. While the work is in the hands of the printers, many things occur, many new impressions are received, which light up some side of the matter he is dealing with, from a new point of view. At the same time, the space for corrections is limited, and there is little time to make them in. And so, checking the flow of his new thoughts, and economizing every proof as far as possible, Count Tolstoy turns the sheets into a regular net-work of inky marks. Exactly the same thing happens with the second proof, and it may be said without the slightest exaggeration that if ninety and nine proofs of one of his works were submitted to him, the same thing would happen nine and ninety times. In this he seems to labor under the same difficulty that made Balzac the despair of his printers, for he runs up bills for changes on proofs that often entirely consume his share of the profits.

In general, a critical attitude towards his own work is very strongly developed in him, and the day after writing he can clearly see his mistakes. But in correcting his proofs, his clairvoyance comes out even more strongly, and some chapters issue from the process changed to the point of unrecognizability.

Once when there was a discussion as to strenuous work on artistic productions, Count Tolstoy said:

"You should not neglect the slightest detail in art; because sometimes some half-torn-off button may light up a whole side of the character of a given person; and that button must be faithfully represented. But all efforts, including the half-torn-off button, must be directed exclusively to the inner reality, and must by no means draw away attention from what is of first importance to details and secondary facts. One of our contemporary novelists, in describing the history of Joseph and the wife, would certainly not miss the chance to exhibit his knowledge of life, and would write: 'Come to me!' murmured she, in a languishing voice, stretching out her arm, soft with aromatic unguents, on which shone a bracelet decorated, and so on, and so on, and these details not only would not light up the heart of the matter more clearly, but would certainly obscure it."

Flushing, Long Island, N.Y.

# 6

# An Interview with Count Tolstoy
## by Edward Steiner

Steiner, Edward. "An Interview with Count Tolstoy." *The Outlook* (New York) vol. 66 (1900): 828–835.

On the main plaza in Tula, the Russian Sheffield, stand hundreds of Russian laborers with saw or pickax, mason's or locksmith's tools, waiting for a chance to earn their daily bread. I stepped among these men, who live but some ten miles from Count Tolstoy's residence at Yasnaya Polyana, and asked one after the other if he knew Count Tolstoy and what he knew about him. One said,

"Yes; I saw him walking in Tula many a time. He is a nice old man. They say he writes books, but I have never read any of them, and I do not know what they are about."

Another, who scarcely knew his name, was very much astonished when I told him that I came from America to visit this man whose name had gone all over the world. Another threw up his hands in astonishment when I told him that Count Tolstoy lives the life of a poor man, though he might be rich, and that he could earn countless rubles by his pen, but that instead, he prefers to let his books go out into the world without money and without price.

The advice one receives in Tula as to the best way to reach Count

Tolstoy's home, varies with the persons you ask about him. The police will tell you that you must not go at all; the hack-drivers will tell you that it is an endless distance out in the country.

The best way to go is to take the train to Yasnaya, where dozens of drivers are ready to take you to Yasnaya Polyana and who instinctively know that you are an American and that you wish to see the Count.

The residence of the Count lies at the foot of the village, buried within the park where giant oaks hide it completely.

I hardly had jumped from my cart when the Count, surrounded by his family, appeared, and after a hearty greeting, asked me immediately to accompany him upon his evening walk. I gladly agreed, and side by side we walked through the park....

The Count seemed thoroughly acquainted with our social conditions in America. How thoroughly acquainted with us he is, is proved by the fact that he knows of Mayor Jones, of Toledo, and his platform, that he has followed the development of the single-tax idea, and, strangest of all, understands the political platforms of both great parties and is acquainted with the personalities of the leaders. He asked me a torrent of questions in regards to everything of importance in America, and I wondered all the time who was the interviewed and who was the interviewer.

"You had a wonderful pleiad in literature," said the Count. "What wonderful men they were! Emerson, whom I love and whom I owe very much, Lowell and Whittier, Theodore Parker, Thoreau and Longfellow. Now," he said, "whom have you? Nothing and nobody. I have sent to you your magazines. They are beautiful picture-books, but they are not literature. Oh yes, there is Howells, and then I suppose there are others whom I do not know."

... There is nothing false, nothing assumed about him, whether you meet him as an author, count, or farmer.

Asking him for a message for his many friends in the States, he said, somewhat reluctantly,

"Tell them to be true, to be loving, to be simple," and that, I believe, is the message of Tolstoy to the world.

# 7

# Home Life of Tolstoy: How Tolstoy and Tolstoy's Wife Wrote Novels

*by John Holmes*

John Holmes was an American journalist and literary critic popular at the beginning of the 20th century. He visited Tolstoy in the 1890s.

Holmes, John. "Home Life of Tolstoy." *Current Literature* (New York) vol. 29 (1900): 149.

"Anna Karenina" is empty stuff. It is tedious and vulgar. What Philistine dared to make such criticisms of a masterpiece of realistic fiction? Why, one Count Leo Tolstoy, who had rather intimate knowledge of the novel in question. He expressed these opinions while he was at work on the book, and after it was completed, according to the reminiscences contributed by his son, Count Ilya Tolstoy, to "The Century Magazine," he said much harder things about it.

Count Ilya's unconventional reminiscences of his illustrious father show that the wife of the great Russian novelist was an industrious and longsuffering person. Some English, and American Tolstoyans are wont to consider their idol a sort of domestic martyr who, dressed in a peasant's garb, did a peasant's hard toil while his family lived in luxurious ease.

It is true that he wore the dress of a peasant, but if there was a martyr in the family it was his wife.

Her work, Count Ilya tells us, seemed much harder than her husband's because she was actually seen at it by the family and because she worked much longer hours than he did.

She spent whole evenings revising his manuscripts and frequently sat up late at night after every one else had gone to bed.

Tolstoy's handwriting, we learn, was very illegible and he had the habit which his son calls "terrible" of writing in whole sentences between the lines, or in the corners of the page, or sometimes right across it. When anything was beyond the Countess's powers to interpret, she would take it to her husband's study and ask him what it meant. He would take the manuscript in his hand and ask, with some annoyance, his son says, "What on earth is the difficulty?" and would begin to read it aloud. When he came to the difficult place he would mumble and hesitate and sometimes had the greatest difficulty in making out, or, rather, in guessing, what he had written. Often, we are told, his wife discovered and corrected gross grammatical errors.

Here is a picture of domesticity that should warn women of the peril of marrying philosophical anarchists:

"When 'Anna Karenina' began to come out in the 'Russky Vestnik,' long galley proofs were posted to my father, and he looked them through and corrected them.

"At first the margins would be marked with the ordinary typographical signs, letters omitted, marks of punctuation, etc.; then individual words would be changed, and then whole sentences, till in the end the proof-sheet would be reduced to a mass of patches quite black in places, and it was quite impossible to send it back as it stood; because no one but my mother could make head or tail of the tangle of conventional signs, transpositions, and erasures.

"My mother would sit up all night copying the whole thing out afresh.

"In the morning there would lie the pages on her table, neatly piled together, covered all over with her fine, clear handwriting, and everything ready so that when Lev, or Lyovotchka got up he could send the proof-sheets off by post.

"My father carried them off to his study to have 'just one last look,' and by the evening it would be just as bad again, the whole thing having been rewritten and messed up.

"'Sonya, my dear, I am very sorry, but I've spoiled all your work again; I promise I won't do it any more,' he would say, showing her the passages he had inked over with a guilty air. We'll send them off to-morrow without fail.' But this to-morrow was often put off day by day for weeks or months together.

"'There's just one bit I want to look through again,' my father would say; but he would get carried away and recast the whole thing afresh.

"There were even occasions when, after posting the proofs, he would remember some particular words next day, and correct them by telegraph: Several times, in consequence of these rewritings, the printing of the novel in the 'Russky Vestnik' [Russian Messenger] was interrupted, and sometimes it did not come out for months together."

And yet, after all this labor, "Anna Karenina" was not satisfactory to its author. "What difficulty is there in writing about how an officer fell in love with a married woman?" he said. "There's no difficulty in it, and above all, no good in it." And his son adds: "I am quite convinced that if my father could have done so, he long ago would have destroyed the novel, which he never liked and always wanted to destroy."

But the Countess Tolstoy was more than a hard-working amanuensis; she was also a housewife of the type that New England somewhat arrogantly claims for its own and she took excellent care of her six children and that seventh child, her husband. Her son cherishes her memory and gives an attractive picture of the energetic, affectionate Russian woman, directing the cook, making clothing, educating her boys and girls, revising manuscript; generally with a baby at her breast. Tolstoy was not an easy husband to feed, it seems. Count Ilya tells one story that is especially significant. There was jelly for dessert one day, and the author of "War and Peace" was not pleased. "All jelly is good for," he said in humorous indignation, "is to glue paper boxes." So the children ran off to get some paper and their father made it into boxes with the aid of the despised jelly. We are not surprised to learn that "Mama was angry."

# 8

# A Visit to Tolstoy
## by John Coleman Kenworthy

John Coleman Kenworthy wrote *Tolstoy: His Life and Works* (1910), one of the first studies of Tolstoy which assesses his novels, renders several personal impressions and dwells on the novelist's relationships with the British and American writers.

Kenworthy, John Coleman. "A Visit to Tolstoy." *The Humane Review* vol. 1 (1900): 262–267.

Before starting on my journey through famine-stricken Russia I had an interview at Moscow with Count Tolstoy, and received from that high-souled man some valuable suggestions as to the conduct of my inquiry. It was only fitting that on my return I should seek out the Count, and tell him what I had seen and heard since I parted from him.

The Count had left Moscow to resume his work of relief in the province of Ryazan, and was at a village of Petrovka, in the district of N., situated at a distance of about eighty versts from the railway.

I was glad to accept the hospitality of Count Bobrinsky, as the weather was very inclement.

A terrible snowstorm raged all day after my arrival at the Count's chateau. The chateau bell was kept ringing. Nevertheless two wayfarers were discovered next morning frozen to death in the snow not far from the house.

Snow was still falling upon the morrow; but, as the weather showed some signs of clearing, I proceeded on my journey in a sledge drawn by two good horses, kindly provided by my host, and driven by a "yamschik" [driver] who knew the road.

It would take too much space, and be foreign to the purpose of this article, to detail the incidents of this journey. I will merely say that to me, used to the sledge traveling, the journey was an exciting and exhausting one.

Several times my driver lost his way, and once we had to stop in a village and take refuge. The latter portion of the journey lay over the upper portion of the ice on the river Don. We were speeding towards the ice to the count's headquarters.

I was received by the Countess Maria (the count's younger) daughter who, to my considerable disappointment, told me that her father was not at home.

Noticing that the Countess and the other ladies of the house betrayed some excitement on my arrival, I inquired the reason.

"The approach of the sledge," explained the countess, "always excites us. Every minute we fear that gendarmes may come to take away our father."

"They would hardly do that," I replied, trying to reassure her. It was impossible, however, for me not to recognize that the apprehensions expressed for the count's safety were by no means groundless. The enemies of the inoffensive count are many, and it is not their fault that his liberties have not already been seriously curtailed. By persistently and maliciously misrepresenting his actions and words, they do their best to stir up public opinion against him.

It appeared from what the countess said that an incorrect translation of the article which her father contributed a month or two before in the "Daily Telegraph" on the social condition of the people, had been published in the "Moscow Gazette," which made it appear that the count had incited the peasantry to revolt, and had in this way brought the Count into bad odor with the Government.

I had previously heard about this article of Tolstoy's. A week before, when I arrived in Samara from Petrovka, I found that the townsfolk were discussing it with some vehemence and excitement. The prevailing opinion appeared to be that the author of the article was mad, and ought to be shut up in a lunatic asylum.

A "tchinovnik's" [officer's] wife exclaimed in my hearing, "He is throwing knives to the people to cut our throats with! He ought to be sent to Siberia, for he is stirring up the people!"

To this an old Samara friend of mine, who has been exerting himself to the utmost on behalf of the peasantry, replied, "Well, if they did cut my throat it would not surprise me, although I have helped them as well as I could. They are unable to distinguish friends from enemies."

Thereupon an official of high rank who over the conversation said, with a frankness which I did not find in one of his class, "I believe that every word Count Tolstoy has written is perfectly true; nevertheless, he has no right to let the common people know the truth."

After my conversation with the Countess Maria I went for a stroll round the house. The dwelling had been the abode of one of Count Tolstoy's most intimate friends, the recently deceased M.N. Raevsky, the first Russian gentleman to start "free tables" for the starving peasantry, and the first, I believe, to lose his life through his efforts to relieve the prevailing distress. He died, I understand, from a fever caught while visiting a starving family. His house is a large and rambling one-storied structure, with an iron-sheeted roof and a balcony in front, and is pleasantly situated on the high banks of the Don. Its appearance in summer would probably be considered picturesque, but at the time of my visit it was not very attractive. Internally, the house was in a state of disrepair; externally, a thaw having set in, it was surrounded by water. At the moment of writing, when the roads all over the country are breaking up, the approach to it must be of a very uninviting character.

The library of the house was interesting, as it showed that its late occupant had been a man of some culture. Amongst M. Raevsky's books I observed a volume of Shakespeare, an old English edition of Virgil of date 1677, "The English Kingdom in Asia," and various works on agriculture and mathematics. Around the walls were hung family portraits.

In the afternoon I had another drive with the Cossack maiden. She had come from Moscow, but was a typical South Russian, being stoutly built, rosy-cheeked, and as brown as a berry.

Nevertheless, she was thoroughly at home with the Riazan peasants. She would have been welcome anywhere, for she was one lump of good-nature.

Tolstoy she worshipped, and would discuss with his daughter his ideas for an hour at a time.

The count did not return at all on the day of my arrival. I discovered, however, that although he personally was absent, he had left behind him in the person of my hostess an excellent representative. Tolstoy's daughter was in fact a small replica of him. To talk with her was to talk by proxy with him. Nor did she merely repeat his ideas; she closely resembled him also in her appearance and disposition. We got on to the subject of music, and she was not long in stating her agreement with the views expressed by her father on that topic in the "Kreutzer Sonata." The tendency of music and singing was, she held, to promote immorality. The net effect on the mind was an evil one. Operas were not good things. We should be better without them.

I could not but express some dissent.

Our conversation on this subject was interrupted by the arrival of the post. The young Countess acts as her father's secretary and opens all of his letters. In the letters that came that night were drafts to the value of $3,000 [to support the peasants in the Russian hunger-stricken districts], two-thirds of this sum had been sent by his English and American friends, and the remainder by Tolstoy's Russian admirers. Every week, the Countess told me, the post brought in as much, sometimes more — a remarkable proof, I thought, of the esteem in which the Count is held. [...]

It was not until the next afternoon that the Count made his appearance.

The count was most cordial in greeting me.

"Is it possible, dear sir," he queried, "that you saw peasants of the Samara province dying of starvation? When I was a young man, I used to go and sleep in houses which were said to be haunted; but I never saw a ghost. Nor have I, as yet, seen a man in this district die of hunger; and yet my friends in many villages of the province of Samara are dying of starvation! Such a spectacle I can hardly think possible in Russia. I cannot think that the Russian muzhik is so hard-hearted as not to help a dying comrade. Besides, every village boasts some wealthy peasants, and these would be ready to help their poor brethren, and to prevent such a state of things coming about."

Count Tolstoy in these skeptical remarks did not in the least surprise me. It is still to the majority of Russians an incomprehensible thing that, in Russia, the country which supplies the greater part of Europe with grain, a single person should die of starvation. Such, however, is the case. There are, undoubtedly, while I am writing these pages, thousands of peasants who are dying, if not of absolute starvation, from diseases directly caused by insufficient nourishment and an injurious diet. Many are subsisting on clay, weeds, on bread mixed with chopped straw, and on weed soup, melon skins, etc.

I explained to the Count that it was quite to be expected that many should die of the effects of hunger when in one province alone there were several hundred thousand individuals who received no assistance whatever from the governor. And as for the wealthy peasants he spoke of, in several of the villages which I had visited, those individuals had found to be themselves in need, having disposed of their animals and consumed their seed-corn.

"When a man eats nothing for months," I continued, "save bread, insufficient in quantity and bad in quality, and such injurious articles as clay, and then is carried off by typhus or some other complaint, directly traceable to this diet, I regard his death as being a death from hunger, although the doctors in this country do not."

In the course of conversation on the following morning, the count showed himself deeply interested in English and American social questions; also in Ruskin and Matthew Arnold. Ruskin he thought one of the greatest men of the age, and it pained him to notice that English people generally were of a different opinion. "But no man is a prophet in his own country; and the greatest men are seldom recognized in their own times, for the very reason that they are so much in advance of the age. Their contemporaries are unable to understand them."

"When Ruskin," continued the Count, "began to write on philosophy and on morality he was ignored by everybody, especially by the English Press, which has a peculiar way of ignoring anybody it does not like. I am not astonished that people speak so little of Ruskin in comparison with Gladstone. When the latter makes a speech they are loud with praises, but when Ruskin — whom I believe to be a greater man — talks, they say nothing."

I confessed to the count that I knew Ruskin only as an art critic....

Here I told him that when in London, I frequently patronized the vegetarian restaurants, and I suggested that if he should ever go to London, he should try those places of refreshment.

"Go to London!" he repeated with a sigh. "I shall soon be going to the next world."

Those who wish to know more about Tolstoy's present religious opinions should consult that remarkable book of his, "My Religion." It is said that when the Count completed this work he called all his family around him, and told them, to their dismay, that he was going to give all his property to the poor. The Countess, so the report goes, on hearing the Count announce this quixotic intention, swooned away. "Sell what thou hast and give it to the poor," was a precept which they had heard often, but to translate it into action was for them too hard a task.

And so the Count left the house, telling his family that they could do what they liked with the money. As for himself, he had no further need of it. A simple blouse and plain food would suffice for him. The Count has adhered to his resolution. He does not, a friend tells me, own now so much as a kopeck. His estates, his horses, his money, everything he possessed have been made over to his wife and children.

My conversations with the Count were frequently interrupted by peasants coming in to ask for aid of some kind; and, once one of his followers, a Moscow gentleman, entered the room. The Count requested the last-named to be good enough to reply to a Jewish student of the university, who had written begging the Count to allow him to come and assist him and to contribute pecuniarily to the good work.

"Tell him," said the Count sadly, "that he cannot come because of his nationality, although he would have been welcome."

Before taking my leave of the Count, I told him the Countess Maria had not converted me from my healthiest opinions respecting the right to resist evil.

"There are many men," I argued, "who are cruel, greedy and aggressive, and if we are not to resist them we cannot preserve our liberty and independence. Even the Huguenots, Puritans, and Covenanters were obliged to resort to force."

"It is a great mistake," replied the Count, "to think that the heart of man is as bad as you believe it to be. There is good at the bottom of the worst men; and we should appeal to the good that is in a man's nature. Harrison and Matthew," he added, "are successfully preaching this doctrine in America; and the Stundists in this country are practically carrying it out."

In support of his argument he mentioned an instance of some peasants, who, to test the sincerity of some Stundists, gradually robbed these of all their movable property. One day they took away the horses, another day the cows, the third day the furniture, until, finally, there was nothing left for them to take. Then they waited a day or two to see whether the Stundists would be false to their professions. Finding, eventually, that the Stundists did not move in the matter, and being conscience-stricken, they returned all the stolen property.

"But those peasants," I exclaimed, "had consciences. What about men who do not possess consciences? Take for example the Bashkirs and Tartars, and other wild tribes of Asia." And I narrated how some of the Mennonite colonists of the province Saratov, who, like the Stundists, believed in the doctrine of non-resistance to evil-doers, had at last been obliged to arm themselves while at work, as some of their evil-minded neighbors, taking advantage of their non-defensive attitude, had begun to plunder and kill them. To this Count Tolstoy replied, "They do wrong to resist."

"What then," I asked, "would you have soldiers do when ordered to kill their brethrens?"

"They should refuse to obey," said the count, who, I may remind my readers, has himself served in the army.

Returning to the subject of war, the Count said, "Several of my friends have been imprisoned for years and others exiled to Siberia for refusing to become soldiers and to slay their fellow-men." I replied that I certainly thought that men of talent and energy could be better employed than in covering the earth with gore and manufacturing widows and orphans; that their strength should rather be spent in reclaiming their country from barbarism, in developing the resources of the country, or in creating beautiful works of art. Only when the soldier was defending the homes and liberties of his fellow-countrymen was he acting nobly. A war of aggression was simply murder on a large scale. It ought to be, and I hoped soon would be, an impossibility with civilized and so-called "Christian" nations.

In parting from Count Tolstoy, he gave utterance to the following remarkable and sad words: "I do not know whether what I am doing is for the best, or whether I ought to take myself away from this occupation. All l know is that I cannot leave this work. Perhaps it is weakness; perhaps it is my duty which keeps me here. But I cannot give it up, even if I should like to. Like Moses on Mount Horeb, I shall never see the fruit of my labors. I shall never know whether I have been acting for the best or not. My fear is that what I am doing is only a palliative."

Surely when the historian comes to cover that canvas of the latter half of the nineteenth century, he will find no more pathetic figure for his painting than that of the great genius Tolstoy, battling with famine and fever, and striving with his might and main to bring about the universal brotherhood of mankind, and yet pursued by doubts as to whether, after all, there is not some better way which he does not see.

# 9

# Russia of To-day
## *by Henry Norman*

Sir Henry Norman (1860–1928) was a British traveler, politician and journalist who wrote *All the Russia: Travels and Studies in Contemporary European Russia, Siberia and Central Asia* (1902).

Norman, Sir Henry. "Russia of To-day (on Tolstoy)." *Scribner's Magazine* (New York) vol. 28 (1900): 387–406.

Russia!

What a flock of thoughts take wing as the word strikes the ear! Does any word in any language, except the dear name of one's own land, mean as much to-day?

What is Russia? The unfettered, irresponsible, limitless, absolute rule of one man over a hundred millions of his fellows — is that it? The ikon in the corner of every room where the language is spoken, the blue-domed basilica in every street of great cities, the long-haired priests chanting in deep bass, the pedestrian ceaselessly crossing himself, the Holy Synod, whose God-given task it is to coerce or to cajole a heathen world to orthodoxy — is that Russia? Or is it the society of the capital, speaking all languages, familiar with all literatures, practicing every art, lapped in every luxury, esteeming manners more highly than morals? Or is it the vast and nearly roadless country, where settlements are to distances like fly-specks to window-panes; where the conveniences, the comforts and the decencies of civilization may be sought in vain outside the towns and away from the lines of railway; where entire villages are the prey of unnamable disease; where seven people out of every ten neither read nor write.

The name of Moscow will always bring back to my mind, before anything else, my visit to Tolstoy. And indeed, he is as much a part of Russia, as significant of Russian character, as prophetic of Russian development, as the Kremlin itself. At the bottom of every Russian is a stratum of enthusiastic idealism, of disbelief in the thing that is and belief in the thing that may be. Scratch a Muscovite and you find a transcendentalist. Drop into conversation with your neighbor in the railway carriage and in ten minutes you will be disputing hotly over some purely abstract proposition.

The typical Russian is doer and dreamer in one, and Tolstoy is the dreamer incarnate in every Russian heart.

Tula, "at once the Sheffield and the Birmingham of Russia," as a guide-book pretentiously informs you, is a night's journey from Moscow, and Yasnaya Polyana, Count Tolstoy's estate, is seven miles from Tula.

It is a delightful drive in the crisp bright autumn morning; there is actually some good farming to be seen — a rare thing in this country — long plantations of little forest trees, miles of half-grown wood. Then over a hill-top comes an aspect of very modern Russia — the huddle of buildings forming a great ironworks, huge chimneys belching smoke, the clang of the rolling-mill, the enormous slag heaps. (...) For six miles a fair road, then our driver turns sharply aside into a mere wheel-track and for a mile the little carriage is thrown from side to side as it plunges in and out of the ruts. At last something which at home would be called a village green, and two little whitewashed towers forming the end of an avenue of old birches. This is Count Tolstoy's famous place — not, by the way, that he is "Graf Tolstoy," to anybody hereabouts, as I found when I hired the carriage. He is just "Leo Nikolaevich," Leo, the son of Nicholas. The birches are hoary as is their master's head, and great in stature even as himself, and their way winds upward, past an exquisite willow grove by a lake, till it brings you in sight of a white low-spreading chateau, with roof painted green, like almost all roofs in Russia, close set round with trees.

Tolstoy works in his room till one o'clock, and nothing is ever allowed by his devoted family to disturb him. Miss Tolstoy, a woman whom it is a privilege to have met even for so short a time, takes us round the farm. It is not like the farms of England, still less like the West; it resembles more the neglected homesteads of New England. The tillage is of the roughest, two ploughs by the barn door might have been fashioned by Cain, there is no stored wealth in a yellow stack-yard, the fields are deserted. No landowner can live by his land, Miss Tolstoy assures me, and estate by estate is passing out of the hands of those who inherited it from a long line of ancestors, into the possession of the rich merchants and manufacturers of the city, who are careless as to produce and seek only the social prestige that land alone gives in old countries. She is pessimistic this morning, for she goes on to say that even of these, the third generation is always ruined and has to begin again.

"No Russian," she said, "ever 'founds a family,' as you say. A man makes a fortune, his son lavishes it, his grandson disperses it." I suggest modern agricultural machinery, pedigree crops and stock, chemical fertilizers. She shakes her head — "It would never pay here." In his youth, Tolstoy was a mad sportsman, from dawn to nightfall in the saddle, or with gun and hound. Then the estate was watched and cherished for the chase's sake; now he thinks of it but as an appendage of the people which he monopolizes. But here he comes, walking sturdily down the narrow wood-way, his dogs leaping joyously about him.

The photograph reproduced here, which he afterward permitted me to take, shows him precisely as he appeared that day. The prophet's brow, the patriarch's beard, the peasant's blouse — they are familiar to all the world. He was wearing an old black cap, round his waist was a leather strap, his shoes were un-blacked and split — a strange negligence in practice for the advocate of manual labor, who made himself a cobbler on principle. But the lens cannot portray the infinite sweetness of his expression, nor the pen convey the exceeding gentleness of his words. For him the law and the prophets, the ten commandments and the categorical imperative, are all comprised in the one word — Love. Who has it, has everything — religion, ethics, law, politics: who has it not, has nothing.

"Write as one who loved his fellowmen," would be also Tolstoy's request to the recording angel, if he were not far too modest to wish to be written down at all. And his devotion to the race marks his attitude to the individual. He greets you with genuine pleasure, he asks your opinion almost with deference, he considers your answer with respect. Your personality is evidently a thing he regards as sacred. You struggle in vain to reverse the relationship, but without much success, for his soul dwells apart and you cannot get on the same plane with him — there is so little common ground between you.

To your question about his view of some matter of current interest he replies as a mathematician might reply to a question about the rotation of crops. I asked him if he sympathized with Mr. Witte's fostering of Russian manufactures at the expense of agriculture. He replied that he did not see what difference it makes to the engine that does the work whether it is painted red or green. Not until next day did I interpret that Delphic reply. He meant that in comparison with the question whether the relations of man to man and man to men are inspired by love, all matters of tariffs and bounties are as infinitely irrelevant as the paint on the boiler is to the stroke of the piston. Then I asked him about the Dreyfus case, at that moment being reheard at Rennes. And to my unspeakable astonishment I found him a believer in the preposterous "secret dossier," a defender of the General Staff, accepting the guilt of Dreyfus as an easier alternative than the conspiracy of his fellow-officers against him.

"The people are hypnotized," he said. "They know nothing and they all shout the same thing. After all, why should I concern myself with Dreyfus — are there no innocent men in the prison of Tula?"

So far as the authorities are concerned, Tolstoy seems to bear a charmed life.

The story about the Tsar meeting him at a railway station and holding a long conversation with him, was a pure invention. Indeed, when an important official from St. Petersburg came to Tula in the course of certain investigations, and desired to ask Tolstoy's advice, the latter refused to receive him. But except the suppression of some of his writings, the authorities leave Lev Nikolaevich alone, though his views must seem to them the quintessence of subversive propaganda.

"Three things I hate," he said to me: "autocracy, orthodoxy, and militarism." — and these are the three pillars of the Russian State. I asked him point-blank, "How is it that the government has not arrested or banished you?"

"I cannot tell," he answered, and then, after a moment's pause he added, slowly, in a tone of much solemnity: "I wish they would. It would be a great joy to me."

The general opinion among advanced Russians is that the police are restrained in this instance by the world-wide scandal that any harsh treatment of Tolstoy would cause. But I am inclined to think that Tolstoy's influence, which is probably greater out of Russia than in it, is almost confined to the spiritual sphere, and not found in practical life.

I have dwelt thus long upon my visit to Yasnaya Polyana partly because Tolstoy is one of the most striking of living figures and anything at first hand about him, especially now that we can hardly hope that he will be included in this category much longer, is probably of interest, and partly because, in his vague and facile idealism, he is the typical Russian.

# 10

# Conversations with Ernest Crosby Embodying Personal Impressions of Count Leo Tolstoy

Ernest Crosby was an American journalist who visited Tolstoy in 1900, as he traveled across Russia.

Crosby, Ernest. "Conversations with Ernest Crosby Embodying Personal Impressions of Count Leo Tolstoy." *Arena* (New York), vol. 25 (1901): 429–439.

**Q.** Mr. Crosby, as one of the American pilgrims who have journeyed thousands of miles to far-away Russia in order to see the great apostle of renunciation, and as a student of his works, you are, I think, among the best qualified of our countrymen to speak of Count Tolstoy and intelligently interpret his social and religious views. Hence, I hope you will tell us something of the man and his theories. What were your impressions of Count Tolstoy? We always like to know whether the prophet who bids us seek the heights has himself journeyed along the steep, rugged, and brier-strewn pathway; whether he is consistent; whether he is a doer as well as a teacher of the higher law. Of course, we know that the illustrious author and philosopher has made what the world considers a great sacrifice, but beyond this is he, in his daily life, in his home, and among his humble neighbors, all that we have pictured him from his writings?

A. Count Tolstoy has often been charged with being inconsistent, and I do not suppose that he would claim that he is consistent; but from my own observation when I visited him at his home at Yasnaya Poliana I should say that he is one of the most consistent men in the world. To abolish at once all the distinctions which centuries of rank, privilege, wealth, and education have made between a man and his neighbors was an undertaking of no small difficulty, especially when his family only agree with him in part. Tolstoy's food and raiment are as simple and inexpensive as those of the peasants around him. He does all the cleaning, sweeping, and chamber work connected with his own room and person. As far as he can, he has banished all luxury from his house. When I was there, there was not even a rug or carpet on any floor that I saw. With the exception of a few family portraits, a piano and a guitar, and some shelves of books, there was nothing visible in the house except necessaries. The service at table was simpler than in many an American poor man's house.

He was not well during my visit of two days, and I did not see him engaged in manual labor; but it is well known that he does as much of it as his age and health permit. He told me that he preferred plowing to any other manual work. Like the peasants, he was accustomed to lead a horse with a harrow, while plowing with a one horse plow. A pair of boots made by the Count are exhibited at the Museum at Moscow. They are doubtless better adapted to a museum than to the human foot, but they show the earnestness of his endeavors to cope with the disadvantages of his education as a man without hands or muscles.

The question of consistency recalls Count Tolstoy's advice to me on that subject. "Speak out what you think," he said, "and you will be furnishing weapons against yourself." It is certainly true that criticisms of inconsistency have the effect of making a man redouble his efforts to be consistent.

I think I have said enough to show that Tolstoy approaches so near to absolute consistency that no American would be likely to find fault with him on that score. But this is not true of the Russians. They are, I think, the most logical people in the world. Persuade a Russian that autocracy is a bad thing, and the chances are that he will at once begin to manufacture bombs for the Czar. Convince him that private wealth is wrong, and in half an hour you may find him on the street-corner with his pockets turned inside out, distributing his money to the poor.

We Americans are not built upon that plan. We sometimes get new ideas too, and more or less revolutionary ones at that, but in our prudence we usually think them over for thirty, forty, or fifty years, as the case may be, and death at last relieves us from responsibility. You may remember the story of the Irishman and the parrot. He heard that parrots lived to be two hundred years old; so he bought a young one to see if it was true. Our ideas usually survive us, like the parrot, and we never put them to the test. There are advantages on both sides, in the Russian and in the American system.

The American is less likely to go off at half-cock, and the Russian is more likely to make valuable contributions to practical ethics.

In judging Count Tolstoy's consistency we must also remember that he is a non-resistant. So far as he can persuade his wife and children to do away with superfluities, he has his way; but when Madame Tolstoy puts her foot down his very principles require him to yield. This undoubtedly accounts for the piano and the guitar. I have sometimes thought that it would be a good plan to have one of the parties a non-resistant in all marriages. As far as my observation goes, it would usually be the husband.

But on one point Count Tolstoy is very strong. No inconsistency on the part of any man, no apparent inability to live up to his ideals, should induce him to modify those ideals or weaken his principles an iota. Opportunism, compromise,—even if they find their way into your life,—must leave your principles intact. He gives as an illustration the case of the straight line. No one has ever drawn a straight line. It does not exist in Nature; yet I must not for this reason alter by a hair's breadth my idea of a straight line. It is true that I shall always draw crooked lines; yet by sticking to my ideal I may approximate the standard more and more. But if in despair I make a crooked line my ideal, there is no hope for me.

The question of consistency is in the last resort one of sincerity, and no one can see Count Tolstoy, as I have seen him, without being convinced of that. The whole man is in his frank, serious, kindly face.

Although he is dressed like a peasant there is not the least suggestion of pose or self-consciousness in his appearance. He never thinks of the gallery. Victor Hugo had many of the ideas of Tolstoy. He rebelled against the distinctions of rich and poor, of governed and governing. He showed his deep sympathy for the poor by directing that he should be buried in a pauper's coffin, and as a matter of fact his body was placed in one while it lay in state in the midst of mourning thousands. But Hugo knew that he could not have dressed as a peasant during his life without becoming hopelessly theatrical. He lacked the simplicity, the single-mindedness, which, in Tolstoy's case, convinces all who see him that he dresses and lives as he does because he cannot do otherwise. His inmost being has revolted against the injustice of the whole gentility business, and he must show it in his life or die of repression.

**Q.** In sacrificing the beauty of his home and insisting on living the rigidly plain and prosaic life of his rustic neighbors, do you think he is accomplishing as much good as he might do if he had retained more of beauty and culture in his home surroundings and sought to enrich and beautify the homes of the peasants and bring into their barren lives something of the joy that comes from an appreciation of the beautiful? I may be wrong, but it seems to me that the Count laid too little stress on the refining, exalting, and ennobling influence of beauty. Stern duty, in her simple and austere mien, appears to have filled his mental horizon. His splendid imagination has in a way been starved, it seems to me. There is a moral grandeur and heroism in this noble apostle of the higher life which calls for the tribute of every high-thinking man and woman, but in spite of this it seems to me that the Count has fatally overlooked the fundamental demand of life: he has not considered the lily, with all that that implies; and, strangely enough, with all his natural wealth of imagination he has failed to learn the lesson that the Creator has striven to impress on the minds of the simplest of his children. Everywhere Nature spells out the word "Beauty," that the imagination of man may be satisfied and that he may learn the lesson taught by a million tongues. To me it seems that he who seeks to divorce beauty from utility seeks to separate what God has joined together. Now, is it not true that Count Tolstoy has in a way repeated the fatal error of the cloister of the Middle Ages and the brutal warfare that Puritanism later waged against the beautiful. He has conceived it his duty to serve his fellow-men. Well and good. He believes it his duty to go to the poor and be as one of them. Well and good, if it is to enrich their hard and prosaic existence, giving them an ampler life, richer in all that enriches being. The spirit of altruistic service, the overmastering desire to aid the poor, as manifested by the great Nazarene, calls for the tribute of our love and admiration; but at the same time I deplore his failure to see that with his rich imagination and strong sense of beauty he might, but for mistaking a partial appearance for the whole truth, have enriched a hundredfold the lives of those about him and inaugurated a movement destined to grow rapidly. Yet here I may be mistaken; but you who have communed with him, and who know the conditions of life environing him, can better judge than I.

**A.** I think there is much force in your criticism. Tolstoy is a great artist, but his revulsion of feeling against the society in which he lived so long has made him suspicious of its art. The art of the day is preoccupied, he says, with three insignificant and worn-out feelings — pride, sexual desire, and weariness of life. He wants a new art built on something higher. "Art is a human activity," he tells us, "consisting in this — that one man consciously, by means of certain external signs, hands on to others feelings he has lived through, and that other people are infected by these feelings and also experience them." "It is a means of union among men, joining them together in the same feelings." If we accept these principles, and to me they seem manifestly true, we can understand how Tolstoy has come to protest against a dilettante art, produced for a small and pampered portion of the community and tending to separate men into classes rather than to unite them. In a new and brotherly world Tolstoy expects a new and real art to arise, of which indeed he is the forerunner crying in the wilderness, "Make straight the way of the Lord!" Meanwhile he is ready to dispense with the half-art that we have. It is another exhibition of relentless Russian logic which leaves us unconvinced although we accept its premises. There are pretty things in life, and it is better to have them around us than ugly things; and, while it is quite true that our education has vitiated our taste, we must make the best use we can of such taste as has survived in us. To beautify our lives, where we can do it even in mere externals (without dealing unjustly with any one), is clearly a duty; and it does seem to me that Tolstoy has failed to see this. He virtually admits the claims of beauty, at least in one passage: "The subject-matter of all kinds of ornamentation consists not in the beauty, but in the feeling (of admiration of, and delight in, the combination of lines and colors) which the artist has experienced and with which he infects the spectator. Among these feelings is the feeling of delight at what pleases the sight." Beauty, then, is a unifier too, and as such a proper element of art.

In considering this matter of art we must remember that Tolstoy is not an "all-round man" by any means, but a prophet; and a prophet must in the nature of things be one-sided: he must lay the emphasis in one direction. It is notable that Jesus showed little interest in external art. He was an artist in literature. (Was there ever anything written more artistic than the first part of the parable of the Prodigal Son?) But when his disciples called his attention to the wonders of the temple architecture, he had no eye for them. Although his father was a carpenter, and he may have worked at the trade himself, yet he never dwells on form. His life work lay in another direction. Tolstoy has not been able to divest himself of his literary art; it was too deeply bound up with his nature. His "Resurrection" shows it in its entire original splendor, and Sir Henry Irving recently said that one of his two dramas was the strongest play of recent times. But he has turned his back on the plastic arts, feeling that a divided world cannot do justice to them. If Tolstoy and William Morris could have been united in one man, we should have had an all-round man indeed. While Tolstoy has shortcomings on the external side, Morris has them on the spiritual. But would a man so balanced have been such a force in the world as either of these incomparable men? I doubt it.

**Q.** Do you think that the views of Count Tolstoy are having as much effect on thinking Russia as upon scholars throughout western Europe and the New World, and that he is producing a lasting impression upon the peasants around him; or do they reflect in a large measure the narrow bigotry and prejudice of the priesthood and regard him as an atheist who, though he may have a kind heart, is nevertheless to be regarded with suspicion and whose teachings are to be shunned as imperiling the soul?

**A.** I have no means of knowing how great the influence of Count Tolstoy is in Russia. I know of individual instances of noblemen who have followed his example and devoted their lives to their fellows. One noteworthy example is that of Vladimir Tchertkov — formerly an officer in the imperial guards at St. Petersburg and a personal friend of the late Czar, with whom he used to play lawn tennis — who has been exiled on account of his democratic and humanitarian activities, and lives in England, where he conducts the "Free Age Press," which prints cheap editions of Tolstoy's ethical writings in both English and Russian. I met Mr. Tchertkov last summer in London — a thorough-going aristocrat in appearance, despite his flannel shirt. It was odd to think that not so many years ago he was attached to the Embassy there and on intimate terms with the great people of London society. It stands to reason that a genuine Russian like Tolstoy must have more influence in his own country than abroad. There is something distinctively Russian in his thought and it appeals to the Russian mind.

As for the peasants, it is not easy to get at them. They cannot read, and depend upon rumor for most of their knowledge. In his own village of Yasnaya Poliana they are devoted to him, and I was told that this village was far superior to the general run; but, as it was the only one I examined, I could not judge for myself. When the peasants do think they think independently in the line of Count Tolstoy's thought. Indeed, he claims to have learned the truth from them. Russia is honey-combed with peasant sects, more or less inclined to non-resistance and fraternal principles. The Doukhobors, of whom we all have heard so much, are a conspicuous example of this. Nine thousand of them are now settled in Northwestern

Canada, largely through Count Tolstoy's efforts, having emigrated to avoid military service, which offends their consciences. Tolstoy has written many tracts and moral tales for the peasants and they have a wide circulation. We may be sure that they have an extended influence, following as they do the natural bent of the people.

**Q.** In his purely religious views, what are his conceptions, as you understand them, of Deity, of the future of the soul, and those questions over which churches have warred and great religious bodies have chiefly concerned themselves?

**A.** Tolstoy's religious ideas have not been at a standstill. It is easy to quote his books for almost any assertion on this subject, but the fact is easily explained when we consider the regular development of his views from the beginning. He was, until he reached the age of fifty, an agnostic if not an atheist. The faith that has grown in him since has been altogether the work of his own experience. The only use he has made of the experience of others has been in inducing similar experiences in himself, and even this he has not done deliberately, but naturally in the search for the truth. "If any man will do his will, he shall know of the doctrine." Tolstoy has found this statement to be true. In the experience of love to God and men, he has become conscious of possessing an immortal soul. He told me, when I asked him, that all true life was immortal. He answers the question specifically in a recent leaflet: "As to the question about what awaits us after death, I would answer by the conjecture that the will of Him who called us into this life for our welfare leads its somewhere through death — probably for the same purpose."

But it is in the apprehension of God that Tolstoy has gained most from experience. I remember that I was delighted with his book on "Life" because it never mentions God and did not postulate what seemed to me an assumption as the best of its reasoning. As the result of reading that book I concluded that love for one's neighbor was the basis of religion, and I told Tolstoy so when I met him.

"Not at all," said he. "Love for God comes first. Why should you love your neighbor, if you do not first love God?" I told him that I thought I did love my neighbor first, but he would not believe it: "No, you don't understand your own sensations." This conviction has grown upon Tolstoy until he has become, what Spinoza was said to be, a "God-intoxicated" man. His recently published "Thoughts on God" shows a realization of the presence of God as striking as is to be found in the Psalms. I give here a few passages:

"Somehow, while praying to God, it became clear to me that God is indeed a real Being, Love; is that All which I just touch and which I experience in the form of love. And this is not a feeling, not an abstraction, but a real Being; and I have felt Him.

"All that I know, I know because there is a God, and because I know Him. Only upon this can one firmly base one's relations with other men and with one's self, as well as with life outside space and time.

"He is the origin of my spiritual self—the external world is only my limit.

"I found Him as it were afresh. And I was filled with such joy, and such a firm assurance did I gain of Him, and of the possibility and duty of communion with Him, and of His hearing me, and my joy grew so great that all these last days I have been experiencing the feeling that something very good has come to me, and I keep asking myself: 'Why do I feel so happy? Yes! God! There is a God, and I need be neither anxious nor afraid, but can only rejoice.' Perhaps this is what some call the 'living God.'

"There is not one believing man to whom moments of doubt do not come—doubt in the existence of God. And these doubts are not harmful; on the contrary, they lead to a higher understanding of that God whom one knew has become familiar, and one no more believes in Him. We entirely believe in God only when He discloses Himself afresh to us. And He discloses Himself to us from a new side when we seek Him with all our soul."

"I too for long did not name Thee ... But Lord I named Thee, and my sufferings ceased. My despair has passed ... I feel Thy nearness, feel Thy help when I walk in Thy ways, and Thy pardon when I stray from Thee ... Lord, pardon the errors of my youth, and help me to bear Thy yoke as cheerfully as I accept it."

**Q.** What would you say were the focusing points of his social theories or upon what chief foundation truths does his philosophy of life in its larger relations rest?

**A.** Tolstoy's great discovery and central theory is the old, old truth that love is the natural spiritual energy of man, and that all circumstances, laws, and institutions must bend before this prime function of his soul. In short, he takes Christianity at its word, not because "it is written" but because he has found its truth attested in his deepest experience. All of his apparent eccentricities become intelligible, or even necessary, when we trace them back to this paramount obligation of loving. While he is not a constructive philosopher, his spirit must underlie any sound piece of construction. "Except the Lord build the house, they labor in vain that build it." Tolstoy's great importance in the bringing in of a new day is his dramatic value. Himself a great dramatist, he has always seen things dramatically, and he has at last become a dramatic representation of the need of the age. Scenes, pictures, and events have always impressed him more than arguments and books. The freezing of his coachman at Kazan, while he was dancing at a ball, first called his attention to the grievances of the working classes. An execution by guillotine, which he attended at Paris, first shook his faith in government. It was his own experience in the Crimean war that revealed the horrors of wholesale murder to him. The contrast between himself and a peasant, as they both dropped a coin in a beggar's hat, opened his eyes to the defects of a rich man's charity. His dramatic instinct made him a great novelist and dramatist, and made him understand the Gospels as few men have understood them. As he explains them you see the events as if they occurred in the streets today, and you comprehend why the Pharisees speak thus and the disciples answer so. And now unwittingly, but by an unerring instinct, he has become himself the protagonist in a great drama. Like the Roman knight he has plunged into the abyss yawning between class and is endeavoring to realize the reconciliation of a world divided against itself. Tolstoy has written many great works, but the greatest is his simple, pathetic, inevitable life. If he could have helped it, we might criticize his role; but it has been as much the work of destiny as Mont Blanc or the Atlantic.

# 11

# Walks and Talks with Tolstoy
## by Andrew White

Andrew Dickson White (1832–1918), American educator, diplomat and minister to Russia in 1892–94, New York Senator in 1864–67, the U.S. Ambassador to Germany, was a close personal friend of Mr. Cornell and the first president of the Cornell University.

White, Andrew Dickson. "Walks and Talks with Tolstoy." *McClure's Magazine* (New York) vol. 16 (1901): 507–518.

Revisiting Moscow after an absence of thirty-five years, the most surprising thing to me was that there had been so little change. With the exception of the new Gallery of Russian Art, and the bazaar opposite the sacred gate of the Kremlin, things seemed as I had left them just after the accession of Alexander II. There were the same dirty streets; the same peasantry clad in sheepskins; the same troops of beggars, sturdy and dirty; the same squalid crowds crossing themselves before the images at the street corners; the same throngs of worshipers knocking their heads against the pavements of churches; and above all loomed the tower of Ivan and the domes of St. Basil, gaudy and barbaric as ever. Only one change had taken place which interested me; for the first time in the history of Russia a man of world-wide fame in literature and thought was abiding here — Count Leo Tolstoy.

On the evening of my arrival I went with my secretary to his weekly reception. As we entered his house, on the outskirts of the city, two servants in evening dress came forward, removed our fur coats, and opened the doors into the reception-room of the master. Then came a great surprise. His living-room seemed the cabin of a Russian peasant. It was wainscoted almost rudely, furnished very simply, and there came forward to meet us a tall, gaunt Russian, unmistakably born to command, yet clad as a peasant, his hair thrown back over his ears on either side, his blouse kept in place by a leathern girdle, his high jackboots completing the costume. This was Tolstoy.

Nothing could be more kind than his greeting. While his dress was that of a peasant, his bearing was the very opposite; for instead of the depressed, demure, hangdog expression of the average muzhik, his manner, though cordial, was dignified and impressive. Having given us a hearty welcome, he made us acquainted with various other guests. It was a singular assemblage: there were foreigners in evening dress, Moscow professors in any dress they liked, and a certain number of youths, evidently disciples, who, though clearly not of the peasant class, wore the peasant costume. I observed them with much interest, but certainly as long as they were under the spell of the master they communicated nothing worth preserving; they seemed to have "the contortions of the Sibyl without the inspiration."

I naturally asked to be presented to the lady of the house, and the Count escorted me through a series of rooms to a salon furnished much like any handsome apartment in Paris or St. Petersburg, where I found the Countess, who, with other ladies, all in full evening dress, received us cordially. This sudden transition from the peasant cabin of the master to the exquisite rooms of the mistress was startling: it seemed like scene-shifting at a theater.

After some friendly talk, all returned to the rooms of the master of the house, where tea was served at a long table from the bubbling brazen urn — the samovar; and though there were some twenty or thirty guests, nothing could be more informal. All was simple, kindly, and unrestrained.

My first question was upon the condition of the people. Our legation had corresponded with Count Tolstoy and his family as to distributing a portion of the famine fund sent from America, hence this subject naturally arose at the outset. He said that the condition of the peasants was still very bad; that they had very generally eaten their draft animals, burned portions of their buildings to keep life in their bodies, and reduced themselves to hopeless want. On my suggestion that the new commercial treaty with Germany might help matters, he thought that it would have but little effect, since only a small portion of the total product of Russian agriculture is consumed abroad. This led him to speak of some Americans and Englishmen who had visited the famine-stricken districts, and while he referred kindly to them all, he seemed especially attracted by the Quaker John Bellows, of Gloucester, England, the compiler of the wonderful little French Dictionary. This led him to say that he sympathized with the Quakers in everything save their belief in property; that in this they were utterly illogical; that property presupposes force — to protect it. I remarked that most American Quakers knew nothing of such force; that none of them had ever seen an American soldier save during the late civil war, and that probably not one in hundreds of them had ever seen a soldier at all. He answered, "But you forget the policemen." He evidently put policemen and soldiers in the same category, as using force to protect property, and therefore to be alike abjured.

I found that to his disbelief in any right of ownership literary property formed no exception. He told me that in his view he had no right to receive money for the permission to print a book. To this I naturally answered that by carrying out this doctrine he simply presented large sums of money to publishers in every country of Europe and America, many of them rich, and some of them piratical,— and that in my opinion he would do a much better thing by taking the full value of his copyrights and bestowing the proceeds upon the peasantry starving about him. To this he answered that it was a question of duty. To this I agreed, but remarked that our disagreement was as to what his duty in the matter really was. It was a pleasure to learn from another source that the Countess took a different view of it, and that she had in some way secured the proceeds of his copyrights for their very large and interesting family. Light was thus thrown on Tolstoy's remark, made afterward, that women are not so self-sacrificing as men; that a man would sometimes sacrifice his family for an idea, but that a woman would not.

He then went on to express an interest in the Shakers, and especially in Frederick Evans. He had evidently formed an idea of them very unlike the reality; in fact, the Shaker his imagination had developed was as different from a Lebanon Shaker as an eagle from a duck, and his notion of their influence on American society was absurd.

He spoke at some length regarding religion in Russia, evidently believing that its present dominant form is soon to pass away. I asked him how, then, he could account for the fact that, while in other countries women are greatly in the majority at church services, in every Russian church the majority are men, and that during the thirty-five years since my last visit to Moscow this tendency had apparently increased. He answered: "All this is on the surface; there is much deeper thought below, and the great want of Russia is liberty to utter it."

In regard to the Jews, he said that he sympathized with them, but the statements regarding the persecution of them had been overdrawn. Kennan's statements regarding the treatment of prisoners in Siberia he thought overdrawn at times, but substantially true. He expressed his surprise that certain leading men in the empire, whom he named, could believe that persecution and the forcible repression of thought would have any permanent effect at the end of the nineteenth century.

He then dwelt upon sundry evil conditions in Russia, on which my comment was that every country has of course its own grievous shortcomings, and cited, as to America, the proverb, "No one knows so well where the shoe pinches as he who wears it." All this showed him that it was the inevitable result of our wretched laxity in the administration of criminal law, which had led great bodies of people, more especially in the southern and extreme western parts of the country, to revert to natural justice, and take the law into their own hands, and I cited Goldwin Smith's profound remark that "some American lynchings are proofs not so much of lawlessness as of the general respect for law."

He asked me where, besides this, the shoe pinched in the United States. I told him that it pinched in various places, but that perhaps the worst pinch arose from the premature admission to full political rights of men who had been so benumbed and stunted intellectually and morally in other countries that their exercise of political rights in America is frequently an injury, not only to others, but to themselves. In proof of this I cited the case of the crowds whom I had seen years before huddled together in New York tenement-houses, preyed upon by their liquor-selling landlords, their families perishing of typhoid and smallpox on account of the negligence and maladministration of the local politicians, but who, as a rule, were almost if not quite ready to mob and murder those of us who brought in a new and a better order of things; that for years the class of people who suffered most from the old, vile state of things did their best by their votes to keep in power the men who maintained it.

We then passed to the subject of the Trans-Siberian Railway. In this he seemed interested, but in a vague way which added nothing to my knowledge.

Asking me regarding my former visit to Moscow, and learning that it was during the Crimean War, he said, "At that time I was in Sebastopol, and continued there as a soldier during the siege."

As to his relations with the imperial government at present, he said that not long ago he had been elected to a learned society in Moscow, but that the St. Petersburg government had interfered to cancel the election, and he added that every morning, when he awoke, he wondered that he was not on his way to Siberia.

On leaving him, both he and the Countess invited me to meet them the next day at the Tretiakov Museum of Russian pictures, and accordingly, on the following afternoon, I met them at that greatest of all galleries devoted purely to Russian art. They were accompanied by several friends, among them a little knot of disciples — young men clad in simple peasant costume like that worn by the master. It was evident that he was an acknowledged lion at the old Russian capital, for as he led me about to see the pictures he liked best he was followed and stared at by many.

His discussions of these pictures interested me greatly. His ideas came out in various striking utterances, but the limits of this article forbid my repeating them.

Our next walk was taken across the Moscow River on the ice, to and through the Kremlin, and as we walked, the conversation fell upon literature. As to French literature, he thought Maupassant the man of the greatest talent, by far, in these days, but said that he was depraved, and centered all fiction in women. For Balzac he evidently preserved admiration, but cared little apparently for Daudet, Zola, and their compeers.

As to American literature, he said that Turgenev had once told him that there was nothing in it worth reading — nothing new or original; that it was simply a copy of English literature. To this I replied that such criticism seemed to me very shallow; that American literature was, of course, largely a growth out of the parent stock of English literature, and must mainly be judged as such; that to ask in the highest American literature something absolutely different from English literature in general was like looking for oranges upon an apple-tree; that there had come new varieties in this growth, many of them original, and some of them beautiful, but that there was the same sap, the same current running through it all; and I cited the treatment of women in all Anglo-Saxon literature, whether on one side of the Atlantic or on the other, from Chaucer to Mark Twain, as compared with the treatment of her by French writers from Rabelais to Zola.

To this he answered that in his opinion the strength of American literature arose from the inherent Anglo-Saxon religious sentiment.

He expressed a liking for Emerson, Hawthorne, and Whittier, but he seemed to have read at random, not knowing at all some of the best things. He spoke with admiration of Theodore Parker's writings, and seemed interested in my reminiscences of him and of his acquaintance with Russian affairs. He also revered and admired the character and work of William Lloyd Garrison. He had read Longfellow somewhat, but was evidently uncertain regarding Lowell — confusing him apparently with some other author.

Of contemporary writers he knew some of Howells's novels, and liked them, but said: "Literature in the United States at present seems to be in the lowest trough of the sea between high waves." He dwelt on the flippant tone of American newspapers, and told me of an interviewer who came to him in behalf of an American journal, simply to know at what time he went to bed and rose, what he ate, and the like. He thought that people who cared to read such trivialities must be very feeble-minded, but he said that the European press is, on the whole, just as futile.

On my attempting to draw from him some statement as to what part of American literature pleased him most, he said that he had read some publications of the New York and Brooklyn Society for Ethical Culture, and that he knew and liked the writings of Felix Adler. I then asked who in the whole range of American literature he thought the foremost. To this he made an answer which amazed me, as it would have astonished my countrymen. Indeed, did the eternal salvation of all our seventy millions depend upon some one of them guessing the person he named, we should all go to perdition together. That greatest of American writers was — Adin Ballou. Evidently, some of the philanthropic writings of that excellent Massachusetts clergyman and religious activist had jumped with his humor.

The next day he came over to my hotel, and we went out for a stroll. As we passed along the streets I noticed especially what I had remarked during our previous walks, that he had a large quantity of small Russian coins in his pockets; that this was evidently known to the swarms of beggars who infest the Kremlin and the public places generally, and that he always gave to them.

On my speaking of this, he said he thought that any one when asked for money ought to give it. Arguing against this doctrine, I said that in the United States there are virtually no beggars, and I might have gone on to discuss the subject from the politico-economical point of view to show how such indiscriminate alms-giving in perpetual driblets is sure to create the absurd and immoral system which one sees throughout Russia — hordes of men and women who are able to take care of themselves, and who ought to be far above beggary, cringing and whining to the passers-by for alms.

But I had come to know the man well enough to feel sure that a politico-economical argument would slide off him like water from a duck's back, so I attempted to take him upon another side, and said, "In the United States there are virtually no beggars, though my countrymen are, I really believe, among the most charitable in the world." To this last statement he assented, referring in a general way to our shipments of provisions to aid the famine-stricken in Russia; but, I added, it is not our custom to give to beggars, save in special emergencies. I then gave him an account of certain American church organizations which had established piles of fire-wood, and thereby enabled any tramp, by sawing or cutting some of it, to earn a good breakfast, a good dinner, and, if need be, a good bed, and showed him that Americans considered beggary not only a great source of pauperism, but as absolutely debasing to the beggar himself, in that it puts him in the attitude of a suppliant of that which, if he works as he ought, he can claim as his right; that to me the spectacle of Count Tolstoy virtually posing as a superior being, while his fellow Russians came crouching and whining to him, was not at all edifying. To this view of the case he listened very civilly.

He spoke with some disapprobation of travel. He had lived abroad for a time, he said, and in St. Petersburg a few years, but the rest of his life had been mainly spent in Moscow and the interior of Russia. The more we walked together the more it became clear that this last statement explains some of his main defects. Of all distinguished men that I have ever met, Tolstoy seems to me most in need of that enlargement of view and healthful modification of opinion which come from observing men, and comparing opinions in different lands and under different conditions. This need has been all the greater because in Russia there is no opportunity to discuss really important questions. Among the whole hundred and twenty millions of people there is no public body in which the discussion of large public questions is allowed; the press affords no real opportunity for discussion; indeed, it is more than doubtful whether such discussions would be allowed to any effective extent in correspondence or at one's own fireside.

I remember well that during my former stay in St. Petersburg people who could talk English at their own tables generally did so, in order that they might not betray themselves to any spy who might happen to be among their servants.

Still worse, no one, unless a member of the diplomatic corps or otherwise especially privileged, is allowed to read such books or newspapers as he chooses, so that even this little access to the thoughts of others is denied to the very men who most need it.

Like so many other men of genius in Russia, then — and Russia is fertile in such — he has had little opportunity to take part in any real discussion of leading topics, and the result is that his opinions have been developed without modification by any rational interchange of thought with other men. Under such circumstances, any man, no matter how noble or gifted, having given birth to striking ideas, coddles and pets them until they become the full-grown, spoiled children of his brain. He can see neither spot nor blemish in them, and he at last virtually believes himself infallible. This characteristic I found in several other Russians of marked ability. Each had developed his theories for himself until he had become infatuated with them, and despised everything differing from them.

This is a main cause why sundry ghastly creeds, doctrines, and sects, religious, social, political, and philanthropic, have been developed in Russia. One of these religious creeds favors the murder of new-born children in order to save their souls; another enjoins the most horrible bodily mutilation for a similar purpose; others, still, would plunge the world in flames and blood for the difference of a phrase in a creed, or a vowel in a name, or a finger more or less in making the sign of the cross; or this garment in a ritual, or that gesture in a ceremony.

In social creeds they have developed nihilism, which virtually assumes the right of an individual to sit in judgment upon the whole human race; and condemn to death every other human being who may differ in opinion or position from this self-constituted judge. In political creeds they have conceived the monarch as the all-powerful and irresponsible vice-regent of God, and all the world outside Russia as given over to Satan for the reason that it has "rejected the divine principle of authority." In various branches of philosophy they have developed doctrines which involve the rejection of the best to which man has attained in science, literature, and art, and a return to barbarism. In the theory of life and duty they have devised a pessimistic process under which the human race would cease to exist. Every one of these theories is the outcome of some original mind of more or less strength, discouraged, disheartened, and overwhelmed by the sorrows of Russians developing their ideals logically and without any possibility of adequate discussion with other men. This alone explains a fact which struck me forcibly: the fact that Tolstoy's love of humanity, real though it certainly is, is accompanied by a depreciation of the ideas, statements, and proposals of almost every other human being, and by virtual intolerance of all thought which differs in the slightest degree from his own.

The next day he came again to my rooms, and at once began speaking upon religion. He said that every man is religious, and has in him a religion of his own; that religion results from the conception a man forms of his relations to his fellow-men and to the principle which in his opinion controls the universe; that there are three stages in religious development: first, the childhood of man, when he thinks of the whole universe as created for him and centering in him; secondly, the maturity of nations—the time of national religions, when each nation believes that all true religion centers in it, the Jews and the English being striking examples; and, finally, the perfected conception—when man has the idea of fulfilling the will of the Supreme Power, and considers himself an instrument for that purpose. He went on to say that in every religion there are two main elements, one of deception and one of devotion, and he asked me of the Mormons, some of whose books had interested him. He thought two-thirds of their religion deception, but said that on the whole he preferred a religion which professed to have dug its sacred books out of the earth to one which pretended that they were let down from Heaven. On learning that I had visited Salt Lake City two years before, he spoke of the good reputation of the Mormons for chastity, and asked me to explain the hold of their religion upon women. I answered that Mormonism could hardly be judged by its results at present; that, as a whole, the Mormons are no doubt the most laborious and decent people in the State of Utah, but that this is their heroic period, when outside pressure keeps them firmly together and arouses their devotion; that the true test will come later, when there is less pressure and more knowledge, and when the young men who are now arising begin to ask questions, quarrel with each other, and split the whole body into sects and parties.

This led to questions in regard to women generally. I explained some features of woman's condition among us, showing its evolution, first through the betterment of her legal status, and next through provision for her advanced education, but told him that, so far as political rights are concerned, there had been very little practical advance in the entire east and south of the country during the last fifty years, and that even in the extreme Western States, where women have been given political rights and duties to some extent, the concessions have been wavering and doubtful.

At this he took up his parable, and said that women ought to have all other rights except political — that they are unfit to discharge political duties; that, indeed, one of the great difficulties of the world at present lies in their possession of far more consideration and control than they ought to have. "Go into the streets and bazaars," he said, "and you will see the vast majority of shops devoted to their necessities. In France everything centers in women, and women have complete control of life, as contemporary French literature shows. Woman is not man's equal in the highest qualities; she is not so self-sacrificing as man. Men will at times sacrifice their families for an idea; women will not." On my demurring to this latter statement, he asked me if I ever knew a woman who loved other people's children as much as her own. I gladly answered in the negative, but cited Florence Nightingale, Sister Dara, and others, expressing my surprise at his assertion that women are incapable of making as complete sacrifice for any good cause as men. I pointed to the persecutions in the early Church, when women showed themselves even superior to men in suffering torture, degradation, and death in behalf of the new religion, and added similar instances from the history of witchcraft. To this he answered that, in spite of all such history, women will not make the sacrifices of their own interest for a good cause which does not strikingly appeal to their feelings, while men will do so; that he had known but two or three really self-sacrificing women in his life, and that these were unmarried. On my saying that observation had led me to a very different conclusion, his indictment took another form. He insisted that woman hangs upon the past; that public opinion progresses, but that women are prone to act on the opinion of yesterday or of last year; that women and womanish men take naturally to old absurdities — among which he mentioned the homeopathy. At this I expressed a belief that if, instead of educating women, as Bishop Dupanloup expressed it, "in the lap of the Church," we educate them in the highest sense, in universities, they will develop more and more intellectually, and so become a controlling element in the formation of a better race; that as strong men generally have had strong mothers, the better education of women physically, intellectually, and morally is the true way of bettering the race in general. To this idea he demurred, and said that education would not change women; that women are illogical by nature. At this I cited an example showing that woman can be exceedingly logical and close in argument; but he still adhered to his opinion. Happening to mention the name of George Eliot, he expressed a liking for her.

On our next walk he took me to the funeral of one of his friends.

He said that to look upon the dead should rather give pleasure than pain; that "memento mori" is a wise maxim, and looking upon the faces of the dead a good way of putting it into practice. I asked him if he had formed a theory as to a future life, and he said, in substance, that he had not, but that as we came at birth, from beyond the forms of space and time, so at death we returned whence we came. I said, "You use the word 'forms' in the Kantian sense?"

"Yes," he said; "space and time have no reality."

We arrived just too late at the house of mourning. The dead man had been taken away, but many of those who had come to do him honor still lingered, and were evidently enjoying the "funeral baked meats." There were clear signs of a carousal. The friends who came out to meet us had, most of them, flushed faces, and one young man in military uniform coming down the stairs staggered, and seemed likely to break his neck.

Tolstoy refused to go in, and, as we turned away, expressed disgust at the whole system, saying, as well he might, that it was utterly barbarous. He seemed despondent over it, and I tried to cheer him up by showing how the same custom of drinking strong liquors at funerals had only a few generations since prevailed in large districts of England and America, but that better ideas of living had swept it away.

On our way through the street, passing a shrine at which a mob of peasants were adoring a sacred picture, he dwelt on the fetish — his definition of religion given me on one of our previous walks, and he repeated it, declaring religion to be the feeling which man has regarding his relation to the universe, including his fellow-men, and to the principle which governs all.

The afternoon was closed with a visit to a Raskolnik, or "Old Believer," a most curious experience, but too long to relate here.

As we came into the road after this visit he suddenly turned to me, and said almost fiercely: "That man is a hypocrite; he can't believe what he has said; he is a shrewd, long-headed man; how can he believe such trash? Impossible!" At this I reminded him of Theodore Parker's famous distinction between men who believed and men who "believe that they believe," and said that possibly our Raskolnik was one of the latter. This changed the current of his thoughts. He said that he had read Parker's biography, and liked it all, save one thing, which was that he gave a pistol to a fugitive slave and advised him to defend himself. This Tolstoy condemned on the ground that we are to resist evil. I told him of the advice I had given to Dobrolubov — a very winning Russian student at Cornell University — when he chose the profession of an engineer. This advice was that he should bear in mind Buckle's idea as to the agency of railways and telegraphs in bringing and extending liberal ideas and devote himself to his profession of engineering, with the certainty that its ultimate result would be to aid in the enlightenment of the empire, but never on any account to conspire against the government; telling him that he might be sure he could do far more for the advancement of Russian thought by building railways than by entering into any conspiracies whatever.

Tolstoy said the advice was good, but that he would also have advised the young man to speak out his ideas, whatever they might be. He said that only in this way could any advance ever be made; that one main obstacle in human progress is the suppression of the real thoughts of men. I answered that all this had a fine sound; that it might do for Count Tolstoy, but that a young, scholarly engineer following it would probably find himself not in a place where he could promulgate his ideas, but guarded by Cossacks in some remote Siberian mine.

He spoke of young professors in the universities, of their difficulties, and of the risk of their positions if they spoke out at all.

I asked him if there was any liberality or breadth of thought in the Russo-Greek Church. He answered that occasionally a priest had tried to unite broader thought with Orthodox dogma, but that every such attempt had proved futile.

From Parker we passed to Lowell, and I again tried to find if he really knew anything of Lowell's writings. He evidently knew very little, and asked me what Lowell had written. He then said he had no liking for verse, and he acquiesced in Carlyle's saying that nobody had ever said anything in verse which could not have been better said in prose.

A day or two later, on another of our walks, I asked him how and when, in his opinion, a decided advance in Russian liberty and civilization would be made. He answered that he thought it would come soon, and with great power. On my expressing the opinion that such progress would be the result of a long evolutionary process, with a series of actions and reactions, as heretofore in Russian history, he expressed dissent, and said that the change would come soon, suddenly, and with great force.

As we passed along the streets he was, as during our previous walks, approached by many beggars, to each of whom he gave, as was accustomed to take provision of copper money with him on his walks for this purpose, since he regarded it as a duty to give when asked, and he went on to say that he carried the idea so far that even if he knew the man wanted the money to buy brandy he would give it to him; but he added that he would do all in his power to induce the man to work and to cease drinking. I demurred strongly to all this, and extended the argument which I had made during our previous walk, telling him that by such giving he did two wrongs: first, to the beggar, because it leads him to cringe and lie in order to obtain as a favor that which, if he does his duty in working, he can claim as a right; and, secondly, to society, because indiscriminate giving causes a multitude to prey upon it who might be giving it strength; and I again called his attention to the hordes of sturdy beggars in Moscow. He answered that the results of our actions in such cases are not the main thing, but that the cultivation of better feelings in the giver is first to be considered.

I rejoined that this had to me a decidedly selfish sound, and then asked him about his manual labor. He said that his habit is to rise early and read or write until noon, then to take his luncheon and a short sleep.

He thinks this good for him on every account, and herein we fully agreed.

On our return through the Kremlin, passing the heaps and rows of cannon taken from the French in 1812, I asked him if he still adhered to the low opinion of Napoleon expressed in "War and Peace." He said that he did, and more than ever, since he had recently read a book on Napoleon's relations to women, which showed that he took the lowest possible view of womankind.

I then asked him if he still denied Napoleon's military genius. He answered that he certainly did; that he did not believe in the existence of any such thing as military genius; that he had never been able to understand what is meant by the term. I asked, "How, then, do you account for the amazing series of Napoleon's successes?" He answered, "By circumstances." I rejoined that such an explanation has the merit at least of being short and easy.

He then went on to say that battles are won by force of circumstances, by chance, by luck, and he quoted Suvorov to this effect. He liked Lanfrey's "History of Napoleon," and Taine's book on the Empire, evidently because both denounce men and things he dislikes, but said that he did not believe it.

We came finally under the shade of the great tower, into the gateway through which Napoleon entered the Kremlin, and there we parted with a hearty "good-by."

The question has been asked me at various times since whether, in my opinion, Tolstoy is really sincere, and allusion has been made to a book published by a lady who claims to have been in close relations with his family, which would seem to reveal a theatrical element in his whole life. To this my answer has always been, and still is, that I believe him to be one of the most sincere and devoted men alive — a man of great genius, and at the same time of very deep sympathy with his fellow-creatures.

Out of this character of his come his theories of art and literature, and, despite their faults, they seem to me in many respects more profound and far-reaching than any others which have been put forth in this century.

There is in them, toward the current cant regarding art and literature, a sound, sturdy, hearty contempt which braces and strengthens one who reads or listens to him. It does one good to hear his quiet sarcasms against the whole "fin de siecle" business — the "impressionism," the "sensationalism," the vague futilities of every sort; the "great poets," with no power over melody or bar; the "great painters," mixing their colors with as much filth as the police will allow. His keen thrusts at these incarnations of folk, and obscenity in the last quarter of the nineteenth century, and especially at those who seek to hide the poverty of their ideas in the obscurity of their phrases, encourages one to think that in the next generation the day of such pretenders will be done. His prophesying against "art for art's sake"; his denunciation of art which ministers to sensual pleasure; his ridicule of art which can only be discerned by "people of culture"; his love for art which has a sense not only of its power but of its obligations, which puts itself at the service of great and worthy ideas, which appeals to men as men — in these he is one of the best teachers of his time and of future times.

Yet here come in his unfortunate limitations. From his substitutions of assertion for inference, and from the inadequacy of his views regarding sundry growths in art, literature, and science, arises endless confusion.

For who will not be skeptical as to the value of any criticism by a man who stigmatizes one of Beethoven's purest creations as "corrupting," calls Shakespeare "a scribbler," and denounces nearly all that he has himself ever written?

Nothing can be more genuine than his manner; there is no posing, no orating, no phrase-making; a quiet earnestness pervades all his utterances. The great defect arises, as I have already said, from his mode of living; namely, that during so large a part of his life he has been wont to discuss subjects with himself and not with other men; that he has therefore come to worship idols of his own creation, and often very unsubstantial idols, and to look with misgiving and distrust on the ideas of others. Very rarely during our conversations did I hear him speak with any real enthusiasm regarding any human being; his nearest approach to it was with reference to the writings of the Rev. Adin Ballou, when he declared him the foremost literary character that America has produced.

A result of all this is that when he is driven into a corner his logic becomes so subtle as to be imperceptible, and he is very likely to take refuge in paradoxes.

At times, as we walked together, he would pour forth a stream of reasoning so lucid and reach conclusions so cogent that he seemed divinely inspired; at other times he would develop a line of argument so outworn, and arrive at conclusions so insane, that I could not but look into his face closest see if he could be really in earnest; but it always bore that same expression, forbidding the slightest suspicion that he was uttering anything save that which he believed — at least for the time being.

As to the moral side, the stream of his thought was usually limpid, but at times it became turbid, and his better ideas seemed to float on the surface as iridescent bubbles. Had he lived in any other country, he would have been a power mighty and permanent in influencing its thought and in directing its policy; as it is, his utterances will pass mainly as the confused, incoherent wail and cry of a giant struggling against the heavy adverse currents in that vast ocean of Russian life:

"The cry of some strong swimmer in his agony."

The evolution of Tolstoy's ideas has evidently been mainly determined by his environment. During the two centuries now ending, Russia has been coming slowly out of the Middle Ages; indeed, out of perhaps the most cruel phases of medieval life. Her history is, in its details, discouraging, her daily life disheartening: even the aspect of nature to the last degree depressing — no mountains, no hills, no horizon, no variety in forests — a soil during a large part of the year frozen or parched; a people whose upper classes are mainly given up to pleasure, and whose lower classes are sunk in fetishism; all their poetry and music in the minor key; old oppressions of every sort still lingering; famine chronic, no help in sight, and, to use their own cry, "God so high and the Czar so distant."

When, then, a great man arises in Russia, if he gives himself wholly to some well-defined purpose, looking to one high aim, and rigidly excluding sight or thought of the ocean of sorrow about him, he may do great things. If he be Suvorov or Skobelev or Gourko, he may win great battles; if he be Mendeleev, he may reach some epoch-making discovery in science; if he be Derjavine, he may write a poem like the "Ode to God"; if he be Antokolski, he may carve a statue like "Ivan the Terrible"; if he be Nesselrode; he may hold all Europe enchained to the idea of the Autocrat; if he be Milutin, or Samarov, or Tscherkasky, he may devise vast plans like those which enabled Alexander II to free twenty millions of serfs, and to secure means of subsistence for each of them; if he be De Witte, he may set an example to American statesmen by a resolute rejection of debased currency and by the reform of a vast financial system.

But when a strong genius in Russia throws himself into philanthropic speculations of an abstract sort, with no chance of discussing his theories or plans until they are full-grown and have taken fast hold upon him, if he be a man of science, like Prince Kropotkin, one of the most gifted scientific thinkers of this decade, the result may be a wild revolt not only against the whole system of his country, but against civilization itself, and finally the adoption of the theory and practice of nihilism, which logically results in the destruction of the entire human race. Or if he be an accomplished statesman and theologian, like Pobedonostsev, he may reason himself back into medieval methods, endeavor to fetter all free thought, and to crush out all forms of Christianity except the Russo-Greek creed and ritual. Or if he be a man of the highest genius in literature, like Tolstoy, whose native kindliness holds him back from the extreme of nihilism, he may rear a fabric heaven-high in which truths, errors, and paradoxes are piled up until we have a new Tower of Babel.

Then we may see a man of genius denouncing all science; urging a return to a state of nature, which is simply Rousseau modified by misreadings of the New Testament; repudiating marriage, though himself most happily married, and the father of sixteen children; holding that Dante and Shakespeare were not great in literature, and making Adin Ballou a literary idol; holding that Michelangelo and Raphael were not great in sculpture and painting, yet insisting on the eminence of sundry unknown artists who have painted brutally; holding that Beethoven, Handel, Mozart, and Haydn were not great in music, but that some unknown performer has given us the music of the future; declaring Napoleon to have had no genius, but presenting Kutusov as a military ideal; loathing science — that organized knowledge which has done more than all else to bring us out of medieval cruelty into a better world — and extolling a "faith" — which has always been the most effective pretext for bloodshed and oppression.

The long, slow, every-day work of developing a better future for his countrymen is to be done by others far less gifted than Tolstoy. His paradoxes will be forgotten; but his devoted life, his noble thoughts, and his lofty ideals will, as centuries roll on, more and more give life and light to the new Russia.

# 12

# A Recent Interview with Tolstoy
## by Th. Bentzon

Thomas Bentzon was an American journalist who met with Tolstoy in 1901.

Bentzon, Th. "A Recent Interview with Tolstoy." *The Critic* (New York) vol. 41 (1902): 570–574.

 I had certain prejudices against the man. I doubted his simplicity and mistrusted his paradoxes. Too many photographs had shown him following the plough, splitting wood, reaping in the fields of Yasnaya Polyana, or else seated before his bench, or writing in the dress of a mujik in a room perfectly bare except for a scythe, a sickle, and a shovel. These sensational portraits, including the last one, a masterpiece by Repine, where he is represented with bare feet, had caused me some perplexity. They appeared to me an unpleasant attempt at effect.

 I could not understand how a man could be so much peasant and at the same time live in a chateau, so detached from the material benefits of the world, allowing his family to profit by his large returns as an author, while denying them to himself. In spite of myself, I remembered an anecdote I had heard of his youth. When he was quite young, a mere student, the story goes, while in the country one time with his cousin, the poet Alexis Tolstoy, he made an impromptu and scandalous appearance in a park, wearing no more clothes than our first father, and mounted astride a cow.

This seemed not inconsistent with my idea of his later desire to astonish. I thought of his weekly receptions at Moscow in an absolutely rustic dwelling where his disciples in blouses surrounded him, contrasted with the salons when the Countess Tolstoy received her guests in evening clothes and silk gowns, and I was only half convinced.

My heart beat with hope and fear as I entered the delightful gardens wreathed with vines surrounding the villa which, at first glance, one would take for an aristocratic residence in the suburbs of London.

"Convalescent" is a strange word to apply to the grand old man, straight and muscular, who advanced to meet me, much finer-looking than his portraits, for those give only the leonine appearance of his face, the bizarre power of his flowing beard, the boldly outlined features under the magnificent forehead of an imaginative thinker, and the bushy eyebrows only half concealing the fire of his glance. But the changing expression, the sensitiveness of this rugged face, escapes the painter. How much kindliness in his smile, and how well does the peasant preserve in his blouse the dignified "mien of the grand seigneur"!

By the side of this blouse, the elegant toilet of Madame Tolstoy is somewhat surprising. I recognized at once the woman of the world, affable, well-poised, opposed to all exaggeration. She is twenty-five years younger than her husband, still youthful, and with a grace which in her permits freedom of speech. Perfectly capable of discussing and of contradicting Tolstoy's ideas, she has, nevertheless, stood by him firmly in his hours of peril. But her natural characteristics are moderation and good sense. One thing that she said paints her marvelously well:

"When I married Count Tolstoy, I had modest ideas, that is, I was willing to be second. He made me advance to the first place. Since then he has desired to make me third. Eh bien, non! I shall hold to second."

The other members of the family whom I met were the Princess Obolensky, the Marie who was the Antigone of her father, Tatiana Lvovna, his secretary, and Prince Obolensky.

I was received in a large, beautiful drawing-room, much too magnificent for Tolstoy's taste, and from which he had had many of the most precious objects removed. But his ascetic tastes had not been allowed full sweep except in his own room, furnished merely with a large divan which he used as a bed. With that was a writing-table as long as a banquet-table, strewn with manuscripts, newspapers, scattered pages over which ran that delicate, rapid, spontaneous handwriting, pages overcharged with erasures which did not prevent his correcting his proofs still further. According to the specimens that I have seen, the printers must have had a hard time to recognize their own work, for Tolstoy is an artist in spite of himself, whatever derogatory utterances he may have made concerning art, and form means more to him than one would believe after his protestations. I had proof of that when he spoke of our younger men of letters, of the "Revue Blanche," etc.

During dinner the conversation turned to literature; first to Rousseau, for whom he evidently feels remarkable affinity in spite of his own superiority of character, then to English writers.

His prime favorite in fiction is Dickens, and it is easy to understand why. Like himself, Dickens loves the insignificant, the poor, humble side of life; like himself, too, he denounces injustice, oppression, and cruelty. He likes the socialism of George Eliot. Apropos this superior woman, I asked him what to think of his own anti-feminine theories, and he replied with the courtesy of a perfectly well-bred man, that he desires the free expansion of every one's characteristics, man or woman, provided that what we call culture does not efface the essential virtues or create pride.

The whole anger of his nature was directed towards Kipling; not only does he detest the "imperialism" of this English writer, but he refuses to grant him any talent, which is going rather too far.

Tolstoy's horror of war is expressed in a pamphlet, "Carnet du soldat," translated by J.W. Bienstock, which he must have been writing when I saw him, for it appeared later, dated from Gaspra. He dictated it during his illness, wishing to use his last strength, as he said, to serve God in that way, not wanting to die before leaving on record a reply to the "Soldier's Manual," which General Dragomirov wrote in quite a different spirit.

The attitude of the Countess Tolstoy when her husband speaks of religion is very curious to observe. We all know with what courage, in an admirable letter addressed to the procurator of the Holy Synod, she protested against the sentence of excommunication. Tolstoy himself never wrote anything more beautiful than this sentence:

"The true renegades are not those who wander away in search of truth, but those who, placed at the head of the Church, act as spiritual executioners."

When I congratulated her on this utterance, she replied very simply: "I could not have spoken otherwise."

Nevertheless, she remains attached to the orthodox church, and wishes that the most solemn events of life, birth, marriage, and death, should be consecrated. Even while recognizing that the law of charity is the greatest of all laws, she respects the exterior forms of worship to the extent that, when secretary for her husband, she refused to copy in the manuscript of "Resurrection" a passage on the mass of which she disapproved.

"It is a good thing," she said to me in recounting this fact, "for men of genius to have near them people of common-sense to oppose them occasionally."

She spoke thus before Tolstoy, who did not reply. Evidently he is accustomed to these criticisms in his family, and knows how to endure them, however alive the sensibilities betrayed in his expressive face.

Indeed, non-resistance is one of the prime virtues that he practices. Consistent with his belief, he permits a footman sent by the Countess to follow him with a pelisse over his arm, while Tolstoy himself walks in peasant's dress. It is perfectly possible for him to allow his indiscreet disciples to use his name in too noisy a fashion. I have seen him at table eat and drink all that his wife put before him with the docility of a child, although prior to his illness he was a strict vegetarian. He excuses himself by saying: "It is the doctors' orders; for the moment, I am at their mercy."

His resignation under his physical sufferings is pathetic. He never complains, although he is afflicted with two or three incurable diseases. According to his belief, serenity and silent acceptance of whatever comes are signs of faith. "I rejoice in having taught myself not to be sad," he says in one of his letters. "The man who believes in God ought to rejoice over everything. To be discontented or sad about anything is not to believe in God."

His feebleness, then, is heroic feebleness. It matters not, he confesses it humbly. He signed himself, "Your feeble brother," in his beautiful letter to the Doukhobors of the Caucasus, those sectarians who call themselves "wrestlers in the spirit," and who, persecuted to act contrary to their conscience in carrying arms, emigrated to Canada. Tolstoy consecrated to them the author's rights of "Resurrection."

He intends some day to finish Madeline's story in "Resurrection," but, he said, "I have so much to write before," and then, with a smile, "enough to fill forty years."

He is preparing his "Journal," which is on the liberty of conscience. I dared not tell him that he would do better to devote his time at once to a beautiful romance, nor how much I wish that he had given only the form of a romance to the thoughts which he has embodied as oracles!

Are not these great plans of work pathetic in an old man whose death has been so many times announced as imminent? He works without any relaxation, invariably setting aside the entire morning for writing. He consented to his Crimean exile only on that condition.

The youthful and charming faculty of enjoyment of everything remains with him, in spite of his age and illness. He drew us out on the terrace after dinner to look at the full moonlight. The perfume of flowers was wafted to us in the silence. Suddenly he exclaimed: "These nights in Crimea — are they not glorious?"

Often his conduct is at variance with his theories. One of his women friends, an excellent pianist, went to see him at Yasnaya Polyana, and he begged her to play to him for an entire evening, forgetting that he had condemned all the musicians from Wagner to Beethoven.

Dare I say that these inconsistencies, which reveal his naturalness and freedom from all partisanship and pedantry, appear to me very attractive?

Tolstoy has no "system." Poets have no such need, and this reformer is only a great poet, an idealist even when he touches the most brutal realities of life.

To any one who suggests that his life and teachings are not always in accord, he invariably replies: "That does not prove that my principles are bad, but that I am weak." And to this weakness, with which he has often been reproached, we give after an hour of conversation the fitting word, kindliness, a kindliness which fears to inflict on others even the smallest pain.

We spoke of Repin's portrait of him. It was bought by the state for the Museum of Alexander III, but now that the clergy have forbidden the faithful to look upon the pernicious representation of an excommunicated being, it is not probable that the picture will be exhibited in a public gallery for many a day.

I remarked on the fidelity with which the painter has caught his habitual attitude, his manner of thrusting his hands, somewhat deformed by rough work, flat through his leather belt.

When the subject of the bare feet was introduced, Tolstoy interrupted me to explain:

"I was going to my bath when Repine, who was then living with me, said, 'Stay just as you are.'"

And I thought, with true repentance, that many people, among them myself, believed they saw, in this fancy of the artist, a voluntary pose of the model, an attempt to have it believed that he is a "mujik" to this degree.

I left him with the belief that he is the incarnation of pity supported by the imperious need of justice. He has the desire of reforming a social condition which is not in accordance with Christ's wish, and he translates this desire into acts. We need not fear that he will have many imitators.

When I remember him, I see him on a beautiful night, with the blue sky full of stars, standing on the terrace that overlooks the sea, the full moon riding high above in the heavens; pensive, his two hands thrust into his belt, his rugged, powerful head — the face indicating better than words the triumph of God over the beast — inclined towards his breast. With sublime inconsistency, he demands for the oppressed, the humble, the ignorant, — the only ones, according to his belief, to whom the Father of all intelligence reveals himself, Liberty and Light, the possession of which, under the conditions of this world, would quickly carry them from his ideal by making them in all ways like other men, full of pride.

# 13

# Tolstoy Today
## *by Edward A. Steiner*

This is the first of a group of articles, by Edward A. Steiner, the result of several months' literary work in Russia as the representative of *The Outlook* magazine. The time was spent wholly in research for his book, *Tolstoy the Man*, in interviews with him and his family, and in gathering literary material from the Tolstoy circles in Moscow and elsewhere. The articles were printed in *The Outlook*; this one is dated September 5, 1903.

Steiner, Edward A. "Tolstoy Today." *The Outlook* (New York) vol. 75 (1903): 35–42.

We hesitated long before asking if we might visit Tolstoy on the particular occasion here described. Rumors of serious illness checked both the artist's and the biographer's desire to see him, and only after we heard that his condition had improved did we venture out.

"Come and bring N. with you," read the telegram we received in answer to our letter. N. is a musician of note, and the feeling that through his playing Tolstoy would receive much pleasure made our coming easier, for we felt that we got nothing in return for the inspiration received.

Inhaling the cigarette smoke which makes the atmosphere stale and thick, is no great pleasure, especially as the train stops longer at the stations than it travels between them, and, being the only so-called fast train, is uncomfortably crowded. No air either enters or leaves the compartment, and when we reach our destination, and can really breathe the fresh, ozone-laden air, it is as exhilarating a moment as if we had stepped from a prison cell into freedom. The little depot is almost covered by snow, and after being wakened for a moment by the stopping of the train it sinks again into the deepest quiet. Here and there from among the white birches the rising smoke tells of some mujik's cabin in which the housewife has bestirred herself and has kindled the fire.

The horse and sleigh of Countess Tolstoy are awaiting us in the station yard, and almost simultaneously we ask the coachman, "How is the Count?"

"Slava Bogu [Praise God], he is much better," answers the faithful servant, whose broad, good-natured face smiles at us from his wrappings of fur, which make him look like an overgrown infant ready to be carried away by its nurse. He remembers the Count's guests, and has a particular smile for those who know that Tolstoy's philosophy about money has not at all influenced his servants, who are just as eager for their tips (Na Tschay-Rus.) as if they were living in the most materialistic atmosphere.

Swiftly we glided along through the increasing quiet; the noise of the passing train had almost ceased, and its deep breathing grew fainter and fainter. From the east a tinge of golden red poured over the silvery landscape; for a moment there was a hovering between twilight and morning, then the sun rose, bringing light but no warmth, and the great conqueror who in the summer colors earth and skies in varied hue seemed unable to affect the mass of white or to change the great shroud into a wedding garment. The noisy crows alone made dark spots upon the landscape and brought discord and disturbance into silence and harmony. No one in the village had yet stirred out of doors; the peasants were hibernating until the moment, when the increasing hunger would drive them out of doors; the windows were kept from being lost in the colorless landscape by the dirt of doors and outer walls. Horses, cattle, and fowl were indoors with the peasants, and within many a hut was heard the faint cock-crow, followed by the grunting of an unfed pig or the hoof-beat of a restless horse. From above the snow, like strange-shaped mushrooms, peeped with their Chinese roofs the white towers flanking the gateway to the Tolstoy estate; and the trunks of the trees within made dark lines upon the whiteness, showing the well-worn road between them. At the door we were met by Maria Lvovna, the Count's favorite daughter, who has been constantly at his bedside, and who at this time was acting as his private secretary and is his confidential friend. Among the Count's children the daughters had the greatest sympathy with his teachings, although since they have married they have gone the way of the world.

When we arrived, Countess Tolstoy was still in her room; she rises very late, her work keeping her up until past midnight. She is now correcting a new edition of her husband's works, and between the struggle with publishers and proof-readers she is taxed to the utmost, although she preserves both her youth and strength in a remarkable way. Any one who saw her a few evenings before at the symphony concert in Moscow, radiant in a light gray silk costume, her bright eyes shining from pleasure, would not have realized how much work and how many years are burdening her.

We were immediately shown to our rooms, but great was our astonishment when we found one of them to be the Count's former study, which had been converted into a guest-room after his removal upstairs during his severe illness. Mr. N. immediately called an indignation meeting to protest against such sacrilege, and we unanimously declared our disapproval of the change. The room should have been kept as it was.

Those scattered books, script, the large ink-pot, the Count's picturesque but crude scythe, and his working garments all are gone; the books are transferred to and straightened out in book-cases, where they stand like soldiers in perfect order, and our unpoetic satchels stand upon the table where he wrote all the books which made him famous. Surely there will be no holy shrine to which enthusiastic Tolstoyans may make a pilgrimage in after years, for the devastation seems complete. A physician who now is a member of the household lives in the Count's former bedroom, but the simple furniture has been left just as and where it was.

At the breakfast-table we find the usual contingent of strangers, and we look at one another in rather an unfriendly way, as much as to say, "What in the world brought you here to trouble a poor old sick man—can't you leave him alone?" We are good mind-readers, all of us, and we stare at each other during the informal meal, drinking our hot tea in silence; and no friendlier look comes over the faces of these somebodies and nobodies when our party is asked to go upstairs to see the Count. The room which we enter is spacious and comfortable; two large windows look out over the tree-tops and upon the silent fields of Yasnaya. The eye instinctively seeks the Count, and we are much startled as we see him. He is so thin that his features stand out with unusual sharpness. The eyes are still searching, but show the effect of much suffering, and a veil like the shadow of a passing cloud hangs over them. His voice, too, has grown weak, and his hand-clasp is like the touch of gloved fingers, without warmth or strength; but the greeting is not less cordial than ever. Now, struggling with approaching death, he is fastening upon paper memories and impressions of bygone years, and when every moment is precious he yet denies himself to no one, and does not stint the time which he spent with his friends. It is such a large welcome as only a large soul can give one. It is in striking contrast to the welcome which one receives from every other member of his household. They make you feel that you are here by grace alone, but it also makes you feel immediately that I have done him a favor by coming.

The conversation first turned upon his own health. He has been near death's door; the heart almost ceased its task of sending blood through his body, the limbs were cold and motionless, and around his bedside through many an anxious night stood loving watchers who feared the coming of a lightless morning. But no fear was his; he was not being dragged to his grave. Calmly he awaited the moment of his departure, and he struggled neither for life nor with death. He dropped no pious phrases as he told us of his nearness to the other world; it was the story of a traveler who came near to the gate of a city whose name and location he knew not, but of the existence of which he was quite sure. He did not tell as much of himself as we should have liked to hear; he quickly turned the conversation to the artist's and writer's work and plans, to N.'s children, whom he loves, and to all the living things which interest him so much.

The praise of Yasnaya's quiet he turned into a sarcastic polemic against the effort in the cities to build houses of entertainment for the laborers. You take the workers out of the pure air into a place crowded by people, you compel them to breathe dust, dirt and disease, and you call that "helping the poor to enjoy themselves." Our praise of the People's Palace in St. Petersburg, built by the present Czar, found no echo in his heart.

Upon our inquisitive looks at his writing-desk, he told us that he was then hard at work writing his reminiscences, and that he had finished a new story based upon his experiences in the Caucasus, and he read us page after page of the simple but beautiful narrative from his life in those wild mountain regions. His style seems simpler than ever; clear and sharp stand out his characters. The background is faint, scarcely touched, but the men and women whom he portrays are alive, and the truth they speak is clear and their words are pure. They are created by his love for all the men he met and knew in those young years of his eventful life.

The manuscript is as unreadable as ever, and Maria Lvovna had to be called upon to decipher those passages in which her father's pen had tangled the thought of the story by successive corrections. He was greatest and most precious when he laid down the manuscript and began to tell of his own feelings and emotions in those days.

How little he spares himself! He gathers up every scrap of the past, even if by so doing he tarnishes his halo; but he tells truth and loves truth, even if truth makes him unlovely.

We know now that the stories of his childhood and youth which were the first products of his pen were not entirely autobiographical; that, in fact, they contained much which, while it grew in him, he did not experience in actual life. He made us all laugh by telling the story of his first dancing-lesson. He was so ungraceful that the dancing-master tied a stick of wood to his back to make him stand out straight. "I could make better use of that stick of wood now," he said, pointing to his limbs, which were wrapped in a blanket. "But I shall surprise you to-morrow. I shall go out for a walk."

After dinner, N. was asked to play. The poor musician was so nervous that he had scarcely eaten anything, and when he sat down to the piano he fairly trembled from stage fright. First on the list were Tolstoy's old favorites: Gluck, Brahms, and Handel. "They are so quiet," he says. "Their passion was lofty and never base." Mozart came next, and changed him most, for he loves him above all the composers. "He never stirs within us," he says of him, "and when he touches the emotions, he does it with delicacy and purity." Chopin Tolstoy enjoys very much, and among Slavic composers he finds him the most sympathetic. During the playing of one of Beethoven's sonatas he grew visibly agitated; and that much-condemned "Kreutzer Sonata" he heard with pleasure. Schumann's songs brought tears to his eyes. "It touched my heart so much," he said, in excuse for his seeming weakness.

What an apt listener he is! how every fiber of his being responds to it, how he draws it in and how it intoxicates him! He knows, as did the Hebrew prophets, how art itself may become man's temple and his God, and he fights against his natural devotion to it, fearing that it might lure him from the narrow path which he has marked out for himself.

Long after the piano has echoed its last vibrant note we sit in silence and muse. The snowflakes fall thick and fast upon the already heavy-laden treetops. The Count sits with his head sunk over his breast, the fingers of both hands pressed against each other, and tears in his eyes.

Schumann's "Du bist die Ruh" has brought them out of his heart. Quiet, quiet everywhere but in our hearts; and is it quiet in his old age, when he feels the approach of death? With peace upon his brow, there is also much pain. The glow of artistic success, the gratitude of those he has helped. Yet each life has its tragedies, and those of us who know realize that he will carry some great sorrows. His tears are for a little boy, "Vantshik," (Little Ivan — Rus.) as they called him, the only one of his thirteen children into whom seemed to have been breathed the same spirit by which he was filled by the Creator. The little one looked into the world with the same clear eyes as did his father, and clung to him conscious of that inner relationship, the kinship of the soul. He died. The hurt in the father's heart seemed healed; but out of the treasure of song which Schumann gave to the world, and to which he listened that afternoon, there came one tender note and tore open the old bleeding wound. Strangers crowd his doorway asking his blessing, and go out into the world to live as he has taught them; strangers listen with reverence to each one of his words and become his disciples; but among his own there is none to preach his message or to live it. No complaint has ever passed his lips, and the tragedy of his heart has no witness except his own great soul, which has taught itself to love, and in love to suffer.

His philosophy of life has not changed, his belief in the efficacy of Christ's law for the salvation of man and of society is as firm as ever, and his theological views have still the same agnostic ring; but he knows God, prays to God, loves God, and truly "loves his neighbor as himself," and does not ask, "Who is my neighbor?"

It would be just a little part of all that he said and how he said it, to narrate his condemnations, or write down what he approved. This was no day for a biographer to make notes or an artist to make sketches, but it was a day for men to look into the great heart of one of God's great men.

Russia knows no spring. April is still only winter painted green, and then all at once it is summer. Long, not over-straight furrows are being drawn upon the great fields which surround Yasnaya Poliana. Patient moujiks are led across the fertile acres by the more patient if not more intelligent horses....

Tolstoy is waiting for the harvest, and although he will not again be able to thrust his sickle into the ripened grain, he believes that God's in his heaven — all's right. He is really aged; his form is bent, his step is slow, but his vision is not dimmed. He is young and vigorous in his condemnations, and younger still in those things which rejuvenate themselves each day, and which never fail: Faith, Hope, and Love.

He is still Russia's greatest living writer, in spite of the new stars which have arisen — Gorky, Chekhov, Andreev. He is still the one bold voice which protests against the wrongs perpetrated by state, Church, Czar, priests, and populace. His name is still the password which leads into the homes and hearts of all the lovers of freedom and believers in the law of Christ, but all he desires is to remain one of the Master's humblest disciples even unto the end.

# 14

# My Last Memory of Tolstoy
## *by Alexandra Nicchia*

Alexandra Nicchia was a traveling American female journalist who visited Russia at the turn of the century, met with Tolstoy in 1903, and described the complex relationship in the writer's huge family, including the growing tension between Tolstoy and his wife.

Nicchia, Alexandra. "My Last Memory of Tolstoy." *The Craftsman* (Syracuse, N.Y.), vol. 4 (1903): 45–48.

"Count Tolstoy, madam, is out cutting hay."

These outwardly respectful words were eloquent of a nameless thing to me, as a deep-shouldered maid-servant stood in the doorway of the man who is great to all the world but his own kin, and allowed a slow smile of remembrance to break over her heavy Slavic face.

I had just driven fifteen long and rugged versts from Tula to Yasnaya Polyana. For all that distance I had been tossed about in a harrowingly antiquated "telega," [Rus. cart], under the sweltering open sun of a Russian summer, to the nerve racking accompaniment of my driver's endless profanity.

The Countess herself, and six of the children, the servant added, were bathing down at the river. I knew enough of that half pagan household to deem it wiser to seek out the Count amid his hay-cocks, than the Countess amid her nymphs.

So, with the deep shouldered servant-maid swinging solidly on before me, I gathered up my dusty skirts — that Russian dust, how deep can it lie — and strode across the open fields, swimming in their mid-day heat.

Count Tolstoy's estate is on rolling land in places, and at last before me, on the crest of a long slope, I could see a little group of laborers where the master was mowing among the men. The hand that penned "War and Peace" was hacking determinedly at a few kopeks (cents) worth of hay-crop. Moujiks and master seemed to stand out before me there, almost Titanic, in the pulsating mid-day heat, silhouetted against the pale blue sky-line.

At a distance, I recognized the scholarly sloping of his shoulders. As I looked at him, swinging that ponderous, primitive, incongruous scythe, outlined against the hot turquoise sky, stubborn even in his defeat, determined in a great man's inward isolation, of his loneliness of soul, of a spiritual despair which he had not always hidden, swept over me.

Just why it did, I scarcely know; but that moment it came to me, and from that moment it has remained with me.

Although we had met before, more than once, the Count did not know me as I came up and stood before him. He straightened his bent back, but not without difficulty, I remember, and mopped his dripping face with his huge "platok" (kerchief).

He leaned on his heavy scythe, his breath still coming in gasps, and looked at me from under his shaggy brows, out of those small, close-set, penetrating, almost wolfish grey eyes. I was about to recall my name to him, embarrassed for the moment, and to explain my mission, when the petulantly wrinkled brow relaxed out of a sudden. He caught up my hand, with what I have every reason to believe was genuine pleasure, dropping his scythe, and leaving it there forgotten for the men to carry back, when, half an hour later, we took our way to the house.

Only that afternoon the Countess had confessed to me, with no taint of bitterness, that with her own hand she had written and re-written for her husband the manuscript of "War and Peace" twenty-one times. And she was the mother of thirteen children, the manageress of the estate, the secretary of a novelist, and the patient wife of an impatient genius!

But, as I was about to write, young people are young people the world over. And six of the Count's nine children, who were born at home, made the company, during their meal, merry enough at times. But the shadow of a life's melancholy, the gloom of a nation's still seemed to dwell in that big, bald, crudely furnished dining-room, dominated by the grim presence of the master himself. It is true he talked a great deal at night; I even remember that he sent me down to the kitchen to have the sugar-bowl refilled. I sat at his side, where the ever-watchful Countess had the habit of placing the honored visitor, and I also ate meat, though I saw that my host was eating what I strongly suspect was a cabbage soup, afterwards heaping his plate with its inevitable buckwheat mush. And as he devoured his dish, he volleyed keen question after question upon me, listening intently his pale grey eyes always alert while doing so, his massive head bowed in what may seem to the unknowing an attitude of humility. This appearance of humbleness, I had noticed more than once that day, as I watched him sit with his lap-board on his knees, looming over a pair of badly-made soles for a pair of badly made boots — and yet I knew it was all a quiet but none the less passionate obligation to those gods whom he held highest and best. Yet at most times it is his impatient strength, his rugged vitality that impressed me.

It was towards the end of that memorable dinner — memorable at least to me — before the younger children had been sent to bed, and the older people had clustered around the samovar of the Countess, that a burst of half-suppressed laughter broke out from the little ones, being away from the Count and myself. The Count talked on, preoccupied and unheeding, until a stern word or two from his wife to the children caught his attention. Then he asked, what it all was about.

The Countess gently protested that it was nothing, and was talking of other things, until a youthful voice popped up (I am translating quite freely), "No, No, we must tell Papa. Oh, mama, we must."

And then, amid some protest, the laughing girl went on,

"It's what Count K. told us yesterday, papa, about you. He said that Our Little Father (Tzar Alexander the Third) had spoke about you to Pobedonostsev (Procurator of the Holy Sinod and the Chief Minister). He said that it's no use bothering about you. He said that you could not help being just you, whatever you were, and that you wanted to be a moujik (peasant) just because you happened to be born a Count! But if you'd been born a moujik, he said, you'd have wanted even worse to be a Count!"

The pale grey eyes looked in studious silence at the girl. They looked at her, I believe, for several moments. I could see the toil-hardened hand drum impatiently on the rough table. Then the great leonine man seemed to shrink back into himself, and once more I had a passing and painful sense of one lonely dreamer's isolation. It was only for a moment, but the memory of it will stay with me for all time.

# 15

# My Last Visit to Tolstoy
## *by Aymler Maude*

Aymler Maude was one of the first translators of Tolstoy into English (highly praised by the novelist), the first Tolstoy biographer and a close personal friend of the Russian novelist, who visited Yasnaya Polyana repeatedly in the 1890s–1900s.

Maude, Aymler. "My Last Visit to Tolstoy." *The Bookman* (New York), vol. 24 (1906): 108–114.

It is now nearly four years since, early one morning in August 1902, I walked across pleasant, in places wooded country from Kozlovka-Zaseka, a small country station on the Moscow-Kursk railway, and reached, first, the long birch alley leading to the house, and then the house itself, at Yasnaya Polyana, where Tolstoy lived.

Five years had passed since I had last visited it and saw him. The place had altered but little; it was still the same plain, substantial country-house, with old-fashioned, rather bare furniture, but comfortable, roomy and well-adapted for its purpose. The large grounds seemed even more neglected and overgrown than of yore, as though announcing that their master was absorbed in matters more serious than the trimness of his gardens.

Tolstoy himself was slowly recovering from a series of illnesses, which had brought him to the death's door. One after another angina pectoris, inflammation of both lungs, pleurisy and enteric fever had been announced by the doctors who almost gave up. Slowly, however, his strong constitution pulled him through, and at the time of my visit he was on the high-road to recovery, though still so weak that he was glad to be helped upstairs after a couple of miles' walk. I noticed that at times he had to leave our company in the large room which served both as dining and sitting room, to go and lie down; and once or twice he even dropped asleep in his chair.

Tolstoy has always been skeptical of the advantages of medicine and of doctors, and it was amusing, how the Countess told of his surprise at finding that it really had an effect, when at the time of his greatest weakness they administered injections of camphor.

Speaking in his humorous way, he said to the three doctors who attended him, "Well, gentlemen, I did you a great injustice. You are really very good men, and you know all your science teaches — the only pity is that your science knows nothing!"

In a similar way, after being visited by an American Senator (or ex-Senator) with whose opinions he had been unable to agree, he once, at dinner, asked his family and visitors whether they knew how the United States is governed. They did not know; so he proceeded to explain that for the government of the country each State of the Union carefully chooses out its wisest men, and these in turn carefully choose the very wisest of all to be Senators. One such Senator had, he said, been to see him. This Senator knew all the sciences and all the languages, and had read all the books; but the pity was that he had not yet begun to think!

The Countess has a habit of telling even casual visitors of her difficulties, and of the opinions she holds contrary to her husband's, but I noticed many signs of her love and care of him; and far from being conscious of discord in the house, I was much impressed by the signs of love and respect that surrounded the old man from his own family, as well as from the retainers, and from the visitors of all classes and sorts who came to speak with him.

That, after over twenty years of married life, Tolstoy changed his views on property and other questions very much, and that this occasioned friction with his wife, whose views had not changed as his had, is a matter of common knowledge. But the fancy sketches that have appeared from time to time in our periodicals as to their relations to one another do him, and especially her, much injustice. With reference to one such article, which appeared soon after my visit, Tolstoy wrote to me: "My relations with my wife, my respect and love for her, and our friendly forty-year family life, are too well known to our acquaintances, and my wife is known to too many people, for the writings of some journalist or other to injure her reputation in any way."

The members of the family would accept all that Tolstoy has written but apart from any question of opinions, there was, in the family group I saw at Yasnaya, evidence of mutual respect and affection, which could not have existed had independence of thought among them been suppressed. Of his three daughters in particular Tolstoy said: "I have to thank God for giving me such daughters."

He has never kept a paid secretary. The work of copying out his manuscripts and assisting him in his correspondence has been undertaken first by his wife, and later on by each of his daughters in succession.

During my visit the youngest daughter, the Countess Alexandra, an attractive, powerfully-built and vigorous young lady, was the only one living in the house, but the second of his two married daughters, Mary, Princess Obolensky, was living with her husband in another house near by, and came over to the big house for most of the meals. This daughter in particular has been much influenced by her father's views. They all share the characteristic Tolstoy manner, and are frank of speech, kindly and sympathetic, and possess that assurance which comes of meeting many people intimately and on friendly terms.

Tolstoy's only sister, Mary, who, since her husband's death, has become a nun at the Shamardino Convent, near Kaluga, was also staying in the house. She had obtained leave of absence from the convent in consideration of the state of her brother's health. Knowing my interest in Tolstoy, she narrated several stories of the days when he devoted himself to educational work and started eleven schools in the neighborhood. On one occasion, soon after the emancipation of the serfs, owing to rumors of further rights the Tsar was said to have granted, the peasants of the district refused to work for the land-owners. Thereupon Tolstoy, his wife, sister and eleven teachers from the schools set to work themselves, and saved his crop by their own exertions.

In those days the boys from all the schools within reach used to collect, on Sundays, at Yasnaya Polyana, and Tolstoy would spend hours with them.

But to return to what happened during the four days of my stay: Tolstoy's two younger sons, with their wives, paid visits to Yasnaya Polyana, and no less than fourteen other visitors came, several of whom remained one or more nights. It will illustrate the diversity of interests that surrounded Tolstoy if I mention some of these visitors.

One was V.V. Stasov, the well-known critic and author, who is at the head of the Imperial Academy Library at St. Petersburg. He is an old friend of the family. His immense knowledge of books, as well as the great library he has at his command, makes him very useful to Tolstoy when the latter is dealing with some fresh subject and wants to see the best that has been written upon it. Stasov by no means shares all Tolstoy's views; but he feels the highest esteem for him. He remarked to me that among her great writers Russia has had three who were prominently intellectual. They were Hertzen, Griboyedov and Tolstoy.

Another guest was the sculptor Ginzburg, who was modeling a bust of Tolstoy. I had met him at the house on a former occasion, and was much struck, both times, by his inimitable powers of mimicry. With a towel and a chair he could give a whole performance of a nurse and the baby she had in charge; or he could become a most life-like tailor stitching clothes. Tolstoy was delighted with this dramatic abilities, and when we were out for a walk one day said to him: "Ah, if only our theatre-realists could be got to understand that what is wanted is not to put real babies on the stage and show the real messes they make, but to convey, as you do, by voice and feature, the real feeling that has to be expressed."

Ginzburg was anxious to interest Tolstoy in the sufferings of the Jewish population, and some of the stories he told him from his own knowledge of the subject were striking. He knew, for instance, of a girl anxious to complete her studies and qualify as a school-mistress, but who was unable to get college training within the place of settlement to which, as a Jewess, she was confined. There was only one possible way for her to procure the legal right of residence in Petersburg.

That way was to become a professional prostitute, and to apply to the police for a "yellow ticket," the special passport issued to the unfortunate class. This expedient she reluctantly resorted to, but was suspected of not following her vocation, and after repeatedly escaping medical examination by bribing the police doctors, she was ultimately expelled from Petersburg. The "yellow ticket" was not enough; nothing but the actual practice of her profession would satisfy the officials.

Another visitor was Stahovich, Marechal de la Noblesse in Orel, who, at a congress of Russian missionaries some time previously, had made a speech in favor of religious toleration. At that time this was an act of unheard of boldness, and produced a great sensation. Sipyagin, the Minister of the Interior, sent Stahovitch a reprimand, which the latter declined to accept unless it came from the Emperor. He thereupon received a letter from the Emperor, who took exception merely to some expressions Stahovitch had used. It was in connection with this letter, and the reply he was about to send to it, that he had come to consult Tolstoy.

In those dark days of bureaucratic despotism, when in Russia few people dared to call their souls their own, Tolstoy always most warmly approved of every assertion of personal dignity in opposition to official arrogance. I heard him tell with satisfaction how years before, when old Prince Dulgorouki, then governor-general of Moscow, sent for him on account of something he had written, he had returned a message that if the Prince had anything to say to him he had better call on him. He heard no more of the affair, which might have sufficed to send a lesser man to exile.

Several young people, relations of Stahovitch, had come with him to see Tolstoy. It was their first visit to Yasnaya, and was evidently a great event for them. Tolstoy did not miss the opportunity of implanting in their minds the seeds of his anti-war, vegetarian and land-nationalization principles. It was characteristic of Russia that members of a great land-owning family should respectfully sit at the feet of a philosophic anarchist, who admitted anything so mild as land-nationalization, only by way of concession to the weakness of humanity; his own principles demanding absolute abolition of every vestige of any government that enforces its decrees and the free yielding up of land to any one who cares to take it.

There was in the atmosphere of the house an infectious feeling of the importance of what was going on; and this showed itself among the visitors. There was plenty of mirth, but its savor came from the strenuous life lived there. It felt as though we were all invited to share in the immediate regeneration of mankind.

On Sunday afternoon a Jewish clerk living in the neighborhood called asking to see Tolstoy. He had read some of his religious writings, and wanted further explanations. To such callers Tolstoy is especially attentive. The man was invited in to tea, and soon a volume of extracts from the Talmud, a New Testament and an English Concordance were on the table in the large room already mentioned, and a series of questions and explanations were in progress. At first I did not follow this conversation, but presently Tolstoy called for attention, saying: "I have just discovered something. Listen to this." He then read out the parable from the twenty-second chapter of Matthew, beginning: "The kingdom of heaven is likened unto a certain king, who made a marriage feast for his son, and sent forth his servants to call them that were bidden to the marriage feast; and they would not come." He then went on from verse two to verse ten — how other servants were sent, and those who had been invited would still not come, and how at last the king sent his servants to the partings of the highways, to gather all they could find, "and the wedding was filled with guests." Stopping here, he asked the assembled company whether that made sense, as a parable of the international democratization of the kingdom of heaven. All agreed that it did. Then he went on to read verses eleven to fourteen, about a man who had not on a wedding garment, and whom the king ordered to be cast into the outer darkness where there shall be weeping and gnashing of teeth. Tolstoy then asked whether that made sense with the rest of the parable, and received a reply that it did not.

"Well," said he, "I have just found where it comes from! It is part of a story in the Talmud, and must have been copied by accident on to the end of the Gospel parable. Some scribe who knew the Talmud story by heart had probably been engaged in copying the Gospel, and coming to words which occur identically in both, has blundered, and writing from memory, put into the Gospels a passage which makes sense where it occurs in the Talmud, but does not make sense here."

A little later some one asked Tolstoy whether he considered that Christianity had any advantage over Buddhism. To this he replied that both religions were equally concerned to prepare man for what will follow after the present life, but that Buddhism gives this world up as a bad job, accepting what is wrong in it as inevitable; whereas Christianity (at its best) trains the soul of man for what comes after by engaging him in the practical work of establishing the kingdom of righteousness here and now.

One day during my stay a telegram arrived from the Grand-Duke Nicholas Mihaylovitch asking for news of Tolstoy's health. This, Tolstoy remarked, was a reminder that he had delayed acknowledging a service the Grand-Duke had done him by handing the Emperor a letter Tolstoy had addressed to him and wished to have delivered into his own hands.

That same day a workman called who had been injured at a factory and wanted to know how he could secure compensation. After seeing him, Tolstoy said: "In such cases I often have contradictory feelings. One sympathizes with the man, but yet one constantly feels, as in this case, that he wishes to take unfair advantage of his inquiry. He makes out that he can do no work at all, while really he could still do something if he wished to."

In each of the two houses on the estate there stood a grand piano. Where the Tolstoys are, music is never long absent; and professional musicians are frequent visitors to Yasnaya Polyana. One such pianist visited Tolstoy during my stay, performed a new piece he had composed, but as it was in the elaborate style Tolstoy discountenances, it received but scanty commendation from him. I asked if he still held quite firmly to the view of Wagner's later operas expressed in "What Is Art?" Yes; he was as resolute as ever. Music acts in two ways; one way is by the transmission of the artist's feelings; that is the real thing, and of that Wagner has comparatively little. The other is the physical effect on the nerves, produced, for instance, by passing from the softest and simplest sounds to the loudest and most complex crash. Of this pseudo-music, which acts strongly on the nerves, but not on the feelings, there is, Tolstoy maintains, a great deal in Wagner.

Only occasionally could one get Tolstoy to speak of such things as his experiences during the siege of Sevastopol, and other personal recollections; but he spoke more willingly about his works.

He regards "War and Peace" and "Anna Karenina" as belonging to that class of fiction which (like music) merely unites people in pleasant feelings without seeking to improve their outlook on life. "War and Peace," he remarked, is somewhat injured by the intrusion of a philosophy regarding the influence of great men, which (though true) is out of place in a novel. It is difficult to estimate the effect a novel will have on different people. "For instance," said Tolstoy, "in the case of 'War and Peace' (which one would think harmless enough) the daughter of a very celebrated Moscow doctor told me, to my distress, that reading it had given her a love of balls and entertainment."

"Resurrection" belongs to a different school of art, which aims at shaping the reader's feelings.

Tolstoy, who is very appreciative of faithful renderings of his works into other languages, seldom allows himself to complain of bad ones. On this occasion, however, he could not refrain from expressing the dissatisfaction he felt with the new complete edition which Stock, in Paris, was then beginning to publish. Of English versions, besides commending what my wife and I have done (French verses in "What Is Art" as being particularly skilful), he also named Mrs. Constance Garnett's work with approval. As it is rather the custom among some English people to pretend that any translation into French is sure to be good, and any translation into English is bound to be bad, it was with satisfaction, that I heard Tolstoy express so different an opinion, based not on the general merits of a language, but on the individual work of different translators.

Of his story, "Work While Ye Have the Light," in which the people converted to Christianity go and live a simple country life and find all their perplexities ended, he said: "I never hear it mentioned without feeling ashamed." This is so, no doubt, partly because of its artistic defects and unfinished execution, but also because he has long since realized that Christians and Pagans must have shaded off into one another and overlapped. Difference of opinion cannot, in real life, have corresponded to a difference of occupation and character as in that story. People's minds are not white and black, but various shades of gray.

While in poor health, Tolstoy allowed himself the luxury of finishing a novel of Caucasian life, the hero of which is Hadji Murat, who, next to the celebrated Shamul, was the most conspicuous leader of the tribes against whom Tolstoy fought when he first entered the army, in 1852. This novel will not, he said, be published during his lifetime, partly to avoid the unpleasantness of the scramble that, owing to his refusal of copyright, would take place among publishers, and partly because, he says, were he to publish it now he would be tempted to spend too much time in polishing it, and this would interfere with the more important matters he wishes to attend to before he dies. The attention a new novel of his receives when it appears would also be a temptation to his vanity ("I have caught myself at it!"), and would engross him too much.

In reply to an inquiry whether he admitted the charge frequently brought against his translations of the Gospels, that he had often misunderstood the meaning of the Greek text, he replied that he had been very conscientious in his study of Greek, and did not think he had made gross blunders. He had consulted an acute critic and a very fine scholar about doubtful passages; but in his efforts to counteract the Orthodox bias apparent in the Slavonic text he had no doubt often fallen into a contrary bias of his own. He compared his work to an attempt to depolarize a magnetized watch. This, I think, accounts for much that has perplexed people in Tolstoy's version. To a great extent it is a polemical work; and Greek scholars who have not before them the Slavonic version, which was Tolstoy's *bête noire*, do not see why he wished to force certain texts in this or that particular direction.

Speaking of Tolstoy's knowledge of Greek led me to ask what other languages he knows. Russian, French and German he has full command of. English he reads with complete facility and speaks well, though with me he preferred to talk Russian. He also knows Italian. Tartar, which he used to know, he has almost forgotten. Of ancient languages, besides Greek, he knows Latin and Hebrew, but the latter not well.

Of the advantage of learning languages he remarked that it helps brotherly intercourse among men. Meeting people one cannot speak with causes dislike. Speech draws us together.

The Countess mentioned that a publisher had recently offered half a million rubles for the copyright in her husband's works, but that the latter held rigidly to his repudiation of all such rights. Another publisher,

Marks, was offering 200,000 rubles for a copyright limited to two years, but with no better success. Yet when I spoke to Tolstoy of my own reasons for not forgoing copyright in the translations I made of his works, he did not object, but only said: "It is a question I have not considered from the side of practical advantage. I can only put a note of interrogation to it." He then passed on to other topics.

One sign of weakness that I noticed on this visit was that, for the time being, Tolstoy had abandoned his favorite game of chess, which he used to play with considerable ingenuity, though he never studied the book openings. I have seen him win a game by an ingenious combination several moves deep, forcing a pawn to queen in a position that appeared to offer little chance of doing so. When serving in the army in the Caucasus, absorbed in a game of chess, he once omitted to go on duty, and was arrested, losing the St. George's Cross he was to have received next day.

Cards he finds tax his attention less than chess, and he played cards each evening of my visit, winning seventy kopecks one day and one ruble and forty kopecks another. The game of Patience, which is played by a single player, is a favorite resource of his when unable to get on with his work. His daughter told me that he played it one day from two till six o'clock in the afternoon. Once, when playing it, he declared he was testing whether the work he was writing would be of any use to the world. The result of the game indicated that the work would not be of use. "But I shall write it all the same," he remarked as he put away the cards.

It is, of course, only when out of sorts that he spends much time at cards. When in fair health his usual practice is to come to breakfast about nine o'clock. He does not remain at table long, but takes some tea away with him to his room. Except for a short walk, or a bath in the pond, he is not seen again all the morning, and the Countess takes pains to prevent his being disturbed. Toward one or two o'clock he reappears for lunch. The afternoon is generally spent in walking or riding, alone or with visitors; but he does not feel satisfied unless he finds some time before dinner for reading. In the evening social intercourse fills most of the time. Late at night the letters arrive from the post, and are read last thing before going to bed.

He spoke frequently of other people's writings very highly, praising Dickens, of whose books and stray articles he asked me to obtain a complete list for him. Of some of Carlyle's minor works he spoke with approval, but said he had not been able to get on with Sartor Resartus.

Gorky being mentioned, Tolstoy expressed the opinion that his powers were extraordinary; while of the imitators crowding in Gorky's wake

Tolstoy spoke with contempt. "They are," he said, "like children telling tales to frighten one another. 'It was in a dark, d-a-r-k room (aren't you frightened?) and a great man came in! (aren't you frightened?)'"

The subject always nearest to his heart, however, and to which he returned oftenest, was religion. Speaking of his illness, he said with a smile that he had gained so much by the experience that "I can only wish you all to be."

He compared his recovery to being painfully dragged out of a bog into which he had nearly sunk, but into which he knew he had to return before long, and again to sink, before reaching the other side.

Speaking of love, he said it was the motive power of life. God is love. We cannot increase the measure we possess of it, and should not try to force it. How can we control that which controls us? We can remove all that hinders it, and can pay attention to it, recognizing its importance.

To hear this rugged old man, with his shaggy, prominent eyebrows, piercing eyes and ruthless criticisms of nearly all the occupations and interests of his fellow-men, so earnestly insisting on the supreme importance of love was rather strange. As in the case of St. Paul (another panegyrist of love), one feels that the tribute is the greater, because uttered by a man who impresses us not by his power of sympathy, but in his intellectual force.

One of the remarkable things about Tolstoy is the many sides of his activity, and his constant readiness to learn by experience. As an instance of this let me here find place for a story relating to the famine years, 1891 and 1892, told me by the banker A.N. Dunaev, an excellent and warmhearted man and an intimate friend of Tolstoy's. Meeting Dunaev at that time, Tolstoy said to him: "Ah, how useful you would be if you could come and help me to organize the relief in the famine districts!"

"Why?" answered Dunaev. "Surely you have plenty of helpers as it is?"

Tolstoy replied, "You know what I have observed? It is that those people who are free, and who come at the first summons, are free just because they have been found useless elsewhere. The useful people always have ties of their own already."

It is impossible adequately to describe the peaceful yet animated atmosphere of his home, crowded with vital interests, throbbing with life, overrun with visitors, but so influenced by the high and earnest tone of the great man they all looked up to that it felt both more bracing and more peaceful than any social circle I was ever in. In my note-book I see that I jotted down my feelings on leaving the place: "A remarkable and kindly family, apart from Tolstoy's genius. His influence is felt in the simplicity, frankness, kindliness and consideration shown toward all in the place."

At last the time came for my return to Moscow. Declining the Countess's offer of a conveyance, I set out on foot.

It was a fine moonlit night. The undulating country looked beautiful, the air was sweet and still; and as, full of thoughts of Tolstoy and of the others I had met and had friendly intercourse with, I walked toward the wayside station, I came to a place near a wood where there was a splendid echo. To test the echo some sweet voice in the distance sang: "I-love-you," and the echo answered clearly: "I-love-you!" It seemed a fitting sequel to a visit which remains in my memory as one of the most delightful and stimulating times in my life.

The stuffy, dirty, unpunctual and overcrowded train which took me back to Moscow seemed specially designed to emphasize Tolstoy's indictment of modern civilization.

# 16

# Tolstoy in 1906
## by Louise Maude

Louise Maude was the wife of Aymler Maude (see page 115).

Maude, Louise. "Tolstoy in 1906." *The Bookman* (New York), vol. 24 (1906): 104–107.

The afternoon was well advanced when my sister and I reached Tula. Our train was an hour late. At best Russians are not known for their punctuality, and now, when lawlessness seems to be in the air, the train service is more disorganized than ever.

As we were standing on the platform waiting for the train for so long, we asked the guard whether we were not losing time.

"Yes," he replied, "but at the next station we are leaving three carriages behind, and shall then catch up."

After the three carriages were left behind, we were still losing time, though instead of three or four, we now only lost one or two minutes on each railway station.

An hour was wasted in looking for a vehicle and horses to take us from Tula to Yasnaya Polyana, some ten miles away in the country; and it was seven o'clock before we arrived, and saw Tolstoy and his family dining at a long table spread under the trees in front of the house. Several persons rose and came to greet us; and we were asked at once to the table, without going first into the house. I threw my cloak and bonnet on a garden seat, and, after an informal introduction to those members of the household whom we did not already know, was given a place at Tolstoy's side. Besides Tolstoy, his wife, a son, three daughters, and a little grandson, there were present an English governess, a doctor, the eldest daughter's husband and step-children, and one or two other people, all of whom were staying in the house, or at the other house on the estate.

Though two men-servants were waiting at table, the dinner was a most informal meal; but perhaps our late arrival had contributed to the prevailing confusion.

We were asked many questions about ourselves and our friends, with that peculiar relevancy which makes you feel that the questioner is really interested in you, your family and life. Tolstoy has this power of remembering and entering into other people's interests to a very high degree.

Both Tolstoy himself, his son Sergius, who is in the Moscow Duma, and his son-in-law, who is in the National Duma, were pessimistic as to the state of affairs in Russia. It was very evident that the recent events had in no wise altered or modified Tolstoy's anti-governmental views. His sister, rightly supposing that newspapers only reach Yasnaya Polyana late in the evening, had one with her. It was early seized by some of the party, but Tolstoy remarked that he did not like reading newspapers. They not only waste time, but are even harmful, full of lies.

"They have promised the peasants land. And if it were possible, why should the peasants again form a separate class, and be the only possessors of land? Why should not a boot-maker, or a nobleman, have the use of land if he needs it? If they really wish to do something, why don't they adopt Henry George's scheme?"

I replied that people in Moscow said that the peasants would not be content with that, and would not understand it, and I asked whether Tolstoy thought they would.

"Yes," he replied slowly; "I think many of them would. Some to whom I explained it understood it perfectly and quite approved of it."

"That is well," I said; "for many educated people don't seem to understand it at all, and think they would lose their little farms and gardens if Henry George's scheme were adopted."

Tolstoy laughed. "Yes," he said; "I have spoken to people who when I advised them to read Henry George, told me they had done so and quite understood him; yet they complained that 'It is not fair to the people for the labor they put into the land!' And still they pretended to understand Henry George!"

"Well, at least you have now got some freedom of the press in Russia. That is something," I remarked.

"Yes," he replied, rather doubtfully; "yes, that is something." But he did not seem very ready to make even this small admission to the utility of the reforms from which so many in Russia hope great things.

When dinner was over, the company did not all rise at once. Engaged in interesting conversation with the host, I had only a vague sense of moving figures, and a feeling that I need not get up yet.

I gave Tolstoy one or two messages from people who had asked me to tell him how much they had been helped by his writings, as well as a resolution addressed to him by a meeting of the Vegetarian Association recently held at Cheltenham. He seemed pleased, and in his straightforward, simple fashion he said that he could not at all understand how it was that so many good people remain meat-eaters.

"The vegetarian diet is more expensive," said he, and paused, as if wishing to hear my opinion.

"Yes, I know," I answered. "I have often heard the same thing said. But of course it is quite a mistake; it is much cheaper when properly managed."

"Just so. Yet my wife won't admit it, and proves her point by giving me dainties — things out of season, and which I do not at all require."

It was rather amusing that the Countess Tolstoy was meanwhile complaining to my sister of her difficulties in providing for the family, some of whom were strict vegetarians, while others ate fish, and the rest were meat-eaters.

Soon after dinner several of the company assembled on the tennis-court, which is merely a bit of ground shaded by tall trees, with the turf removed, covered with sand, rolled or stamped down to a degree of smoothness which would hardly satisfy English players. On one side of the ground is a long wooden bench, and on it I sat down beside Tolstoy. He watched the game with interest, and the players, among whom was his youngest daughter, seemed very keen on it. It was amusing to hear the familiar English words "game," "love," "play," called out with Russian accents, and intermingled with comments in Russian. A consecutive conversation was impossible, especially as the people who watched the game kept coming and going, now sitting down on the bench, now rising to give room to some one else, or to take their turn at the game. But Tolstoy, though following the game keenly, put in a word every now and then, or made some remark which showed that he listened to what was being said, and again showed that he had not altered or modified his views on the use of physical force, on private property, or on Christian duty. When the Doukhobors happened to be mentioned, his second daughter, Princess Obolensky, remarked that it was the fear of forgetting their ideals and becoming self-satisfied by a life of material prosperity that led them to start on pilgrimages in search of the Messiah, and other eccentricities. Tolstoy began to say something which sounded like approval. Then a village beggar went up the path to a few feet behind our bench, and stood in that peculiar attitude of humility and resignation a Russian beggar can assume, holding his limp cap in his hands, which lay crossed on the knob of his staff; and bowing low his bare head, waited in silence. I turned to look at the beggar, and did not see that Tolstoy's hand felt for his pocket, as mine and those of most of the people present did, but I heard him ask his daughter if she had anything, and saw a hand pass a silver coin to the beggar. It made me think of what Tolstoy says in one of his books about it being a matter of politeness not to refuse a trifle to a man who asks you for it.

The beggar bowed and went his way, and Princess Obolensky told us a story about a woman she had heard of in Paris, who had given away everything she possessed, until she had nothing left but the dress she was wearing next her skin, and that then her relatives had her shut up in a lunatic asylum. There was a ring of pity and indignation in the speaker's voice, and her father again began:

"Yes, it is strange."

But there was another interruption, and I did not hear the rest.

It was a warm evening, yet Tolstoy soon began to feel chilly, and though an overcoat was brought him, he said he would go in, and I thought he seemed to be in pain.

The doctor, whom I had met in England some years before, now offered to show me round the park. I accepted, and followed him down the shady path to the pond, which, he said, had been recently cleaned, and from the banks of which the brushwood that had been allowed to grow for many years had been cleared at the same time. Tolstoy had had this done because in his mother's days these banks were open, and he wanted the ponds to be as they had then been. It was growing dusk beneath the tall, closely planted lime-trees which grew down both sides of the long avenues, at the end of which the evening light appeared, as through a small Gothic window. These avenues, as far as I could make out by the fading light, are intersected in several places by paths. After an extremely hot day, it was still very warm beneath the trees, but now and then there came a delightful, soft, balmy and refreshing breeze. The air was full of the song of nightingales. They seemed to be on every side and above us, as we walked along the soft, sandy, slightly humid footpaths. I had never before visited Yasnaya Polyana, or, indeed, any of those Russian estates, far away in the country, which both Tolstoy and Turgenev describe in their novels, and I could hardly tell whether it was the resemblance to some of the parks nearer Moscow or these vivid descriptions that gave these new surroundings that familiarity which adds a charm to the most beautiful, as well as to the most ordinary, scene. However, I had not much time to spare, nor did I feel sentimentally inclined, and we walked quickly, only stopping for my guide to point out different places mentioned in Tolstoy's novels; for instance, the wood where Kitty and her baby, in "Anna Karenina," were during the thunderstorm, while Levin was both vexed and anxious about them.

When we came up to the house, past the now deserted tennis-ground, we met the Countess, who was taking my sister the same round that I had just gone; and from a balcony Tolstoy called to me to come up if I wanted to talk. The doctor showed me the way up, and I found Tolstoy and his son-in-law on the balcony playing chess in the twilight. Tolstoy asked me to excuse him, as his son-in-law was going away the next day, and this was their last game, and would be finished in a few minutes. After a few moves his son-in-law was checkmated, because (as they both said) his eyes were weaker than the old man's, and he could no longer distinguish the pieces.

When his son-in-law had left us, Tolstoy spoke very kindly about a book of his stories, "Twenty-Three Tales by Tolstoy," which my husband and I had just translated into English, and a copy of which I had brought him. He said he had already had time to read my husband's short preface, which he liked very much, and that he thought the way the book was arranged was excellent.

He then fetched a book he had been compiling, "A Circle of Reading," a collection of thoughts by great thinkers and teachers (including many of his own), grouped according to the lessons they contained, and arranged for every-day readings, with a few short stories by himself and by other writers. He told me he considered that reading some of these thoughts, and thinking them over, was most useful; and that to read them to, and talk them over with, a child was the best form of education.

"Children," he said, "understand many of them." He knew this by experience with his little children, who gladly and regularly came to him every day, to hear some of these thoughts read out and talked over. He said he was compiling a second volume, simpler and even more suited for children and uneducated people.

We went on to talk about a child we both knew, and were interested in; and about a mutual friend I had met in Moscow a few days before, who had nearly got into trouble and lost his place, being accused by the gendarmes, quite unjustly, of carrying on revolutionary propaganda.

"Ah, yes," said Tolstoy despondently, "I have just been thinking how fortunate your old father and I are to be so near death."

It had grown dark; the nightingales never ceased their songs, and from downstairs came the sound of a human voice, singing snatches of songs to the guitar, in a subdued tone, as if observing a natural desire, prompted by the mood of the moment.

"How lovely," said Tolstoy. "Those are my daughter's step-children; they don't know that anyone is listening; that is why it sounds so beautiful."

It was time to go in. Tolstoy took the book he had given me, wrote an inscription on the fly-leaf, and returned it to me. Then he showed me some portraits on the wall of his study.

Among them was one of Henry George, and we passed into the next room, where a long table was spread. We had just enough time to drink a cup of tea before taking leave and starting on our return journey to Moscow.

# 17

# Tolstoy Prophesies the Fall of America
## by Stephen Bonsul

Stephen Bonsul was a prominent American journalist and writer who wrote for the *New York Times* from 1900 to 1910. He is the author of two books, *Unfinished Business* and *Suitors and Suppliants: The Little Nations at Versailles*. He met with Tolstoy during his trip to Russia in 1906–1907.

Bonsul, Stephen. "Tolstoy Prophesies the Fall of America." *New York Times*, 7 July, 1907.

We had talked about my prospective interview with Count Tolstoy so many days and many nights, that I had begun to feel that that was all there was to be of it. [...] Last week Dmitri Ivanovich visited the count and found him distressed.

"He told me with tears in his eyes that he could not work all day as he had done for forty years. 'Why is this?' — he asked me. I said that I could not imagine. Who would venture to tell the great man the truth? Then he said, 'You know, for the first time I feel as though I were seventy years old.' And there was nothing to say except, 'Lev Nikolaevich, you are lucky, for you are within six months of eighty, unless the parish registry lies.' And of course no one would say that."

What happened when the Count first felt the grip of old age upon him I must tell shortly, therefore it will be impossible to use the words of

Dmitri Ivanovich. The morning after he felt it, he rose early, and saddling his own horse traveled to Tula to talk politics with the Governor. Arrived before the palace, he was placed under arrest for a few minutes by the guard, who liked not the looks of this man with the strangely refined face and manner, and clothed in peasant's garb. After his political talk, the Count mounted again and rode a wild round-about way to his home. He must have covered forty miles or more. As a result, the old hunter had colic, and was very leg weary. Then the Count lost his appetite, and went two days without even the vegetarian diet that has sustained his iron fame and tireless industry for the last ten years.

The news that Tolstoy was ill attracted attention throughout the land in the throes of revolution, and the papers were filled with bulletins, real and imaginary, as to the great man's condition. Then suddenly, as suddenly as he had fallen ill, the sage of Tula recovered and adjusted himself to his eightieth year as easily as the conditions by which in an arduous life he has been confronted.

He consented to walk only five hours a day, and to read only four. The farm he would let take care of itself. On the following day, he wrote finis to the first volume of his memoirs, and then embarked upon a volume of fairy tales, a sequel he wrote two years ago.

Dmitri Ivanovich brought the good news and at the same time hustled me to the situation.

"Hurry," he said, "the way is paved for you." And I certainly hurried, at least until I caught the train.

Our engine was built in America, but the engine driver was not. That Tartar took nine hours to drive us a hundred and twenty miles. Ours was indeed a plebeian train, unlike the Siberian express that puffed and snorted on an adjoining track. The express was carrying Generals and Governors to the Far East, but our train was filled with drovers and emigrants, and wandering bands of unemployed peasants. It was composed of the second and third class carriages, and I sat in lonely grandeur in the only second-class coach....

We came into Tula about eight, and I went directly from the railway station into a little "traktir," or inn famous for its horses, for I was still fifteen miles away from the home of Tolstoy....

The three blacks, harnessed abreast in the troika fashion, carried us along the Kiev highway at a sparkling pace. Spring had come at last, and all mankind as well as nature was awakening to the New Year. The driver halted... At last, however, he spied a narrow wagon track that skirted along the birch wood.

That's the way to the village and the lands of his mightiness, he shouted exultantly, and down we plunged.

Whatever else the Count may be, he is certainly not a good road builder. For something over two miles we plowed and plunged our way through flooded woodland and marshy meadow.

More often than not the mud oozed from the bottom of the wagon, and the water of the spring-flooded streams reached the horses' bellies. The track we pursued became more and more faint; the driver wiped his sweaty face with the back of his hand, and every now and then pulled away at a tousled lock of his carroty hair in ever deepening perplexity.

Suddenly two great brick pillars rose before us, upon which once long years ago a vanished gate has hung.

"Oh," shouted the relived driver, "we are at the grounds of his highness. You see, I do not always lose my way." ...

There, right before us, rose the home of the sage, sitting there in the sunny clearing in the woods, from which Yasnaya Poliana has its name. I had only caught a glimpse of the low rambling house of brick, covered with stucco broken away in patches, and the vine covered verandas, when my survey came to an end. I heard the click of the window latch, and looking up I saw Tolstoy as I had seen him a hundred times in his pictures, only a hundred times more vivid.

He stood watching my approach from a Venetian window in the second story, without head covering. He wore a white tunic buttoned up closely around his neck, high boots to the knee, and English riding breeches, dilapidated and scratched by briers, but still in excellent shape. These little things I can describe, but not the hawk-like gaze with which the forest philosopher looked out from his study window at the man who had come on a frivolous errand — and for a moment I thought of flight! Could I hope to conceal from eyes like these my philosophical unworthiness? Would he not see that I have no proper appreciation of people who feed exclusively on vegetables and delight to run about in their bare feet?

Would he not see that I am one of those degenerates who take Emerson as a sleeping potion, and that I had come to the pleasant clearing in the woods in hero-worship of the author of "Anna Karenina" and "War and Peace," masterpieces which the sage of Tula regards as indiscretions of his youth which, if the world were but charitable, would long since have been forgotten.

As these thoughts crowded upon me, I saw my unworthiness plain, and I think I would have had the courage to bolt out, but the young butler opened the door of the manor house with a smile. Here was a gentleman's servant whose services could not be obtained at the employment bureau. He cheered me on with cheering words and reassuring smiles.

"The count has talked about your coming all the morning," said the butler and pushed me in.

For a moment the same eager look came into Tolstoy's eyes that I had seen there from the road below. He remembered, it seemed to me, the long line of bold faced men from America who had come to him in pilgrimage; perhaps in his incurable optimism he had recalled the words of his favorite Emerson, "When half-gods go the Gods arrive." Perhaps he had had hopes. Be this as it may, when I stood before him in the guise of an imitation European, his countenance fell. Then, as though he wanted to laugh at something and yet recognized his present duties as host, he said,

"You see this pencil? It was left me by an American statesman who called some months ago to consult with me about affairs of state. I shall always remember that man. It is the best pencil I ever had."

Then we both laughed, and the Count was so unexpectedly human for a few minutes, that I came within an ace of telling him my trip adventure. And so it was, that suddenly our conversation lost its momentum. It was the first warm day of a wintry spring, and the sunshine poured in through the south window in life-giving streams....

I found myself talking leisurely about Indians; the Indians I had met skulking along the shady sides of Siberian rivers; more Indians I had met upon the sawdust of our circuses, and a few upon the borders of our vanishing wilderness. I spoke about the some images I have seen on the Ussuri, a handwork of Gyliiaki and of some in Mexico, and how curiously alike they were. The Count listened to my babble, and used it against me when the proper time came. When the talk came back to Russia, the Count asked me what signs of hope I saw in the present situation here. I told him — Duma is the first assemblage of Russian men ever met to discuss their own affairs, and to exercise an influence, however slight, upon the Government under which they lived."

"I have no hope in this Duma," reported the Count. "I have no hope in any form of parliamentary Government. Parliamentarism means simply crying over old sores. I am against the Duma because Parliamentarism is not an instinct of Russian people.

"Look at your own Congress and State Legislatures. You Americans had a new and beautiful land out of which your fathers thought to realize a heaven upon earth, and how has it ended? You have reproduced European conditions, in their most exaggerated forms, thanks to what you call representative government, and the national selfishness you call patriotism. How can you take interest in Duma? And you say that people in America take interest in it, too!"

I said, "We seek to alter conditions rather than ourselves. I suppose because we find it easier. Now, why are you interested in Duma?"

This time the Count would take no denial, and I forged ahead, realizing that I was a worm about to be crushed. I told him that I had sat in the Duma for six weeks and had found it to be a deliberative assembly, much more orderly than the most, in which all classes of the empire were more or less fairly represented, including perhaps even the terrorists and the expropriators. I told him I had been struck by the sound common sense of many of the speakers, particularly of the peasant members, whose constituents number four-fifths of the inhabitants of the Empire. I thought that it was possible that in the Duma a fair statement of just grievances might be reached, and that a man might be found capable of redressing them.

"Of course in America," I said, "we do not know whether a large number of the Russian people are fit for self-government. Outside of the Duma they seem to be furnishing much evidence that they are not. Yet in the history of your once great and free cities, such as Novgorod, Tver and Pskoff, it is demonstrated that representative institutions were entirely successful, and that there was much happiness and prosperity in these regions in Russia until Ivan the Terrible and others of his kind reduced free citizens to slavery. Then of course you must remember that we take a sentimental interest in the spread of manhood suffrage. Three hundred years ago we Americans were a band of exiles cast upon an inhospitable shore. We have grown great and strong, and we believe that, under God, thanks are due to our representative institutions."

"Great and strong! Great and strong!" Tolstoy pounced upon my commonplace before it was uttered. "Who besides you futile politicians says that you are great and strong? I grant you were great and strong in the days of Emerson and Thoreau, but today you place your trust in the treasure that is in your vaults.

"Great and strong! Oh! I think not. A nation, like an individual, is strong by the faith that is in it, and today I fear the faith of America is on the almighty dollar. All man's work is the reflection of a man's soul. All man's soul is the conception of his Maker, the Supreme Being. Of course, I do not know but I think that rude images of the Indians of which you spoke are more grateful to Deity than your rushing railways and never-resting factories which have enslaved the freest people. At least the Indians had some vague idea of eternity and of a God, and with rude, trembling fingers tried to incorporate it, but you think only of time, and of big man."

In his earnestness the Count now rose, and forgetting his years walked up and down his study with the stride of a young man.

"Prosperity, prosperity!" he repeated. "What a shameful plea that is, which your American platform-makers address the voters. They do not say, 'we will give you an honest rightful government,' but they say, 'We'll make you all fat and sleek. If you vote for me, you will have a double chin!' And no one arises to say, 'What will your full dinner pails profit if while gorging your bellies you lose your immortal souls?'"

Then the Count stopped and gazed at the photographs which adorn his study, speaking likeness they were of Emerson, Thoreau, Channing, Bryan, Henry George, and the late Ernest Howard Crosby.

"Oh! I thank you for what your country has given the world in the lives of those men. I thank you for what you have given us in the past. But for the future I have my fears. I see no one to follow in their footsteps." There were tears in the Count's eyes as he spoke of his love and affection for those great Americans. Of Mr. Bryan's visit to the farm he spoke with gratitude. But of the rest of our statesmen he made it quite clear that they are outside of the Tolstoyan pale.

"The fall of America," he continued. "When I see the deserted shrines of your forefathers, I think it will come more swiftly than came the fall of Rome." ...

Then with an acrobatic mental jump the Count returned to the Russian situation. Here his criticism of the leading men of all the parties was quite as sweeping and much less courteous than had been his characterization of our political leaders in America. Then for one moment, his iron mood relaxed and relenting, he said,

"No, no, forget that I had the temerity to say that. They are not all bad men; I pray not, but hopelessly misguided. Of course, as you must know, the vital phase of our situation in Russia is the land question, and yet no man, much less a party, not those who say 'yea' to confiscation anymore than those that say nay, dare to approach it with frankness and sincerity. In this very Duma the agrarians of the liberal groups stand convicted of bad faith or of ignorance. There is but one solution of the land question in Russia as well as elsewhere which can be regarded as just and equitable, as far as anything can be final in this transitory world, and that is, of course, the land law as preached in their modern form by Henry George. But our wily agrarians never mention this solution because it promises no class advantage, and I take it as a recognized axiom in politics that if you want to secure votes and get into office you have to compromise.

"Then, of course, Henry George was an honest man, and the world of practical politics rejected him; our agrarians are not so honest, and they won't be rejected if they can help it."

When I saw the Count later that afternoon, his day's work was done, and the plough men and women were returning from the fields singing and laughing. They are a merry happy folk among the Russian peasants, as is their former landlord among his class. He carried in his hand a little weekly paper published in Portland, Oregon. He had his finger on a paragraph, and hastened to say,

"You see the news from Chicago, with its revelations of corruption and rottenness. It is not the only American paper that I read. See, here, is this not beautiful? It is from the "Key Thoughts" of Lucy A. Mallory, and I read them every week. While people in America write as she does, I know the salt has not yet lost its savor. Listen: 'We who know the truth, must first change the world in ourselves internally, before the world can be changed in others externally. If we know the truth of life, and do not live it, we are as a lighthouse set upon a hill in which the light has gone out.'"

Then, with impressive earnestness, he said, "Forgive me if my judgments have been harsh, or have seemed so. Only remember that you live in a light-house set upon a hill, and that in the last few years, it has seemed to many watchers that the light which was once the light and hope of the world, whose rays penetrated into the uttermost parts of the world, was about to be overwhelmed by shadow.

"Pray that young Americans would see to that light, and keep it day and night. It is the flame that their fathers lit, and it has become the light of the world, as well as yours. It would be a dark world without it."

I rose to go, and the Count accompanied me a few steps to where my troika was waiting. The little children now rushed forward and stood around the great tree, each in its accustomed fashion.

"Except you become as little children, you shall in no way enter the Kingdom of Heaven," said the Count with a warm pressure of his hand, as we parted. The black horses darted forward, and soon they were rushing through the streams out on the great highway which leads from the home of "the pleasant clearing in the woods," back to Tula and to the living world.

# 18

# Tolstoy in the Twilight
*by Henry George, Jr.*

"Tomorrow I die, meanwhile, I have another book to write."—Tolstoy.

Henry George, Jr. (1862–1916), was one of the last Americans who saw Tolstoy alive. Tolstoy greatly admired the works of his father, Henry George (1839–1897), American economist, founder of the single tax movement. Born in Philadelphia, George moved to New York City in 1880 and spent the remainder of his life writing and lecturing. He supported the Irish Land League and various economic and political reforms. In 1886 he ran for mayor of New York, running ahead of the Republican candidate Theodore Roosevelt. His son, Henry George, Jr., was a representative from New York in 1911–1915; between 1881 and 1897 he was a journalist with the *Brooklyn Eagle*, and managing editor of the *Florida Citizen* and *North American Review*. He published the biography of his father Henry George in 1900 and met with Tolstoy in 1909.

George, Henry, Jr. "Tolstoy in the Twilight." *The World's Work* (New York), vol. 18 (1909): 12144–12154.

    For me the visit to Tolstoy was like a pilgrimage, yet it was more than a visit to a holy man.

    It was to meet for the first time the man of the greatest moral influence in Russia, and perhaps in all North Europe, despite his excommunication by the Russian State Church.

    I had wired from [the] taiga [spruce and fir forest], Siberia, on my way from Japan, asking if he would receive me, for the newspapers had reported him in feeble health. At Samara, three days later along the line, I received the answer:

"I shall meet you with joy."

Tolstoy lives on his ancestral estate, a few miles out of Tula, in the prefecture of the same name. The Trans-Siberian Express put me down there in the morning. I confess to some feeling of consternation that English would not pass here in Russia. Nothing so disconcerts an Anglo-Saxon as to find himself in a place where his language is disregarded. Thus far I had gone around the world with no other equipment than English. It had served all ordinary purposes. Where an interpreter was needed, someone would always turn up.

But in Russia it was different. Not only did English not meet the common exigencies, but of the outside languages it had less vogue than German and French. However, a young newspaper man, who had heard of my coming and was on the lookout, took me in hand; and although we were separated by tongue — for he could speak only Slavonic — I resigned myself to him and soon was being driven at a mad pace in a three-horse drosky for Tolstoy's home.

Of all the drivers of the world, perhaps the Russian drosky driver is the most brilliantly reckless. One of our horses was hitched between a pair of shafts; the other two swung clear on either side; and, whether over cobbled streets or macadamized roads, they sped with a fiery impetuosity that vividly pictured in the mind the chariot races in the Roman days....

Leaving the open country, our road all at once cut through wooded tracts; and suddenly, without the slightest preparation, I was impressed with the feeling that we were on enchanted ground — the home of fairies and elves, once perhaps the scene of knightly valor. Great firs — the finest and oldest I had ever seen — mixed with ancient cedars and pines, threw their points defiantly to the sky. Deeply buried in the darkened heart of the woods, I pictured in imagination the ruins of a castle....

## *Tolstoy's Beautiful Estate*

It seemed a fitting preparation for the approach to the Tolstoy estate, of which we caught first sight from a hilltop on leaving the woods. To the northeast, a single line of trees marked its nearest border.

The estate goes by the old name of "Yasnaya Polyana," which means, if I am correctly informed, "Clearing in the Woods." It is more than 2,000 acres in extent, and comprises agricultural lands, woods, and a small park set off for the household. The park is on the south side, and there the house stands, two or three hundred yards back from stately brick and stucco posts that mark the main entrance. A huddle of straw-thatched farmers' huts are passed to the left as you enter.

The perfume of flowers came with a spray of raindrops from overhanging boughs as we passed up a winding driveway. The gray mirror of a small lake shone on one hand, and on the other a picturesque brook. Rounding between two huge clusters of white and purple lilacs, we came upon the house — white, ample, two-storied, solid, with a curious border of doll-babies and Noah's Ark animals outlined with a saw in a porch balustrade.

A couple of stone steps and a small platform were in front of the doorway where we drew up. At the sound of our horses' bells several men came forth, two in blouses of some blue stuff. Word of our leaving Tula had been sent, so that we were expected.

Presently Count Leo Tolstoy, the namesake and third son, appeared in a business suit of mixed cloth. He is something past forty and has a striking head and personality, with fine, large, brown, luminous eyes. He wears a reddish beard, and his hair is thinning on top.

He gave me a cordial welcome in English. I presently found that all the members of the family spoke English — easy, ready, fluent English — although at times, from a delicate politeness, affecting to apologize for it to soften a compliment.

Young Count Tolstoy said that his father was waiting; after laying aside our outer things we proceeded upstairs.

The stairs and the floors generally were of unvarnished and unpolished wood, but spotless. There were few rugs. The walls were mostly white; in places, they carried a soft, unobtrusive color. Everywhere you caught the feeling of simplicity, utility, and strength. Everywhere you also caught the feeling of art and literature, although many of the pictures were only photographs, and portraits, at that. But there were books, anywhere, everywhere; not for show, but obviously for use.

At the top of a winding stairway there was a turn, and going through an anteroom, we entered the Tolstoys' work-room at the presence of the seer himself.

He was seated in a wheel-chair, which he had begun to use at the Crimea some six or eight years ago, when seriously ill at that time. His feet were on a level with his hips, and were covered with a rug. He wore the long peasant's blouse of light yellow, coarse material, such as appears in his latter-day pictures, and on his head was what does not so often appear: a skull-cap of the same material. The face was the one familiar the world over — gray eyes sparkling through shaggy, overhanging brows; seamed forehead; thin, floating gray hair; thin, flowing moustache and beard around a restless mouth that seemed sharp and at times flat.

## Working to the Very End

As he sat there in the chair, age seemed to have placed its hand heavily upon him; yet he appeared not so feeble as delicate. But the eyes revealed the keen, buoyant spirit within. It was a life joyously spending itself to the very end, undaunted by the approach of death.

Tolstoy had a peculiarly kind expression; he offered me a very cordial and personal welcome, during which I noticed my father's portrait holding a place of honor on the wall.

"Your father was my friend," he said with singular sweetness and simplicity.

I asked after his health. "I was troubled to read in a Japanese newspaper a report that you had not been so well," I ventured to say.

He answered with the frankness that I found a characteristic of the whole family: "I am now quite old — eighty-one. I do not expect to stay much longer. One of my feet has to be nursed. But I am keeping at work."

He gave me a smile as if the matter of his death was nothing at all; as if he said: "Tomorrow I will die. Meanwhile, I have another book to write."

What could death be to such a man? His business is to work while life is in his body.

As to the work, I said I had heard that there was another book under way. Did it deal with political economy?

"No," he answered; "this is not on political economy. It treats of moral questions, which your father put first."

## Tolstoy Endorsing Henry George

This led him to refer to an article on my father's teachings, for which my visit had served as a pretext, and which he had just sent off to a St. Petersburg newspaper. "Perhaps the paper will fear to print it, for we have little freedom here, and there is little discussion. But if that paper will not print it, then I hope to get it into another." He handed me a copy of the article....

In connection with this unqualified espousal of what he was pleased to call "the teachings of Henry George," my host directed that the translations of the George books into the Slavonic (Russian) tongue be brought to him. They proved to be all of the principal books except "The Open Letter to the Pope" (obviously inappropriate for Russia, where the Greek Church holds sway), and the unfinished "Science of Political Economy."

He also showed me a large number of translated pamphlets and lectures — all in cheap form for popular circulation. The translator and popularizer of the works is his intimate friend and neighbor, Sergei Nikolaev, who, as he said, would come to the house in the evening.

Tolstoy talked with the utmost fervor and enthusiasm of the truth, as if the matter was impersonal to me, suddenly tossed the rug off his feet and got out of his chair to go over to a table, and write his name on some of the copies. The ease and certainty with which he moved was quite bewildering, yet I noticed that he wore a pair of old-style high boots, with the trousers tucked inside. The handwriting had a clearness and firmness that was truly wonderful for a man of eighty-one.

And, even as he wrote, his mind indicated its variety and range. For instance, he touched upon Japan, whence I had just come. "I want to know many things about that country," he said. "I believe the Japanese are a great people."

It was the time of afternoon for the daily nap, which is part of Tolstoy's present necessary routine — for the family watch his health with loving care — we withdrew. There is now no laboring in the fields or cobbling of shoes or strenuous physical toil. While not ailing in any alarming way, except for the swelling of the feet, Count Tolstoy, with his crowded life of more than fourscore years, is in very delicate health; and for a man of his high-strung temperament, he yields to medical advice with surprising docility.

## Tolstoy's Interesting Family

While our host was sleeping, I strolled across the gardens with the son, Leo Junior, whom I found to be delightfully companionable — full of reading, wide-visioned, and arriving at his conclusions by independent thought.

Proving that he is not a mere follower in the footprints of his famous father, he has an artistic bent, and, without any instruction whatever has taken sculpture as a pastime, having a fine bust of his father in process when I visited Yasnaya Polyana. He was pleased to allow my photographer friend to take for me a picture of him standing beside the unfinished bust of his father.

But young Tolstoy's serious business in life is as a playwright; and, like his father, he serves to make his writings teach things. One of his plays deals with Russian politics. He knew well that if he placed the scene in Russia the play would never pass the censor. So he laid it in America, and used American names. Its application to Russia was obvious, but it passed the censor, and had a very successful run in St. Petersburg.

As we walked in the garden on the south side of the house, under the old boughs and trees, I looked at the window above, and imagined how Tolstoy wrote here "Anna Karenina," or set down the self-interrogatories of "My Religion," or wrote with lava heat "War and Peace," or poured out his heart's sympathies in "Our Slavery of Today."

That south garden must have had a part, and a large part in all this.

# 19

# Tolstoy at Home
## *by Kellogg Durland*

Kellogg Durland (1881–1911), a popular American journalist in the 1900s–1910s, is the author of *The Red Reign: The True Story of a Year in Russia* (New York, 1907), which included interviews with Tolstoy; it was the most widely known book on Russia and Russian conditions written by an American of the time, after George Kennan's books on Siberia and the exile system. Durland spent all of the year 1906 and part of 1907 in the empire of the Czar. It was at this time that he visited Count Tolstoy at his home, Yasnaya Polyana.

Durland, Kellogg. "Tolstoy at Home." *The Independent* (New York), vol. 69 (1910): 1191–1195.

Tolstoy was enjoying a horseback ride the afternoon we reached Yasnaya Poliana. It was a clear day in early December. Snow softly blanketed all the country and the tree branches were white against a cobalt sky. All the way from Tula station we heard about Leo Nikolaevitch, for our "yamschik" (horse driver) was one of Tolstoy's peasants. "He knows what is in our hearts," the "mujik" (peasant) said, in explanation of his love for the count. Later I heard from the old man's own lips about the peasants he had visited that day. The life Tolstoy led in his home was infinite in its variety.

So many aspects and activities go to make up the picture. During the several days of my visit, I saw many sides of his existence, and I heard much more from his own people—his wife, his family, his friends, his peasants, and his disciples. It was a wondrous world of itself, this Tolstoy home. And not so small a world by any means as the word implies.

"Yasnaya Poliana," which is interpreted "Pleasant Clearing in the Woods," is set on a knoll that might approximately mark the heart of Russia. It is almost the geographical center of the Russia that lies in Europe, and there dwelt the man who above all others knew and understood the heart of the Russian people. Here came, as it must often have seemed to the Tolstoy family, all the world. Most of us journeyed thither in the spirit of pilgrims, some who came to scoff and some to see. All were welcomed. Day after day thru all the months of latter years streamed visitors from every province in Russia, from every land on earth. Yet for each there was a room and a bright welcome, and a place at the hospitable table. No other spot has drawn so many different kinds of people from so many different places. Yet it is not on any highway, easy of access. A visit to Yasnaya Poliana entails long travel, and herein lies the greater tribute. Moscow is a long night's ride from St. Petersburg, and Tula is another night's ride from Moscow, and Yasnaya Poliana lies fourteen versts from Tula. But the weary distance was compensated when one felt the cordial grasp of the great warm hand and stood before the snapping, metallic eyes that twinkled deep in the cavernous sockets overhung by Tolstoy's beetling brows. The rugged frame, plainly hung with a loose peasant's blouse, sheltered a personality that did not disappoint. In the atmosphere so pregnant with the domination of this man we forgot about "Anna Karenina" and "Resurrection"; we ceased to be perplexed by moral doubts and creeds and theories and all the polemics he had launched upon the world. Here was Tolstoy. That was all.

Yet not all. For there in his shadow lurked another, one who thru near a half century had hovered by him, about him ever watchful, always discerning, never wanting, until this second had become so much a welded part of the first that few of us remembered until afterward that there were two, and that the first without the second would not have been what he was.

At the long table in the great dining hall Tolstoy's place was at one end, and at the other sat the Countess. The line of her guidance has not been set down on any chart, nor written down in any book. Even Tolstoy himself forgot, so part and parcel of his life had she become. In the home this was clear to even the guest of an hour.

It was a crude, hand-hewn sledge that drew me over the crisp snow from Tula station to the Tolstoy estate. The sledge had only one horse, and, as time had little meaning to the mujik, we dawdled along and talked about the famine and the late war and the man I had come so far to see.

This peasant had been drafted for service in the war and he took keen delight in telling us how Tolstoy had been helpful to the soldiers of his own village who were in Manchuria. None of the men wanted to go to war. They did not know what it was all about nor whom they were fighting for. After the first battle this man and seven of his comrades from the same village got together to talk it over. They were all agreed that a battle was not at all to their liking. But how to escape further battles? "Let us write to Leo Nikolaevitch about it," suggested one of them. The suggestion was accepted. It was in line with what they had been doing all their lives when they were perplexed and in trouble — they would go over to Yasnaya Poliana and have a talk with Leo Nikolaevitch. The letter was laboriously written, they all signed it, and it was started to its destination so far away. In due time it came to Tolstoy, who, touched by their simple faith, wrote back at length telling them that all war was wrong, that the army was not to be in Manchuria on its mission of slaughter, and if their consciences were against it, they did wrong to shoot their fellow human beings. The peasant continued:

"After that we always knew what to do. We knew in our hearts that it was wrong for us to fight. We marched into battle because we were made to do so, but after a few minutes the officers would go away somewhere and then we would run away. We always ran after that."

My invitation to Yasnaya Poliana was for several days. I wandered off across the field with one of the household after I had been settled in the room I was to occupy and so I did not see Tolstoy come in from his ride. Indeed, dusk, which settles early in that northland, in winter, had already descended when we returned. The house seemed to typify serenity, peace, and comfort. It was hard to realize that we were in the very heart of a land seething with revolt; that at that time the grip of reaction was tightening as never before in the whole tragic history of that unhappy country, and that from border to border was wretchedness, misery and suffering. Pleasant it seemed standing there among the snow-coated trees in the quiet of the early evening hour; still and restful. Lights burned brightly within, and as we drew near the door a black poodle came to bark his playful, friendly welcome.

A man servant helped us unburden ourselves of our fur greatcoats and snow boots. At the head of the stairs the Countess stood waiting to take me to her husband, who was then resting in his study. She opened the door and motioned me to enter, then she turned and left. There he sat — Tolstoy! There was a thrill as the realization flashed upon one. "Good evening," he called in a cheery voice. "Come and sit near me," and he held out his heavy, toil-hardened hand. How warm it felt! The grip was firm. He said something about forgiving his not rising. I was too intent upon scanning his massive features to notice the first exchange of pleasantries, though I was impressed by the friendliness of the greeting.

"Tell me about my friends in America," he began as soon as I had drawn my chair near to his. "How is Ernest Crosby, and Henry George's son?" Several others he inquired in rapid succession. Happily I knew some of those he wanted to hear from. A half hour must have passed before I had time to glance about the room and observe its orderly confusion. His plain desk was littered with papers, correspondence, pamphlets and books. Around the rooms were many shelves of books extending from the floor to eye level, while above, on the walls, were pictures and many photographs of men whom he had known and admired or whose work he appreciated. The photographs, like the books on the shelves, bespoke the universality of his acquaintance, his knowledge and his interests. There were photographs of friends in many lands, books in several languages. To me he spoke in English, at least at first. Later he dropped into French without apparently being conscious of the change of tongues. Never from the first minute did he treat me as a stranger whom he was receiving for the first time. His manner was rather that of one seeing again a friend after a lapse of time.

"Do you young men in America read Channing, Thoreau, Emerson?" he asked. "Do you read Garrison? All young men of the present day should read the writings of those four great Americans."

Repeatedly he went back to Henry George and Ernest Crosby. Those two, above all Americans whom he had known, he seemed to admire.

He talked on many topics, naturally including the unsettled situation in Russia at that time, and always coming round to his own religious views of life. A well-worn copy of Rousseau's "Emile" was on his desk and he read me many striking passages that expressed his own beliefs and teaching. One sentence that he reread several times has always remained with me: "Si l'on n'eut écouté que ce que Dieu dit au coeur de l'homme, il n'aurait jamais eu qu'une religion sur la terre." And he added:

"The great lesson that we have all to learn is to listen to the words God speaks to us in our hearts. We need no other religion or philosophy than this. We need no institution like a Church. This message is for the people of America as well as for the people of France or of Russia. The whole significance of the present terrible situation in Russia is that Russia is now tending toward an abyss — moral, economic, political — and not until we are at the very bottom of that abyss shall we awake. But when the awakening comes, it will be the greatest awakening the world has ever known for the whole people will turn to God as the only and direct salvation."

When Tolstoy grew tired and his conversation grew slow I withdrew from the room. At the evening meal in the dining-hall he also joined the company.

A meal at the Tolstoy table was a memorable experience. There were always a dozen or fifteen to sit down together, and when I was there nearly every one represented a different political and religious opinion. In the immediate family was reflected almost every shade of opinion. There was Tolstoy himself, the avowed "anarchist"—was ever such a gentle, sweet, pure, kindly anarchist before? One son was not only a monarchist, but a supporter of autocracy, of the Czar, of Reaction in all its blackest forms. Another son was a Conservative.

One daughter supported her father, while another agreed with her conservative husband, who was an Octobrist deputy in the Duma. Next to me sat a social revolutionist who supported terrorist tactics. Each was perfectly frank as to his own convictions, and open discussion was carried on every minute with utmost animation, sometimes in Russian, sometimes in English or again in French, and now and again in German. The Count did not often participate in these remarkable forums, but he listened with closest attention. Sometimes he would get up from the table, and with his hands clasped behind his back and his head bowed, slowly paced up and down the room, never letting anything escape him.

Yasnaya Poliana is a big house, without being grand or imposing, with rather comfort than luxury. The self-imposed asceticism of the Count and the elegant indulgence of the rest of the family have both been exaggerated. Tolstoy in his later life undoubtedly reduced his life to complete simplicity, but there could scarcely be real hardships when ever by his side was the one who, as has been so beautifully expressed, "always managed to slip a piece of velvet under his crown of thorns at just the place where he wanted it to press hardest." His regimen was plain, but it could not smack of the pain of poverty. There were always loving ones to contribute to making the atmosphere sweet and placid. It was, in every sense, a unique home.

There never was one like it before, nor will be again. Prince and peasant were welcomed alike and every guest shared with all the family. Every one who came, from East or West, from North or South, brought something with him: news, ideas, seeds of thought, and each took away impressions that influence and last.

The son whom I met had recently had a period of worldly dissipation. His career had been eventful and far from the path his father desired him to walk.

He would say, "When my father was my age, he was a great deal worse, according to his own 'Confessions,' so that ends it!" And, perhaps, that was the secret of Tolstoy's broad humanism that each one who met him recognized and marked. He had lived completely. He had drunk of every cup, tasted every joy, every grief and every bitterness. So was he able to enter into the life and experience of every human being.

During the days that I remained on the estate many things happened, much was said, that I should like to share with all who are interested in this towering figure who so recently wandered away from the Pleasant Clearing in the Woods to so calmly, so unostentatiously, yet so dramatically meet his end; but for the now this brief and hasty glimpse must suffice, of the picture that must always be treasured in the memory of those who ever were privileged to look upon it — the picture of Tolstoy in his home.

# 20

# The Last Days of Leo Tolstoy
## by Alexander Kaun

Alexander Kaun (1889–1944) was a professor of Russian literature who was born in Russia and emigrated to the United States in the 1900s; he taught at the University of California in the 1920s and 1930s.

Kaun, Alexander. "The Last Days of Leo Tolstoy." *Atlantic Monthly* (Boston), vol. 129 (1922): 299–306.

  Eleven years ago, on a dark November night, the sage of Yasnaya Polyana gave the finishing touch to his life's work. At the age of eighty-two, Tolstoy found that his indefatigable striving for inner harmony, for consistency between word and deed, could not be triumphant as long as he lived on his family estate. His personal simplification, his personal relinquishment of private property, his personal vegetarian diet, bore the aspect of a whim, condescendingly tolerated amid the conventional surroundings of a Russian "nobleman's nest." A hater of sham and compromise, Tolstoy felt keenly the artificiality of his position; and to his close friends he expressed his hope, a number of times, that God would make him strong enough to break away from the roof of cozy lies. This spiritual strength came to him with the ebb of his physical strength: during the night of November 10, he fled from his home, in quest of harmony and truth; and ten days later the tortuous path of his earthly quests came to an end.
  Tolstoy's flight was greeted with joy by his friends and followers, as

the crowning pinnacle of his significant and instructive life. But the circumstances immediately connected with this event were known only to a very few persons. Tolstoy's last secretary and devoted disciple, V.F. Bulgakov, in his most interesting "Diary" for the year 1910, had an enthusiastic entry on the morrow of his master's exodus, which he concludes thus: "But precisely what were the mental motives that impelled him to this deed? What did he experience in the hidden depth of his soul at the moment of leaving Yasnaya Polyana? Of this we are unable to speak as yet. And not a little time will pass before men will arrive at a more or less correct solution of this unusually complex question."

At that time it was difficult to foresee that a revolution would take place in November 1917, which would sweep aside many conceptions of space and time. The unfastidious Bolshevik commissars have shocked not a few sensitive natures by unearthing and proclaiming, *urbi et orbi*, various secret documents, treaties, and memoirs, letters and diaries. Thus we now have access to the contents of former state and private archives, supervised at present by a group of specialists, who publish from time to time their discoveries. The chairman of the "Glavarkhiv,"—which is the abridged title for the main Administration of Archives,—A.S. Nikolayev, has made public two sets of documents re: Tolstoy, found in the archives of the former Ministry of Education and of the Holy Synod, respectively. These documents illuminate the circumstances of Tolstoy's last days, and incidentally enable us to fathom what Mr. Bulgakov considers an "unusually complex question."

As is generally known, the Russian Church, through its governing body, the Holy Synod, excommunicated Tolstoy by a decree issued in March, 1901. The decree contained a provision to the effect that the Orthodox Church would not regard him as a member "until he repented and renewed his communion with it."

Tolstoy replied to this act in a dignified statement, summarizing his religious views, and emphasizing his conviction that his disloyalty to the Church emanated from his loyalty to what he regarded as true Christianity. "I began by loving my orthodox faith more than my repose," ran the conclusion of his reply to the Holy Synod; "then I came to love Christianity more than my Church; and now I love Truth more than all else in the world. And for me Truth still coincides with Christianity, and in the measure in which I profess it I live calmly and joyously, and calmly and joyously I approach death."

The official Church, however, did not abandon its hope of bringing Tolstoy back to the fold. A report to the Holy Synod, now published for the first time, states that Father Dimitri Troitsky, of Tula, "undertook, with the blessing of Bishop Pitirim, the task of exhorting Count L. Tolstoy." He performed his mission from 1897 till the very death of the Count, visiting him twice a year, conversing with him, and even partaking of meals, though Tolstoy "declined to talk on religious questions." In October, 1910, learning of Tolstoy's illness, Father Dimitri wrote to him a letter, exhorting him to seek succor and healing in the Church. Two days later, Tolstoy replied. This characteristic letter appeared recently among the published documents of the Archive of the Holy Synod:

"October 25, 1910,

"Yasnaya Polyana.

"Dear Brother Dimitry,

"I am a very sinful person, and my only occupation consists in mending myself, in the measure of my power and ability, from my numerous sins and sinful habits. I beseech God to help me in this cause, and He helps me. Though at the pace of a turtle, still I advance with his help.

"In this advancing I find the sole sense, purpose, and benefit of my life. The Kingdom of God is within us, and the Kingdom of God has to be won by force (that is, by effort). I believe in this, and exert all possible efforts for this; and here you come to offer me the performance of certain rites and the utterance of certain words, which would show that I consider as infallible truth all that which men who call themselves Church consider truth, and in consequence of which all my sins would be pardoned — pardoned somehow and by someone; and that I shall be not only exempt from the inner, hard,— but, at the same time, joyous,— spiritual work of self-improvement, but that I shall be somehow saved from something, and shall receive some kind of an eternal bliss.

"Why, dear Brother Dimitri, do you address me with such a strange proposal? Have I tried to convert you, have I counseled you to rid yourself of that, in my opinion, pernicious delusion which you profess, and into which you painstakingly lure thousands and thousands of unfortunate children and common people, perverting their minds? Then why do you not leave me in peace, a man who, by his age, stands with one foot in the grave, and who calmly awaits his death? My conversion to the Church faith might have had sense, were I a boy, or a grown-up atheist, or an illiterate Yakout who has never heard about the Church faith. But I am eighty-two years old, was brought up in the very same deception which still dominates you, to which you are inviting me, and from which, with greatest suffering and efforts, I freed myself many years ago, adopting a Christian, not ecclesiastic, point of view, which gives me the possibility of a peaceful, joyous life directed toward self-perfection, and the readiness for as peaceful and joyous a death, in which I see a return to God of love, out of whom I issued forth.

"With brotherly love,

"Leo Tolstoy."

To this characteristically Tolstoyan letter of loose, hurried, long periods, came a lengthy reply from Father Dimitri, which began with apologies but proceeded to admonish softly the recalcitrant heresiarch. He tactfully reproached Tolstoy for presuming to have found the true path, and in conclusion pleaded for frankness: "A candid exchange of opinions is always agreeable for sincere people; and therefore I hope that I shan't disturb your peace; but, if I do disturb it, then I say that there will be plenty of peace after death, but now we need ever more and more disturbance."

To this Tolstoy answered, five days before his flight, with the following brief but kind note:

"November 5, 1910, Yasnaya Polyana.

"I have received your letter, Dimitri Yegorovich, and thank you for it. I perfectly agree with you that humility is the greatest and most needful virtue. As I always say, man is like a fraction, in which the denominator indicates his opinion about himself. It is best for this denominator to be zero (complete humility), and it is terrible when it is augmented to infinity. In the first case, man has a true significance, whatever the denominator; but in the second case none.

"I am sending you my books 'For Every Day,' in which the reading for the 25th day expresses my opinion about this greatest of virtues. One point on which I do not agree with you is where you advocate hope in external help for determining one's perfection and one's nonentity, in place of relying on one's inner effort, which must never weaken, and which alone brings us a little closer to perfection, or at least delivers us from depravity: the Kingdom of God must be won by force. Again I thank you for your good letter, and greet you brotherly. Lev Tolstoy."

As soon as the news of Tolstoy's flight became known abroad, the official Church instructed its emissaries to watch every step of the fugitive, and to report everything he said or did to the ecclesiastic authorities. Bishop Benjamin of Kaluga communicated to the Holy Synod detailed information concerning Tolstoy's doings, from the reports of his subordinates.

On the evening of November 10, Tolstoy arrived at the Optina Pustyn Monastery, where he stopped at the inn of the monastery, and said to the keeper: "Perhaps you are displeased with my arrival — I am Lev Tolstoy; was excommunicated by the Church. I have come to discourse with the old monks, and to-morrow I shall go to Shamordino, to see my sister." In spite of his opposition to the established church, Tolstoy had visited the Optin Hermitage several times after 1877, conversing with holy hermits and ascetic monks. About eight miles from Optin lay the convent of Shamordino, where Tolstoy saw occasionally his favorite sister Maria, a nun.

On this last visit of his to the hermitage and to the convent, his every step was recorded by the watchful clerics. On the thirteenth of November the Count, accompanied by his daughter Alexandra and his physician, Dr. D.P. Makovitsky, suddenly left Shamordino, boarded the train at the station of Kozelsk, was taken ill on the train, and removed, on November 15, to the station house of Astapovo, where he died five days later.

Bishop Marphenius of Tula, and other dignitaries of the Church, were instructed to hasten to Astapovo, and exert their efforts for the salvation of the soul of the sick man. The only cleric who arrived at Astapovo before the death of Tolstoy was Abbot Barsonophius. From the moment of his arrival, on the evening of the eighteenth, he endeavored to see the dying man, in order to carry out the instruction of the Metropolitan, namely, "to offer the ailing Count Lev Tolstoy a spiritual talk and religious consolation, with the aim of reconciling him with the Holy Orthodox Church."

The Count's son, Andrey, promised him to employ his best efforts to enable him to carry out his intention; but Dr. Mikitin categorically refused to admit anyone to his patient, even the Countess. Yet with Tolstoy remained constantly his daughter Alexandra, Vladimir Chertkov, his biographer Sergeyenko, and of course, Dr. Makovitsky. The Abbot's written request to Alexandra for an audience was rejected. The Abbot's statement is corroborated by Bishop Parphenius, to the effect that, in the words of Count Andrey Tolstoy, his father was, in his last days, "surrounded by persons extremely hostile to the Church."

On the death of the Count, at five minutes past six in the morning of November 20, 1910, Abbot Barsonophius called on the widow and her sons, and was informed that the wish of the deceased was to be buried without church rites and ceremonies. On the evening of the same day, an extraordinary session took place at the home of the Petrograd Metropolitan, attended, besides himself, by the Metropolitan Bishops of Moscow and by the Archbishop.

The assembly resolved to send throughout Russia the following laconic telegram: "The Synod has decreed to forbid all services or prayers for Count Tolstoy."

Thus ended the long conflict between the Church and Tolstoy. As on many other occasions, the Russian Church acted in opposition to the sentiments of the majority of the Russian people.

In the report of Bishop Parphenius to the Holy Synod, there is a curious and illuminating passage:

On September the 16th [1910] the wife of Lev Nikolayevich, Countess Sophia Andreyevna, invited into the Count's home the parish priest, Father Tikhon Kudryavtsev, and requested him to serve "Te Deum" with consecration by water, and to sprinkle the house with holy water, in order, as she expressed herself, to drive out the spirit of Chertkov. The priest complied with her request.

Count Lev Nikolayevich was visiting at that time with his elder daughter Tatyana Lvovna Sukhotin, while at Yasnaya Polyana remained the Countess and some of her sons. After the service, Father Kudryavtsev learned, from his conversation with the family of Lev Nikolayevich, that they were indignant at Chertkov, who, in their opinion, had held Count Tolstoy for more than ten years under his strong, almost hypnotic, influence. In their opinion, almost everything which the Count had written during the last years was due to Chertkov's influence. If Chertkov changed or rewrote Tolstoy's works, when publishing them, the Count had no strength of will to protest against it. In order to save him from such an evil influence, the family refused to receive Chertkov, and decided to resort to the prayers of the Church, in order to drive out of the house the very spirit of Chertkov who published abroad those of the Count's works which were either altogether forbidden in Russia, or were mutilated by the censor. Chertkov also maintained a depositary in England, where he kept originals or copies of Tolstoy's manuscripts. He and Alexandra were the persons in whom Tolstoy had the most confidence, and whom he entrusted with his intimate thoughts and plans. In his will, signed August 4, 1910, Tolstoy explicitly transferred the property rights in all his printed works and manuscripts to his daughter Alexandra. She found in Chertkov an eager and devoted co-worker during and after the death of her father.

It was only natural that Countess Sophia Tolstoy, for forty-eight years the devoted wife of the Count, should feel hurt at the preferences her husband showed in selecting his trustees. She was particularly hostile to Chertkov, resenting his influence on the Count as well as on her daughter Alexandra. She contested the right of Alexandra to those of Tolstoy's papers and documents which her mother had collected for years in a special room of the Historical Museum at Moscow. A controversy arose between the mother and her daughter, Chertkov presenting the interests of the latter. The case came up before the Minister of Education, before the Emperor, before the Senate. It appears that sympathy for the widow prevailed against the uncontestable legality of the daughter's claims, and in December, 1914, the Senate ruled in favor of the mother.

Among the documents of this case, which had been kept in the Archives of the Ministry of Education, there is a long memorandum by Vladimir Chertkov, presenting arguments in favor of transferring the papers from the Historical Museum to Countess Alexandra.

Sophia had no right to keep these papers. Among the fourteen we find Countess Olga Tolstoy, Countess Tatyana Tolstoy, and Count Sergey Tolstoy; which goes to show that the "family" of which Father Kudryavtsev reported was not quite unanimous in its support of the mother. Of the other names, it is worth noting those of Tolstoy's secretaries Gusev and Bulgakov, of the secretary of the Countess Mlle. Teokritov, of Professor A. Goldenweiser, and of two family physicians, Dr. Nikitin and Dr. Makovitsky.

It appears from most of these testimonies that the Countess systematically tried to remove her husband's manuscripts from his study to the Historical Museum, mainly in order that they might not fall into the hands of Chertkov, as she stated to various persons. Furthermore, Chertkov expressed his anxiety in regard to some of Tolstoy's diaries of an intimate nature, concerning which Alexandra received from her father secret instructions. The Countess, who, even during the life of her husband, had modified his writings on several occasions, might be suspected of tampering with the contents of the diaries. Chertkov accused the Countess also of having secretly appropriated Tolstoy's pocket-diary, which he did not show to anyone, but kept as a personal secret. He further stated that, in the last ten years of his life, Tolstoy did not trust his wife with his diaries, but deposited them at the State Bank of Tula, with the explicit instruction that they be delivered to no other person than his daughter Alexandra.

(In Bulgakov's Diary, for October 9, 1910, the loss of this diary is mentioned. He quotes Tolstoy: "My regular diary is read by Chertkov and Alexandra; but this was a most secret little book which I do not let anyone read."—The Author).

The morbid jealousy of the Countess was evidently a symptom of her mental derangement. Both P.A. Bulanger, a close friend, and V.F.

Bulgakov, Tolstoy's secretary, mentioned her illness in their testimony. Her elder daughter, Tatyana, wrote in a letter dated August 7, 1910: "One must regard her as altogether sick and irresponsible.... If you look up in the Encyclopedia the word "paranoia," by which her illness has been defined, you will see how all this suits her." In Tolstoy's diary for August 20, 1910, we read: "Read in Korsakov's (book), 'paranoia': Just as if drawn of her." Professor Rossolimo, a famous psychiatrist, diagnosed the condition of the Countess in July, 1910, at the request of the family. To Alexandra he wrote:

"My opinion about the state of Sophia Andreyevna, which I expressed personally both to the late Lev Nikolayevich and to you, is that, under the influence of the declining period of her life and its concomitant exhaustion of the regulating mental forces, the basic peculiarities of the character of the Countess began to appear more and more on the surface. Her character presents the combination of two degenerative constitutions: an hysterical and a paranoiac. The first manifests itself in an especially bright emotional coloring of all her experiences, in the concentration of all interests on her own personality, even to the point of sacrificing truth and fine feelings, to the point of utter unscrupulousness in means for the achievement of her aims. Her second constitution reveals itself in her excessive suspiciousness, and in its resultant wrong conclusions, in everything which concerns Lev Nikolayevich: his teaching, her relations to V.G. Chertkov, and so forth."

Tolstoy's own attitude to his wife is clearly shown in his letter written to Alexandra the day after his flight:

"November 11, 1910, OPTIN HERMITAGE MONASTERY.

"I will tell you everything about me, dear friend Sasha. It is hard. I cannot help feeling a great heaviness. The main thing is, not to commit a sin; here is the difficulty. Of course I have sinned, and shall sin yet, but if only a little less of it!

"And this is what I chiefly and foremost wish for you, too. The more so, since I know that a terrible task has fallen to you, beyond your strength and your youthful age. I have not decided anything, and do not wish to decide. I am endeavoring to do only that which I cannot help doing, and not to do that which I can avoid doing.

"From my letter to Chertkov, you will see how I regard the matter, or rather how I feel. I rely very much on the good influence of Tanya and Seryozha [his children].

"The main thing is that they should understand, and should persuade her, that such a life, with spying and eavesdropping, with perpetual reproaches, disposing of me at her will, everlasting control over me, capricious hatred for the man who is my closest and most useful friend, with obvious hatred for me and simulated love — that such a life is, for me, not disagreeable, but simply impossible; that it is I who should think of drowning myself, if anyone should; that I wish only one thing — freedom from her, from the falsehood, pretense, and malice, with which her whole being is permeated.

"To be sure, of this they cannot persuade her; but they may persuade her that all her actions toward me not only do not express love, but appear to have an obvious purpose to kill me, in which she will succeed, since I hope that with the third attack which threatens me, I shall release both her and myself from this terrible position in which we have lived, and to which I do not wish to return.

"You see, my dear, how bad I am. I do not hide myself from you. I am not asking you to come to me as yet, but will do so very shortly, as soon as possible. Write me about your health. I embrace you.

"L. Tolstoy."

This illuminating document simplifies the problem, and disperses the doubts of Count Ilya Tolstoy, who, in his "Reminiscences" of his father, queries in bewilderment: "Could my father really have fled from home because the wife with whom he lived for forty-eight years had developed neurasthenia and at one time showed certain abnormalities characteristic of that malady? Was that like the man who loved his fellows and knew the human heart so well?"

Were it not for his filial partiality toward his mother, Count Ilya might have found an answer to his question in his own book, a few pages farther on. On November 11, 1910, he asked his sister Alexandra, who was about to join her father at Shamordino, whether Count Leo was aware of the pain he was causing his wife. He quotes her answer: "Yes, he has considered all that and still made up his mind to go, because he thinks that nothing could be worse than the state that things have come to here."

Tolstoy looked upon himself, his words and actions, as belonging to humanity, and he knew that every utterance of his would be recorded for eternity. Hence his letter to Alexandra is inestimable for the understanding of the manifold tragedy of his life. Perhaps still more precious may be considered the following pages from Tolstoy's diary, also found among the Archive papers:

"November 7, 1910.—Sophia Andreyevna continues to be restless.

"November 9.—Rose very early. All night long saw bad dreams. The heaviness of our relations is increasing.

"November 10.—Went to bed at eleven-thirty. Slept till after two. Woke up, and as on previous nights, heard the sounds of opening doors and of footsteps. On previous occasions I had not looked toward the door of my room; this time I looked, and noticed through the cracks a bright light in my study, and heard rustling of papers. Sophia Andreyevna is searching for something, and reading, probably.

"Last evening she begged of me,—demanded,—that I do not close my doors. Both of her doors are left open, so that she can hear my slightest movement. Both day and night all my movements, my words, must be known to her and be under her control. Again footsteps, cautious opening of the door, and she passes.

"I do not know why this provoked in me an irresistible revulsion, indignation. Tried to fall asleep, could not, tossed about for nearly an hour, then lit a candle, and sat up. The door opens, and S.A. enters, inquiring "about my health," and wondering at the light which she has noticed here.

"My revulsion and indignation grow. I suffocate, count my pulse: 97. Cannot lie still, and suddenly make a definite resolution to go away.

"I write her a note, begin to pack the most necessary things, just enough to depart with. I wake Dushan, then Sasha; they help me pack. I tremble at the thought that she may hear the noise, come out—a scene, hysterics, and then I shan't depart without theatricals.

"Toward six o'clock everything is somehow packed. I go to the stable to order the horses harnessed. Dushan, Sasha, Varya finish up packing. Night, pitch-dark; I lose my way to the rear court, wander into the thicket, get caught and bruised by trees, fall, lose my cap, cannot find it, with difficulty disentangle myself, go to the house, I take a cap and a lantern, reach the stable, and give the order. Sasha, Dushan, Varya. I tremble, expecting pursuit.

"But lo, we depart. At Shchekino we wait for an hour, and every minute I expect her appearance. But Lord, we are in the railway car.

"The fear passes. And pity arises for her, no doubt as to whether I have done the right thing. Perhaps I am mistaken in identifying myself, but it seems that I have been saving my self, not Lev Nikolayevich, it that which at times abides in me, in however small a measure....

"November 11.—Shamordino.... While traveling I have been thinking about some way out of my position and hers, and could not think of any, and yet, to be sure, there will be one, whether you want or not, and the one which you foresee. Yes, the main thing I must think about, is how to avoid committing a sin. And let there be what will be. This is not my affair. I have obtained at Mashenka's the "Circle of Reading"; and, opening the book for the 10-th, was struck by the direct answer to my problem: I need the trial, it will be beneficial for me...."

[The Countess gave this letter for publication. I am citing it in the version of Professor G.R. Noyes: "My departure will grieve you. I am sorry for this, but pray understand and believe that I could not act otherwise. My position in the house is becoming unbearable. I can no longer live amid those conditions of luxury in which I have been living; and I am doing what old men of my age usually do. They retire from the life of the world, in order to live in solitude and quiet the last days of their lives. Please understand this, and do not follow me if you learn where I am. Your coming will not change my resolution. I thank you for your honorable life of forty-eight years with me, and I beg you to forgive me for all the wrong that I may have done you, just as I with my whole soul pardon you for whatever wrong you may have done me. I counsel you to be reconciled to the new position in which my departure places you, and not to have any unkind feelings for me."

[This letter confirmed the general view of Tolstoy's flight as being an act motivated by ethical principles, and not by any personal reasons. On the basis of precedents, it is not improbable that the Countess "revised" her husband's note.]

It is worth while consulting the "Circle of Reading" — that remarkable collection of thoughts by various men, which Tolstoy arranged into special readings for every day of the year. The material set for the tenth of November is gathered from the works of Marcus Aurelius, Thomas Kempis, Pascal, Kant, Schopenhauer, and others, including his own thoughts. The keynote is struck by his words: "As the sensation of pain is a necessary condition for the preservation of our body, so is suffering a necessary condition of our life, from birth till death." From Schopenhauer he quotes the famous passage about the need of adversity in men's life, lest they be "swollen with arrogance" and go mad. The other passages exalt suffering, and they conclude with Tolstoy's aphorism: "As just as the legend of the Eternal Jew, condemned in punishment to everlasting life without death, would be the legend about a man who, in punishment, was condemned to a life without suffering." It is a curious coincidence, that Tolstoy undertook his last trial on the very day for which he had arranged the reading advocating suffering. "And let there be what will be. This is not my affair." What profound resignation, combining the fatalism of the Slav with the firm conviction of the Believer, that the will of God must be done.

Thus we are brought a little closer to the personality of Leo Tolstoy. Interest in his life is remote from curiosity for scandalous gossip. One must take Tolstoy's life, art, and thought as one gigantic mosaic, no single particle of which is dispensable. His eighty-two years are revealed for humanity, entirely and instructively, through his largely autobiographical works of fiction, through his religious and ethical writings, through his letters and diaries. In all of these expressions Tolstoy sought the one "hero," who had attracted him since his Childhood, Boyhood, and Youth — Truth. Every detail in his life and work illuminates the difficult road which he followed in his quest of this "hero." His unreserved candor and profound introspection leave not one recess of his mind hidden or veiled. He fixes the powerful search-light of Truth at himself, and we see revealed with even clearness his greatness and occasional smallness, his harmony and his discords, his failures, his happy moments of peace and mutual love, and his multiple tragedies of being, now the cause, now the victim, of misunderstanding, enmity, persecution. And amid these tragedies his family tragedy, his personal Golgotha, is not the least significant and instructive.

# 21

# Talks with Tolstoy
## by *Richard Baeza and Alexander Goldenweiser*

Alexander Goldenweiser, a famous composer and pianist, published in 1921–22 two volumes of reminiscences, entitled *Near Tolstoy*, selections from which have been translated in English. These reminiscences record conversations with Tolstoy during fifteen years of intimate companionship ending only with the great writer's death. Journalist Richard Baeza prepared and edited Goldenweiser's firsthand memoirs for publication.

Baeza, Richard. "Talks with Tolstoy." *The Living Age* (Boston). vol. 319 (1923): 70–75, 127–132.

Like Goethe, Tolstoy was a marvel of vigor in his old age. Goldenweiser describes him to us breaking a fractious colt and as an excellent horseman who thoroughly understood his mounts and personally taught them their paces. On another occasion I was struck with his physical vigor. One of his sons was trying unsuccessfully to perform a difficult gymnastic feat. Tolstoy watched him for some time and then, unable to contain himself longer, said, "Let me try it," and to the surprise of everybody present performed it successfully.

"His mind was as vigorous as his body. We all know that his literary productivity did not cease until his death. When seventy-three years old, he mastered Dutch in a little more than two months — a detail that recalls how Goethe learned Persian in his old age in order to read Hafiz and Saadi. Tolstoy's favorite textbook for studying a foreign tongue was the New Testament, which he would translate with a dictionary in his hands....

When we consider the vast volume of Tolstoy's literary works, we naturally assume that he was a rapid writer; but Goldenweiser tells us that he wrote and rewrote every page with almost as scrupulous care as Flaubert, and never was satisfied with what he had done. He used to say: "I cannot understand how anyone can write without rewriting more than once. I almost never read over my printed works. But if for some reason I have to do so I invariably say to myself: All that ought to be written over. It should be put this way...."

Whenever a thought or a word escaped him, Tolstoy would stop writing and go off by himself until what he was seeking came back to him.

Another trait of Tolstoy's was his passion for personal liberty, his love of a free and wandering life. Dostoevsky says that the typical Russian is the vagabond, "that Russian vagabond whose thirst for happiness can only be quenched by the felicity of the universe." Tolstoy was in this respect a typical Russian. The dream of his life, which he tried to realize on the very eve of his death, was to become a wanderer, to be a pilgrim with script and staff. Goldenweiser tells us how he would visit every band of Gypsies that passed by Yasnaya Poliana, and relates of one such occasion: "When he saw them, Tolstoy seemed transfigured, and involuntarily began to dance to the rhythm of their songs, and to shout encouragement to them."

"What a marvelous people!" he exclaimed. All the old Gypsies knew Tolstoy and liked to hold long conversations with him. Tolstoy was fond of Gypsies from childhood, and knew all their habits and customs.

Frequent references to Tolstoy's ideas upon art occur. It is well known that he was extremely fond of music, but we learn here that his favorite composer was Chopin and that he had an invincible antipathy for all modern music. "Chopin's greatness lies in the fact that the simplest passages in his music never lack content, and the most ornate and complicated passages never suggest the virtuoso."

His favorite Russian authors were Pushkin, Lermontov, Gogol, Gertzen, Tutchev, and Dostoevsky. He said of the last of these: "When we scrutinize him closely, we see that Dostoevsky wrote badly, that he lacked force from the technical point of view; but how much he always had to say! Taine said that he would trade all the French novels for one of his pages." And speaking of Turgenev: "I am very fond of him personally, but I do not rate him especially high as a writer."

On the other hand, Countess Tolstoy seemed to cherish a certain fondness for Turgenev, and told Goldenweiser this charming anecdote. The last time he came to Yasnaya, not long before his death, she asked him: "Ivan Sergeevich, why don't you write any more?" He said: "In order to write I have always had to be a little in love. Now I am too old to fall in love, and so I have stopped writing...."

Referring to Shakespeare and Goethe, Tolstoy said: "I have read both of them from cover to cover three times during my life, and I have never been able to understand where they get their reputation." This opinion, which was unquestionably sincere, will astound many, but we must bear in mind that Tolstoy was judging them from the moral standpoint. On the other hand, he was very fond of Schiller and remarked: "There's a man for you!" He differed from Dostoevsky in detesting George Sand, and could not understand how anyone could read that author's writings.

In general he was indifferent to contemporary writers, except Anatole France, whom he esteemed highly. At the time when Maeterlink was all the vogue, he was most frank in his low estimate of that writer, notwithstanding the admiration that the Belgian dramatist professed for his own works. When someone told him that Maeterlink had written, in the preface to his dramatic works, that "The Power of Darkness" was the greatest drama in the world, Tolstoy laughed sardonically and asked: "Then why doesn't he imitate it?" On another occasion, when somebody asked him if he had read "Uncle Vanya" (a play written by Chekhov — ed.), he replied: "Why should I read it? Have I committed a crime?"

Tolstoy's hatred of modernity prejudiced him against every form of contemporary art. He considered present-day music empty and chaotic. He tried to study modern writers conscientiously, and confessed one day to Goldenweiser: "I am trying to understand and appreciate these moderns, but it costs me tremendous labor." Another day, in speaking of modern art in general; he said: "They have lost all sense of shame. I cannot express it in any other way ... the sense of esthetic shame, artistic modesty. I am not sure you know what this sentiment is, but I feel it intensely every time I read anything artistically false."

On another occasion he observed shrewdly: "Speaking generally, modern writers have lost the idea of drama. Drama, instead of tediously describing to us the whole life of a man, ought to put him in a position where he is so stripped of all that is adventitious that we see him at a single glance as he really is. I have ventured to criticize Shakespeare. But all of his characters are alive, and we can see clearly why they act as they do. In Shakespeare's time they put signs upon the stage, saying, 'moonlight,' 'interior of a house,' and the like, in order — thank God! — that the whole attention of the audience might be concentrated upon the substance of the play. Now it is just the reverse."

On another occasion he said: "Modern art often affects us the way an irritant affects our sensory organs — just as mustard pleases a depraved palate, but is disagreeable to a healthy palate. It is the same with the arts. We must draw a line showing where artistic mustard begins, and in my opinion this is a problem of enormous importance. In painting, especially, it seems to me particularly difficult to draw that line."

Referring to the absurd fad of becoming "an artist" overnight so common nowadays, he said wittily: "If you were to ask a person if he played the violin, and he were to answer, 'I don't know, I never tried,' you would laugh at him. But when it comes to writing, anyone may say, 'I don't know, I never tried,' as if trying were all that was necessary to become an author."

We should bear in mind that the modern writers whom Tolstoy condemned belong to the generation of symbolists and neo-romanticists that we now consider almost classical — some of them, indeed, quite properly as masters. What would he have said of our present ragged army of cubists, futurists, Dadaists and all the rest! On the other hand Tolstoy was not primarily a critic, although he expressed himself with extraordinary acumen regarding certain books and authors. In the first place, his point of view and his standards were strictly moral. He subordinated every aesthetic consideration to ethical canons. Art for art's sake was to him a pernicious doctrine. We can easily see that criticism is impossible with such a critic. Indeed, Tolstoy has not left a single work on literary criticism, for his book, "What Is Art?" and his volume on Shakespeare are both ethical works.

More than that, Tolstoy was altogether too extraordinary a personality to be a good critic. Great creative geniuses, those men who stand head and shoulders above other men, live too much in the world of their own creations and ideals to busy themselves with the creations and ideals of others — especially when these do not harmonize with theirs. This explains the strange cases of misunderstanding and injustice that we find in the greatest men. In fact, genius and intelligence are quite distinct. A very intelligent man is seldom a genius. Genius seems to involve a large measure of obstinacy and stupidity. In some cases, for instance in that of Victor Hugo, the imbecility seems greater than the genius. Goethe, who combined vast creative genius with eminent intelligence, is unique.

Furthermore, the critical faculty demands a certain humility and love for the works of others, which a genius is seldom capable of feeling. He is wholly wrapped up in his own creations. How can we expect a creator to be humble? More than that, we should not be surprised at Tolstoy's hatred of the new, for that is a universal weakness of human nature. Every generation creates its own ideological and sentimental environment; it has its own system of weights and measures. Often the next generation, through a natural reaction, swings to the opposite extreme. It would be folly to expect a man of letters to play false to his time and generation in order to justify his inferiors. Even to expect him to devote much attention to them, and to try to understand them, is asking too much. In this case, likewise, Goethe was unique. We must also remember that no man of letters has ever occupied such an Olympian throne, ever rose so high above his contemporaries, as Goethe, who passed judgment upon the men of his time like a sovereign ruling his subjects.

However, we meet in Tolstoy's books excellent observations on the functions of the critic — for instance the following: "The value of criticism consists in pointing out what is good in a work of art, and thus guiding the opinion of the public, whose tastes are generally uncultivated, and the majority of whom have no true sense of beauty. So it is difficult to be a really good critic; but at the same time it is very easy for the most stupid and narrow man to pose as a critic. Bad criticism is as great an evil as good criticism is a blessing...." On another occasion he said, "If everybody abuses my work, it means there is something in it; if everybody flatters it, it means that it is bad; but if some praise it highly, and others abuse it bitterly, then it is of the first quality."

Speaking of art in general, Tolstoy remarked: "The most important thing in a work of art is that it should have a kind of focus — that is, a centre where all the rays meet and from which they all disperse; and this focus should not be specifically described in words.... Rubinstein said to me one day that his emotions were so powerful when he played in public that he could not communicate them to his hearers. This proves that a work of art is not possible until the soul of the artist has mastered his emotions."

Tolstoy talked to me with exasperation of literature as a trade. I have seldom seen him so agitated. He said:

"No one ought to write unless he leaves a fragment of his flesh in the ink bottle every time he dips the pen. All the *quid* of the author consists in perfecting himself. But why chase after new forms? If anyone has something to say, all he needs is time to say it. I think that in the course of time we shall cease to 'invent' works of art. People will come to look upon it as disgraceful to invent a story about an imaginary Mary or John.

Authors, if there are still any, will describe only interesting and significant things that it has been given them to observe in their own lives."

It is odd to hear the greatest feminist of the century say: "If you won't repeat it, I'll tell you confidentially: women are generally so evil that there is scarcely any difference between a good woman and a bad one."

Soon after their acquaintance, Tolstoy took Goldenweiser by the arm one day when bidding him good-bye, led him aside, and said: "All this time I have wanted to say to you, and now that you are going I will say to you: great as may be your endowments as a musician, and much as may be the time and labor that you have devoted to this art, remember that the most important thing of all is to be a man. It is necessary to bear in mind constantly that art is not everything. In your relations with others endeavor to give them the most in your power, and to receive from them the least that you can. Pardon me for saying this to you, but it was necessary." Words of good advice that show him to have been a shepherd of souls, tenderly concerned for his flock. Few men possessed as he did the art of entering into the hearts of men; and whoever once received him there never dismissed the guest. No man was less egotistic or strove more sincerely to be humble. He once said to Goldenweiser: "The 'I' is a temporal thing that limits our immortal essence. To believe in personal immortality has always seemed to me to betray lack of understanding." At another time he said: "Every day I grow more convinced that the really sensible man shows that quality by his humility. Pride is inconsistent with understanding."

He was frequently afflicted with black pessimism, and seemed to despair of the world's ever becoming better. One day, when speaking of revolutionists, he said: "Their capital error is their superstition that we can regulate human life." And on another occasion: "Possibly it is because I do not feel well, but there are times when I grow desperate over all that is happening in the world. I cannot comprehend how men can continue to live thus, with such horrors following on each other's heels. I have always been shocked and bewildered by the slight value we place on man, even if we consider him simply as a useful animal. A horse that can draw a cart is worth a certain price to us, and we pay that price. But a man, for instance, can make shoes, work in a factory, play a piano; and yet fifty per cent of them die unnecessarily. I remember, when I was raising live stock, if the mortality rose to five per cent I got angry and accused my herdsmen of neglecting their work. Yet fifty per cent of the human beings born are dying unnecessarily."

If Tolstoy felt so then, what would he have thought to-day, when civilization is going to the dogs! During the war and the shameful years that have followed, we have sadly missed a commanding, fearless voice with the authority of Tolstoy's. The world would not have listened to it; I am not so simple as to imagine that. But it would comfort all future generations if history could have recorded some great protesting outcry of the human conscience — if there had been a prophet to mourn over Europe's ruin.

And indeed Tolstoy, with that prophetic instinct with which all great Russians have been endowed, — as were so many of the writers of his epoch, — seems to have foreseen Russia's ruin. One day he said: "I have no doubt that, with all this turmoil at home and abroad, before long, on some fine morning, Russia will go to destruction. Sic transit gloria mundi. To-day she is a vast and powerful State, to-morrow she will suddenly fly to pieces."

Yet he sometimes seemed to contradict himself. For instance, such expressions as this are surprisingly apposite to-day: "The present movement in Russia (Socialism and anarchy) is a world movement, the importance of which is not fully understood. This movement, like the French Revolution before it, will perhaps be the impelling force of the coming centuries. The Russian people possess in a high degree a capacity for organization and self-government. They entrusted their power to the present regime and hoped, as they did when the serfs were liberated, for a distribution of the land. But the land has not been given them. They will have to carry out that great reform themselves. Our revolutionists have not the slightest understanding of the people, or of this sentiment. They might aid, but they will only be an obstacle. The Russian people as I see them — and I do not think I am mistaken — preserve more of the spirit of Christianity than other peoples. Probably the reason is that the Russian people learned the New Testament five centuries before the rest of Europe, which knew practically nothing of it until the Reformation."

This idea of the super–Christianity of the Russian people was a favorite theme with Tolstoy, as it was with Dostoevsky, and he often recurred to it. After the war between Russia and Japan, where the Russian army made such a poor showing in comparison with the Mikado's troops, he said: "The consoling aspect of this debacle, is that no matter how badly the true teaching of Christianity has been distorted, its essence has none the less captured the conscience of the people to such an extent that war cannot be for them, as it is for the Japanese, a sacred cause that makes a hero of the man who dies for it. Fortunately this idea of war as an evil is sinking deeper and deeper into the public mind." That is a profound and logical observation, which all those Christians who extol military virtues should ponder.

The Christ of Tolstoy was not the God of violence that he is represented to be in every Christian confession, but the God of love and pity, the Christ of the Sermon on the Mount. In this volume there is a touching and appealing passage in which Tolstoy speaks of Him.

The God of love filled him with a deep, pantheistic feeling for nature, and suggested some of his most tender and gentle effusions.

"All the world is alive," he remarked one day to Goldenweiser, in sketching a projected work on a philosophical theme that, so far as we know, was never written. "All that seems to us dead appears so merely because it is either too large or too small for us to comprehend. We do not see the microbes; the planets appear to us inanimate for the same reason that we appear inanimate to an ant. Beyond question, our earth is alive, and a stone upon the earth is like the nail on a finger. Materialists make the material the basis of life. All the theories of the origin of species, of protoplasm, of atoms, have their value so far as they help us understand the laws that control the physical world. But we must not forget that they are working hypotheses, and nothing more. The astronomers in their calculations assume, for the purpose of making reckonings, that the earth is immovable, and later correct the error. Our materialists likewise set out from a false premise, but they do not admit it and recalculate their problems upon a true and corrected basis. In reality materialism is the most mystical of doctrines. It assumes dogmatically a mystical matter that creates everything out of itself, and is the foundation of everything. It is something as impossible of concrete visualization as the Trinity itself."

Of all the time I have spent in Moscow, the hours passed in the Tolstoy Museum remain most vividly in my memory. After the inferno of hunger and chaos into which the Soviets have plunged their country, it was like an oasis saved from the fearful wreckage that surrounded it and dedicated to the higher attributes of man.

This museum is certainly the most complete that has ever been established to perpetuate the memory of an individual. Tolstoy's whole life is recorded in its cases and shelves. For example, most of his manuscripts are preserved there, from his copy books in school to the last page that he ever wrote. Countless articles associated with him are carefully catalogued. Suits of clothes, from those he wore in childhood to those he wore in his old age, his cadet uniform, his black peasant blouse, the pen and inkstand that he used, the felt slippers that he wore, the skin of a bear that he shot in the Caucasus, some of the paintings and carvings that he made, his library, the first editions of his works, and other things too numerous to enumerate. Under a crystal globe there is a miniature model of Yasnaya Poliana. In a neighboring room is an exact reproduction of his sleeping chamber with the original furniture: the narrow iron bed on which he did not die; his table, a petroleum lamp, a cane chair, or black crucifix that was the sole adornment of the whitewashed walls; and in one corner — his old leather valise.

But the most interesting feature of the museum for me was a collection of photographs of Tolstoy and his family that cover the walls of several rooms. They enable one incidentally to follow the development of photography from the processes that preceded the daguerreotype, and to see Tolstoy at every age.

Naturally those taken during his later years are more numerous, for scarcely a visitor came to Yasnaya Polyana without his kodak camera, and most of them later sent to the family prints of the pictures they took.

I have spent long hours meditating over these later photographs — those from 1900 to 1910 — and I do not think it is possible to study them with an adequate comprehension of their meaning without being thrilled to the marrow. They all show the same Tolstoy, venerable, withered, wrinkled, tanned, with twinkling eyes and a long scraggly beard; and year by year the wrinkles grow deeper and the expression more self-accusing and hopeless. One sees that a secret and terrible sorrow is gnawing at his soul. In the end it is appalling. There is an enlarged photograph from the year 1910 that is truly horrifying. A strange frenzy that I cannot describe shines, like two glowing coals, in his eyes which were always a trifle monkish beneath his shaggy brows. One feels that he was utterly submerged in implacable despair, almost on the border of madness, dwelling on the verge of shadows and vertigo. One cannot conceive a better figure of King Lear wandering in the wild ... Tolstoy was the victim of his wife and that preyed upon this Prometheus.

Consciousness of this terrible contradiction was never veiled for one moment from Tolstoy's self-accusing inner eye. It kept him on the rack night and day. Another man might have been content to preach what is right; but such halfway virtue could never satisfy a Tolstoy.

Most men have no conception of such tortures of the conscience. Tolstoy lived like an ascetic, not from natural inclination, but by a stern effort of will. He did whatever good was in his power to those about him. He was gentle, kindly, abounding in love and mercy. What more could be asked of him? Everything. Because such a man is under irresistible compulsion to live a life of sanctity in all its fullness. He knows where he fails to measure up to his own ideal, and this knowledge flagellates him day and night. The thought of his wealth, of the money that kept accumulating in the bank while he preached poverty and the abandonment of all temporal riches, became to him an obsession. No other text of the Bible pursued him so constantly as that one in which Christ bade the young man who would follow him to divide his possessions among the poor. The young man departed in sadness and gave up Christ. Tolstoy followed Christ burdened by his riches.

The Tolstoy Museum at Moscow has another collection of photographs of great significance. They are family groups or else pictures of Tolstoy and his wife alone. He is seated; she is standing at his side with her arm around his shoulders. The attitude needs no explanation. It is not an attitude of love, but of domination; one sees at once who was "boss."

In all of them Tolstoy has the distraught, sad expression with which we are so familiar in his later pictures. She alone is smiling.

It is impossible to say whether his family really loved Tolstoy. But none of them understood the last phase of his moral and religious evolution.

The literary glory of Russia, that people made pilgrimages to see from the most distant parts of the earth. But they did not find it agreeable that he should be a prophet and an evangelist.

Sofia Andreevna took every precaution to check any manifestation of his apostolic spirit. It is to be said in her defense that she had married a great writer, a wealthy aristocrat, and not the saint that he wished to become; and it is certain that the vocation of holiness is not mandatory. That is the opinion of the world, and the people of the world will believe that Sofia Andreevna was right. But we cannot think without disdain and distaste of a woman to whom fate had given the mission and privilege of sharing the life of such a man, yet who refused the honor. Furthermore, at times she betrayed positive malice and baseness. Persons who knew the Tolstoys intimately, and frequently visited Yasnaya Poliana, have told me that Countess Tolstoy dealt most harshly with the peasants — the very peasants whom Tolstoy wished to convert to the "true life." For example, she would fine them mercilessly every time their cows trespassed upon her land. It seems that the neighboring villagers, unable to understand Tolstoy's subservience to his wife and supposing that this was all done with his consent, decided that he was a faker, and included him in their general aversion for the family. We can well imagine how a knowledge of this afflicted Tolstoy.

The rest of his torment will be understood by every person who has a sensitive and complex conscience — the struggle to decide how far one's own soul is honest and how far it is merely histrionic. Few problems of conscience are so terrible as this. We know that Tolstoy was tortured during the last years of his life by a desire for liberty, for emancipation from his own family.

More than once he made preparations to escape. After his death a letter was discovered written to his wife on such an occasion. Romain Rolland prints it in his charming "Life of Tolstoy." In this letter we can read between the lines of kindness and moderation a tremendous accusation against Sofia Andreevna. But apparently Tolstoy renounced his intention to flee at the last moment, and postponed the parting. It is usual to attribute his resignation to weakness. But the true motive was quite different. There is a phrase in a letter to a friend that discloses the ultimate reason for his conduct: "I have always given up escaping because I have thought that Sofia Andreevna would hate me, and that everything would therefore be worse." In other words, he might have saved himself, but the soul of Sofia Andreevna would be lost through her hatred. We approach here an ineffable mystery of humanity and love. To comment upon it would be to profane it.

However, shortly before his death, when his mortal illness was already upon him, Tolstoy did flee from his home. Much has been said of this sudden flight, and it has never been fully explained. I report what family friends of the Tolstoys, with whom I have conversed, have told me, without vouching for more than the fidelity with which their words are here recorded. It seems that Tolstoy himself related the occurrence to his physician, who told it, in turn, to a few close friends. One night, shortly before dawn, when Tolstoy was already ill, he heard something rustling his papers in the next room. At first he thought it was a cat; but when the noise continued he rose cautiously and surprised Sofia Andreevna in the act of carrying off his will, for the sake of giving his property to the poor. The next day Tolstoy, horrified by this discovery, fled from the house.

# 22

# Three Evenings with Count Leo Tolstoy
## by N. Everling

N. Everling was an American journalist and literary critic who visited Tolstoy in the 1900s.

Everling, N. "Three Evenings with Count Leo Tolstoy." *The Nineteenth Century and After* (New York), Vol. 93 (1923): 786–792.

During the winter of 1905 Count Leo Tolstoy resided at Moscow, in his house at Khamovniki Suburb. It was at that time that I happened to make the acquaintance of the famous writer. I was introduced to him by the Annenkovs. Mr. K. Annenkov, a well-known and learned man of law and landed proprietor of Lgov, imbued with the ideas of 1860, could in no way be looked upon as being a partisan of Leo Tolstoy's; his wife, Mrs. L. Th. Annenkov, on the contrary, was a zealous disciple of Tolstoy's teaching. An independent landowner, she led a life of absolute simplicity, and followed Tolstoy's literary activity most fervently, so that one could be certain of always finding his latest work, copied in her own handwriting, on her table.

Every winter, as soon as the sledge-roads were trafficable, the Annenkovs would leave their country solitude (the village of Tunisia, in the Lgov district, at a distance of about fifteen miles from Lgov) for Moscow, where they remained for two or three months, so as to see their intimate friends and acquaintances and to gain new impressions. During these visits, when the Tolstoys themselves resided at Moscow, that frequent intercourse between them became established which served as the chief attraction for Mrs. Annenkov in Moscow.

The entire so-called "Tolstoy circle" could be met with in the evening in the two small rooms which they usually occupied for the time in Tchizhov's furnished lodging on the Mokhovaya Street, opposite the University. Mr. Boulanger, Dunaev, P. Sergeenko, Biriukov, and, if I am not mistaken, Kulikov, and Gorbunov-Posadov were amongst the well-known disciples of Tolstoy. The hospitable and social lady of the house, Mrs. Annenkov, who treated her guests to various home-made sweets and pastry, was the center of this small party. The conversation invariably referred to the periodical question of Tolstoy's literary teaching, and to the various public lectures of his partisans and adherents. Faithful to her habits, however, she never remained idle. She would always be busy at some handwork, which generally consisted in knitting woolen scarves, gloves, mittens, socks, and caps intended for Count Leo Tolstoy, whose name she pronounced with special reverence. Her husband, Mr. Annenkov, sometimes jokingly made fun of her handwork, remarking that her knitting was evidently very precarious, judging by the short time Tolstoy was able to wear her work. The Annenkovs, who were vegetarians, always brought their own petroleum kitchen with them from the country, and were accompanied by their own maid-servant, a young and good-natured little Russian, who, as Mrs. Annenkov asserted, was likewise a follower of Tolstoy. The characteristic peculiarities of this village proselyte of the great author consisted in a perpetually swollen cheek and feet clad in huge felt boots.

The Annenkovs remained at Moscow longer than usual during the winter I am speaking of. I had for a long time wished to become acquainted with Count Tolstoy personally; he had already heard of me many years previously through Professor Nicole Grott, had read several of my literary trials and had even once given his approbation, which was flattering to me, but that was all. I must candidly confess now that, owing to my youthful infatuation, I disliked the idea of paying my obeisance to Tolstoy, and preferred to wait until I might chance to make his acquaintance through Grott or some other mutual friends.

I vividly recollect a vexing incident on having, at Professor Grott's request, read through the proof-sheets of Tolstoy's "What Is Art?" (a work, to which, as is generally known, the author lent great importance), which was at the time being published in the periodical review, "Questions of Philosophy and Psychology," edited by Grott. I happened one evening to call on him to return him the sheets, and was met, to my utter vexation and distress, by the words, "Had you come half an hour sooner, you would have met Count Leo Tolstoy."

Thanks to the Annenkovs, a favorable chance of getting acquainted with Tolstoy in suitable circumstances lay in store for me. They proposed to come and fetch me so as to drive together to the Tolstoys', at Khamovniki, in the evening. This was on a cold February day. Mrs. Annenkov drove ahead alone in a cab, whilst her husband and I followed in another. The weather was infamous; a regular snowstorm was blowing, and I was surprised at my companion's stoicism; he was clad in a simple autumn overcoat without a fur collar, and smoked all the way. His endurance was due to the excessive training he had always submitted himself to, bathing as he did in the open air until the beginning of October.

I remember to this day how confused I felt as we drove up to the Tolstoys' house, which was surrounded on all sides by factory buildings. We turned into the courtyard, past the house porter's lodge and the sidewings, and stopped at the entrance door. I remember having pulled the brass door bell myself. A tidily dressed servant instantly opened the front door leading into the brightly lit hall, and politely said, "Please come in; the Count and the Countess are in," as he made room for us to pass and proceeded to brush away the layer of snow which covered our fur coats and caps. We were ridding ourselves of our coats when we heard the sound of voices coming from the upper flat. We ascended the carpeted staircase with its banisters, covered with red cloth and fringes, and were shown into a spacious hall lighted by wall lamps. To the right stood a grand piano, and to the left were a long dinner-table and old-fashioned furniture, such as is met with in most of the country mansions of the second half of the nineteenth century. There was no one in the hall. However, when the flunkey had announced our arrival, an elderly Lady with eye-glasses made an appearance in the doorway, and I instantly recognized Sophia Andreyevna, the great writer's wife, whose portrait I had often seen. Involuntarily I looked for the Count to appear. Sophia Andreyena informed us that her husband was in and would soon join us. There were two ladies, besides us, in the sitting-room.

One of them, the older, was the wife of the famous physician Pogoev; the other, quite a young girl, was M.A. Maklakova, a sister of the Lawyer V.A. Maklakov, Plevako's assistant, who was then beginning to get known. The countess and Mrs. Annenkov sat down on the sofa and picked up their handwork by the light of a lamp screened by a large shade, whilst the rest of us seated ourselves in arm-chairs. Ten minutes had hardly elapsed, when Count Leo Tolstoy made his appearance in the doorway leading from the hall into the sitting-room.

The guests, amongst whom I remember the figures of V.A. Maklakov, N.N. Raevsky, M. Goldenweiser, the sculptor Prince Pavel Trubetskoy, gradually made their appearance. The assembly was fairly numerous. Shortly after we were all asked to pass into the hall and have tea and "zakousska" (hors d'oeuvres).

Tolstoy did not sit down at the large table, but placed himself at a small round table with a cane sofa and a couple of cane armchairs, to the left of the sitting-room door. A small circle formed around him, consisting of V.A. Maklakov, K.N. Annenkov, Gorbounov-Posadov and myself. Tolstoy helped himself to tea, honey and light pastry (he never took any sugar). The conversation broached various social topics and events of the day, amongst others the question of lectures for the workmen; Maklakov spoke with great animation, whilst Tolstoy listened.

The questions of so-called "Government Socialism" were being warmly discussed in all those corners of Moscow where the pulse of social life was beating. The echoes of these interests were noticeable in the conversation which took place. I remember Count Tolstoy's remark on the question of a series of lectures on social questions announced to be delivered at the Historical Museum: "Not worth to come to it all," he said, "because the only vital point won't be mentioned, the questions of real Christian morality, of the mutual love of mankind."

"You go in for philosophy,— could you kindly explain to me what is it that Prince S.N. Trubetskoy has written about Logos in his last book," he said.

Although Tolstoy was well acquainted with Prince S. Trubetskoy's dissertation, just then published in the twenty-ninth number of "The Scientific Notes" of the Moscow University, and despite my having been present at its public delivery, which took place with great solemnity in the public auditorium of the University, Tolstoy felt rather concerned at first by the question. However, I got over the first feeling of uneasiness, and gave a short and, I believe, satisfactory exposition of the principal thesis of that work.

I had to add that I only knew of him by hearsay, but had never read any of his works. "I advise you to read him," Tolstoy said amusingly. "He is certainly of interest you, and you won't regret having given him your time. Have you got his book?"

I replied that I could fetch it at the University library, whereupon he said: "That's not even necessary; I can make you a present of one copy."

So saying, he rose from his seat and went into his study, through a dark passage, which the members of the family had nicknamed "Our Catacombs."

I was surprised at the elasticity and firmness of his gait considering his advanced age. Tolstoy reappeared shortly with four small volumes in a light yellow binding. "Here are the books," he said. "I made notes in them of those passages which pleased me most." I thanked him most warmly.

"When you have read them," he went on with a kind smile, "I will have a talk with you about them; I shall be curious to hear from you what impression they have made on you."

Meanwhile K.N. Annenkov had called his wife from the sitting-room, and we proceeded to take leave of our hosts for fear of tiring Count Tolstoy by our long visit. He saw us off as far as the top steps of the staircase, bidding us farewell in a most affable way. Gorbounov-Possadov and Mrs. Pogozheva likewise left at the same time.

The snowstorm had calmed down, but we were obliged to wade through very deep snow, which lay specially thick on the "Devitchie Pole" [Maiden's Plain], and had not been cleared away owing to the advanced hour. There was always very little traffic in that part of the town.

After having taken leave of Gorbounov-Possadov and Pogozheva at the end of the street, we again hired two cabs and drove to our respective homes, the Annenkovs to the Mokhovaya Street, where I lived at that time.

On my way home I was in an elevated frame of mind and felt so happy and bright at heart. My wish of many years had been fulfilled. I had made Count Tolstoy's acquaintance, and further conversations of the greatest interest, on philosophical and religious subjects, lay in store for me, which would most likely prove very instructing and elevating.

# 23

# A Vacation with Tolstoy
## by Theodore von Hafferberg

Theodore von Hafferberg was a French and English tutor at the Tolstoy estate who taught Tolstoy's nephews.

Hafferberg, Theodore von. "A Vacation with Tolstoy." *Living Age* (Boston), 1923, v. 391 (8): 311–316, 359–361, 406–410.

My visit to Yasnaya Poliana occurred during my student years at Petrograd. One day an announcement posted at University caught my eye, saying that a student with a knowledge of foreign languages, and particularly of French, was wanted as a tutor during the summer upon an estate in the government of Tula. I promptly applied at the address given, which proved to be Senator Kuzminskii's house. His wife was Countess Tolstoy's sister and his family was preparing to spend the summer, as was its usual custom, at Yasnaya Poliana. I was engaged as French tutor and companion for the Senator's son. My duties also included preparing him for admission to the Law School.

On May 10, 1887, I arrived at Yasnaya Poliana at about eight o'clock in the evening, and was shown to my lodging — a cottage in the ancient park adjoining the Count's residence. The upper rooms of the cottage were occupied by the Senator's family. The lower rooms, which had been prepared for my use, were generally called "the School"; for Count Lev Nikolaevich had been accustomed to teach personally the village children there.

I had scarcely had time to glance around my new quarters when I was notified that the Count's family expected me to tea in the big house.

Lev Nikolaevich and the whole company would be delighted to meet me. I was therefore to be presented at once to the greatest literary light of the world! The very thought frightened me, and I had to muster all my courage to overcome my nervousness. I left my best clothes in my trunk,— I should not need them here,— put on a black sack suit, and promptly at 9 p.m.— it was already dark — strolled down the magnificent shaded avenue to the Count's house.

The whole company was already present. Lev Nikolaevich was the first to rise, and greeted me most cordially. I was then presented to the rest of the circle, at least fifteen people. In order to do this, I had to walk around a long table. A place was made for me in their midst, directly opposite Lev Nikolaevich. I was at once impressed with the kindness and gentleness of his eyes — under his powerful, bushy brows — even when they seemed to pierce through the person to whom he was speaking and read his inmost thoughts.

He seized at once the substance of whatever one tried to say, no matter how awkwardly and ambiguously it was worded, restated the thought briefly and to the point, and developed it fully and gracefully. Sometimes the Count's own thoughts seemed to burst forth from him in almost torrential abundance — or like the sparks of electricity from a powerful generator — and stimulated his listeners to quick responsiveness.

During a pause in the conversation, Lev Nikolaevich turned directly to me and said he thought he could pay me quite a compliment: that my slight figure and black suit, and in fact my whole manner and appearance, reminded him strikingly of his old friend, Prince Gorchakov, with whom he had been very intimate in his younger years, especially during the Crimean War.

He added with a touch of irony:

"Finally he became Imperial Chancellor, and died a great political light."

Meanwhile it had been growing late. At about eleven o'clock the party decided to break up and go to bed.

"Anyway, Fedor Fedorovich must be tired from his journey and the rest will do him good. Since you are sleeping over there in the School, you'll surely have pleasant dreams," commented the Count with a smile. He accompanied the party to the door and looked on benignantly as the young ladies kissed each other good night. It suggested to him a farewell thought with which he sped our departure:—

## 23. A Vacation with Tolstoy (von Hafferberg)

"Who can give me the mathematical formula for the number of kisses that have just been given?" We thought for some time, and then someone suggested this formula:

$$\frac{n(n-1)}{2}$$

"Quite right," said Lev Nikolaevich: "So now that these six young ladies have kissed each other, what's the total? Six by five divided by two: fifteen kisses. Absolutely accurate!" And the Count laughed happily, still laughing, he wished us again a good night's rest.

Lev Nikolaevich was a very vigorous man for his age. This was largely due to the importance he attached to physical exercise, which he considered indispensable for a sound body.

In the morning, before coffee, when I and my young student walked through the woods to take a swim in the neighboring river, we generally found Lev Nikolaevich already in the water. He would flounder around, puffing and swimming sometimes on his back and sometimes on his chest. Occasionally we saw him on horseback, though more rarely. From 2 to 6 p.m. we were always sure to find him laboring in the fields, one day at one place, another day at another, wherever there was work to be done.

Mowing was his great delight, and he readily undertook to teach me this art. As I watched him, rhythmically swinging his arms following the scythe with a light, elastic, dancing step, his brilliant description of mowing in "Anna Karenina" involuntarily recurred to me.

One day when my pupil and I were trying out a country horse that he had bought for forty rubles, we met Lev Nikolaevich at about a half-hour's walk from the house, striding along toward home with a scythe over his shoulders.

"Hello!" he shouted at us from a distance. "Where are you going?"

"We are just driving to try out the horse."

"So you have time to waste like that, while an old chap like me is breaking his back in the fields and then has to walk home afterward by foot! You're just in time. You can take me with you. I'll sit back so my scythe — it won't bother you." So the Count perched himself directly behind me, and his talk, as we drove along was indelibly imprinted upon my memory.

"Yes," he said, "young people live blindly for the day without thinking what time is worth and how important it is to use it profitably. In the cities people live either by brain work or by physical labor. It never occurs to them, however, that the first is utterly insufficient and the latter only partly sufficient. Then the city man comes into the country "for recreation," and does not know how to kill his time. Indeed, he generally ruins the real workers by his bad example.

"Tell me, please, has it never occurred to you that a man cannot work with his brain or with his muscles a whole day without a change? If a man works with his brains, his brains should be fresh and rested. If he works with his body, his body should be fresh and rested. If either is fatigued he is no longer a worker. After a man has worked hard with his brain, there is no better recreation than physical labor. Everyone knows it, but no one will practice it. In order to make it a success, a person should divide his time as rationally as possible and live as regularly as possible. Fix a maximum for effective brain work and for effective physical work — let us say, for example, four hours. After four hours your brain begins to tire, and after an equal period your body becomes fatigued with labor. Each needs a change. According to my opinion, the most rational, normal division of time is the one I am following now: a healthy man needs eight hours' sleep, which leaves him sixteen hours for other things.

"Let us take, for example, first: from 6 to 10 a.m. light physical tasks such as easy handicrafts, bathing, and sports that are not of a violent character; second: from 10 a.m. to 2 p.m. brain work such as studying and writing; third: from 2 p.m. to 6 p.m. hard physical labor such as mowing or ploughing; fourth: from 6 to 10 p.m. social intercourse, music, playing chess, and the like."

By this time we were close to the house, in fact just passing through the gateway to the park, so that the long avenue of trees was directly ahead. Tolstoy continued: "Such a division of time is impracticable in a city, especially in a big city. But city life ruins a healthy organism anyway. Every man knows it, and yet no one has the courage to reform and live rationally."

"Yes, yes," I answered, a little embarrassed, "that may be all right in theory, especially for well-to-do people who own land. But poor people in the cities must first organize to bring that to pass, or else hire out as laborers to the peasants. But city people won't do that."

The Count made no reply, for we were already at the house. He merely jumped out of the sulky and said in his jovial way: "Many thanks for bringing me. You must be driving farther. Au revoir."

On another occasion Count Tolstoy came along just as we were starting on a sulky ride.

"Where are you going?" he called, starting in our direction.

"To the store," I said. "I've got some purchases to make and want some tobacco."

"Well, you might bring me some tobacco too. What do you pay for yours?"

"Fifty or sixty kopecks a quarter pound."

"No, no — that's luxury. I can't afford that. Buy me a quarter of a pound please, but do not pay more than thirty-six kopecks. Get it cheaper if you can, but don't pay more. Please buy it for me, I'll pay you later."

The Countess, who attended to Lev Nikolaevich's business affairs, permitted him one silver ruble pocket money a day. He was gratefully contented with this, and every morning distributed seventy or eighty kopecks to the poor and the passing pilgrims who presented themselves regularly at the house about 9 a.m. Pilgrims on their way to Kiev were very numerous, for the highway from Moscow to the latter city runs close to Yasnaya Poliana. He kept only twenty or thirty kopecks for his own private use mainly for his tobacco, which he still smoked.

The Count had his troubles at home over smoking even this cheap tobacco. Once I was at what they called "children's tea," which was served in the big dining room every day between three and four o'clock by one of the governesses. Any of the older people who came in were always welcome. On this particular afternoon I took my cup of tea and sat down opposite the Countess. After I had finished my tea and smoked my cigarette, the Countess noticed how I extinguished the stub on the bottom of the cup and laid it down in the saucer. She felt it necessary to call my attention to this: "No, Fedor Fedorovich, we do not consider it good manners to use a saucer as an ash-tray."

I blushed and begged pardon with the utmost confusion.

"Do not imagine," continued Sofia Andreevna, "that I am offended with you personally. Not in the slightest. Only that is not considered good form in our circles, and it is my duty as the mistress of the house to see that we do not fall into peasant ways, and that keep up our standards and appearanccs. Do you imagine that I would let Lev Nikolaevich commit such an offense against good etiquette? Never! I am just as strict in making him conform to the usages of good society."

Lev Nikolaevich rolled his own cigarettes and smoked them in a holder. I often noticed that when he had finished one and an ashtray was not handy, he would blow the stub out of the holder into his hand, and hold it in his clenched fist.

The Count was very fond of music. Toward the end of May a violinist, young Lassota, a student at the Moscow Conservatory, arrived at

Yasnaya Poliana. He had been engaged for the summer chiefly to teach Lev Lvovich, the Count's son, to play the violin. He lodged in "the Pavilion," which stood on one side of the park, between the School and the main residence, and contained a piano. During the day he gave lessons there in both piano and violin, but evenings he was generally to be found at the Manor House itself, where we had almost nightly concerts in the big living-room on the second. Those present — invariably including the Count — sat either at the big table in the middle of the room or at a small round table in a corner.

At Lev Nikolaevich's wish Beethoven's sonatas were always played. He would listen with great attention. The Kreutzer Sonata seemed to be his favorite. He asked for it almost every evening, so that it was soon played with great readiness and careful phrasing. The Count seemed to bury himself more and more in the harmonies of this sonata. It was clear that they called up pictures in his vivid imagination that were steadily growing stronger and more distinct.

Finally his idea was matured, and he at once set to work. The following winter his "Kreutzer Sonata" appeared. For a time the Russian censor disapproved of it so strongly that the first edition was printed in Paris.

Now and then the Count himself would sit down at the piano, mostly for four-handed pieces. He would also play accompaniments if they were not very difficult, for instance to Braga's serenade, "The Angel," and a trio where Lasotta played the violin and Mme. Kuzminskaia sang.

I had brought my cornet-a-pistons, and was sometimes invited to perform. I occasionally played Fesca's "The Maiden at the Window," "The Wanderer," or "The Postman in the Forest." The Count always applauded vigorously. One glorious morning, when the "Quality" were taking their morning coffee in the park, I played to them from my lodgings and wound up with the accompaniment to some of Heine's songs, which I repeated from memory. Lev Nikolaevich rose from the breakfast table where he was sitting and walked up and down the avenue.

When I had finished one of the little songs, he came up to me and said, with a meditative and slightly melancholy air, that he knew all those songs and that Heine was one of his favorite poets. Then, gazing dreamily into the distance, he began to recite:

"O sah' ich auf der Haide dort im Sturme dich, im Sturme dich,
Mit metinem Mantel nor dem Sturm' beschitzt' ich dich, beschilzt'
  ich dich —
Und war' die Krone mein, die Krone mein,
Du warst in meiner Kron' der schonste Stein, des schonste Stein."

Suddenly he roused himself as from a dream, saying: "Yes indeed, glorious words of a glorious poet! But do not let me interrupt you. Keep on playing; it sounds charming here in the open air."

Then he walked slowly away.

The park avenue that led from the main residence to the cottage occupied by the Kuzminsky family bent down the latter building, and continued on to the so-called "Cattle Yard." In one of the stables there was a room that formerly served as the estate office and still kept its old name. One day I chanced to enter it and found there a haggard old woman, with a bushy stubble of white hair and a toothless, fallen-in mouth, who surveyed me from head to foot with a malicious, glassy stare. Apparently she lived there and I had surprised her just as she had enticed a number of rats and mice upon a purple coverlet spread on the floor, and was feeding them there. I learned later that she had formerly been a servant-maid in the Count's family, and was given lodging in the "office," besides her pension from the estate. She was Agafia Mikhailovna, or "Agasha" as she was called for short in some of Tolstoy's books, for instance in "Childhood" and "Youth."

In mentioning the incident to the Count, I said I supposed she was given her lodgings in return for exterminating the rats and mice instead of feeding them. Lev Nikolaevich nodded attentively to what I said, and then answered good-naturedly: "Yes, yes, from your point of view that would be the thing to do. But I see it differently. Everybody is trying to exterminate rats and mice; but they never are exterminated and continue to be just as much of a pest as ever. But Agasha's case is unique. She has lived her life, she is now lingering in twilight. Her eyes can no longer stand the glare of day, and her soul can no longer stand the sunlight of the world. The only thing that still binds this soul to life is the thought of caring for, and having dependent upon her, some living being. All her years she has been looking after other people, and without having something to look after her last days would be sad indeed — the little life that is left her would lose its content."

The Count drew a deep breath, and after reflecting a moment continued thoughtfully: "We have here, in our village, a very old man — I think he carries a full century on his shoulders. He is a living monument to the past. Since my earliest memory he was cook in my father's house, and later in our own family. Now he, too, has his pension and is living in the village, and comes to us only now and then when we have a great family celebration. These two old people have seen and experienced much. They must have seen more evil than good, because evil outweighs good in the human race, especially in the higher circles of society where the Devil's hold upon men is in proportion to their wealth and honors. Among the humbler classes good seeds fall on more fertile soil. And what illumines — yes, enlightens — the evening of life for these two old people is taking care of some living being, if it is only a dog, a cat, or rats and mice."

A mad beggar, who except for his mental malady was a vigorous man in his forties, haunted the country around Yasnaya Poliana. He was half-clothed in filthy rags. He would often come to the Count's house and, as he was harmless and inoffensive, food would be passed to him through the kitchen window.

The Count tried on many occasions to bring him back to sanity. He would say to him: "Abandon this folly. Look at your dirty rags. I will clothe you from head to foot in new, clean clothes if you will go to work."

The tramp would be silent for a time and then stammer: "No, no, I can't," adding mysteriously: "You do not know to whom you are speaking, and who I am. I am a Romanov of the Imperial blood. Wagonloads of gold have been sent to me. I expect them to arrive every day — and you want me to work at rude, peasant labor! I, a Romanov, work! No, you can't expect that of me. No, no, do not talk like that."

Tolstoy has described such a person in his writings. Once when we were alone together, he spoke to me confidentially of this queer customer. "If he's crazy, so are the ideas and creeds of our best society. Its members do not think physical labor is fitting for them. They regard it as debasing, beginning with the Tsar and his ministers. If you talk to them of physical labor, they will not deign to answer you. All our nobility are permeated with the idea that they are born to be brain workers, and that brain work and physical labor do not go together. If one of their members does forget himself so far as to do manual work, they think him ridiculous and eccentric."

Just when the evenings began to grow longer and darker, a visitor from Petrograd was announced. She was a Countess Tolstoy, a lady-in-waiting at the Court, and wished to spend a couple of days at Yasnaya Poliana. She must be received with due honor, and so an ancient "kolymaga" [carriage] was rummaged out of the coach house. Six horses were hitched to this antique family-caravan, and linkboys rode astride them, since it was already growing dark. Thus the lumbering affair set off to Tula for our distinguished visitor. She was received and brought back with due formality, and decided the following day to favor us with a French reading. The Court lady had discovered in that aristocratic semiofficial French paper, "Journal de St. Petersburg," which was sent to me daily at Yasnaya, but was more frequently to be found in the salon than in my room, a feuilleton article by Guy de Maupassant, "Au Ballon," which she wished to read aloud to our whole circle.

We were duly notified that the reading would occur at eight o'clock that evening in the second-story reception-room adjoining the big living-room. Before describing this reading, however, let me first tell you how the gentlemen and ladies at Yasnaya Poliana were accustomed to dress, for my attire on that evening was the occasion of a mortifying episode.

The Count wore on all occasions, in the summer, a shirt of yellowish-gray unbleached linen or, if it were cooler weather, of un-dyed wool. Most of the young men dressed like the Count, except that their shirts were of thin summer material of various bright colors, generally light blue or white with black dots or other patterns. They all wore belts. Since I had no shirts of this kind in my city wardrobe and yet wanted to dress lightly and comfortably, I looked for a suitable shirt in town; but I could not find one that fitted me, and decided offhand to wear a light shirt of cotton "kumach," of the fiery-red hue so popular among the peasants.

Since the day of the lecture had been fearfully warm and I had worn the red shirt since morning, I kept it on that evening, feeling perfectly certain that I should be permitted to wear a red shirt in the home of Tolstoy, the great friend of the people. The old Countess Tolstoy read the feuilleton by Maupassant very expressively, with easy self-possession — in fact, gave us as much of a treat as if we actually made a trip in a balloon. Nobody commented upon my red shirt, so I thought everything was all right.

But the next morning Madame Kuzminskaya read me a lecture: "I wish to call your attention in the interest of good form, to a circumstance that pained me deeply last evening, but which I refrained from speaking about to you before the whole company. The way you dressed last evening in that red shirt was decidedly unbecoming and utterly out of place in our social circle."

"What?" I exclaimed in surprise. "I thought just the opposite — that in Leo Nikolaevich's home this popular red color would be just the thing."

"You are merely making insincere excuses," the lady replied indignantly. "You know well enough that when you are at the home of Lev Nikolaevich, you are not his guest but the guest of Countess. You have no occasion to act the Tolstoy disciple and wave a red shirt as a Tolstoy banner. Wear what you want during the day, but you must not again enter our company in that challenging garb, especially when have such an aristocratic visitor as we had last night."

One evening our whole company was sitting upstairs in the big room. On the round table in the middle of the room a huge lamp with a dark shade. Everyone was busy — some reading, others writing, one or two drawing and painting. But I was playing checkers with Lev Nikolaevich. At every move he made I heard him mutter: "No, better die on the spot." When he had done this several times, always repeating, "No, better die on the spot," I ventured to ask him what he was saying. He answered, smiling, as if rousing himself from a profound mediation: "That is a favorite expression of an old acquaintance of mine. It delights me greatly. It contains a grain of deep wisdom: 'No, better die at once, than live an unworthy life without object and purpose!'"

As he said this he lifted his eyes, and I read under his high vaulted brow, in his deep tolerant glance, his true thoughts: "Is this not an unworthy life that I am leading, with the constant knowledge that all my teachings, my efforts to benefit mankind, are in vain? Will not all my labors prove fruitless through my powerlessness to add actual deeds to my empty words? Am I bringing up my children in the truth of my doctrine? Have I the courage to renounce this family circle and to go out among the common people and put my doctrines into practice?"

I was once lamenting to the Count how little, relatively, I had read, and told him I did not want to read omnivorously, or at random. I asked him if he could suggest a course of reading or if there were books he would especially recommend me to read before others.

"You have exactly the right idea," he answered, "in not wishing to read everything at random. The system I should recommend is this: wait until you feel a spontaneous interest, whether in a science or in a special social, philosophic, or other question. Then get the books you need, and your reading will bear fruit."

On another occasion I asked him what method he would recommend to me to master a foreign language in the shortest time. I had a school knowledge of English that I had acquired at the University, but I could make big progress in its practical use.

"My dear Fedor Fedorovich," said the Count, "I can recommend with confidence to you, who already know German, French, and the ancient languages, and have a school knowledge of English, the method by which I learned enough Hebrew to read the Old Testament in the original.

"In the course of three days I had the Hebrew alphabet and the fundamental grammatical rules of the language taught me. Then I started out alone to study Hebrew texts, comparing them with their translations. In that way I reached a point where I could read and understand any texts that I wished. For English, too, you cannot do better than take the Gospels, for the translation that we have of them is the most exact and lucid."

One afternoon, when I was again going to the station for the mail, the Count joined me. He was on his way to call upon a relative, and as we walked along together we conversed of several more or less important matters. When we were about halfway to our destination, we saw a flock of sheep grazing near the road and a shepherd boy sitting on the edge of a ditch, busily braiding a wreath of the wild flowers that grew in abundance around him. When we drew near, the lad scarcely glanced at us and continued his occupation. However, the Count lifted his linen cap and greeted the youngster like an old acquaintance, so that the boy had no recourse but to lift his cap likewise and respond. I was rather surprised at the incident, and asked Lev Nikolaevich why he had greeted the boy first.

"Is it not our duty," he said, "to instruct the unlearned, and especially the young, in the truth and meaning of love—above all in love for their neighbor? Who is to teach the uneducated unless it be the educated? And is not the best way of teaching by good example? Should we, who enjoy the advantages of education and culture, not conduct ourselves during our whole life so that we may be examples for the uneducated classes? And are we, the educated, not indebted to the uneducated to an extent that we can never even approximately repay? The least that we, who are convinced of this, can do, is to show them our regard—to give them our moral support by kindly counsel, and to prove to them that we are trying to live in the way that they should live.

"Yes, when I think of all this," he added after a few moments' silent meditation, "I realize how much I have upon my conscience, how much I have still to make good. When a man has such a long and active life behind him, he involuntarily asks himself what I ask myself now: What sins of omission and sins of commission have I been guilty of? And the answer is: I have done all things that I should not have done. There is none of the Ten Commandments that I have not broken. Even the Fifth Commandment—"Thou shalt not kill"—I have cruelly and repeatedly broken. During the Crimean War I fought at the front, and I have many human lives on my conscience. Moreover, in my private thoughts I have many times been a murderer. For all that, I must repent and do penance, else I cannot escape the eternal hell-fire of my own conscience.... But come along with me. I'll go with you to the post office, and we shall go down to the Shidlovskys' (his relatives) together."

At the Shidlovskys' we found the "Clover Leaf of Three Creeds" together — the three Veras — inseparable companions who had thus been christened. Vera Lvovna, the seventeen-year-old second daughter of the Count, was trying conscientiously to follow her father's teaching and wherever possible to win converts for the coming "Tolstoyism."

Vera Alexandovna Kuzminskaya, who was about the same age, was attracted by the beliefs of her cousin, but seemed to cherish, nevertheless, certain social prejudices that prevented her from being a whole hearted disciple — she was a kind of broad churchman, so to speak.

The third cousin, Vera Petrovna, evidently could not tell what she did believe, was uncertain whether to steer to the right or to the left, and put off her decision for the future. Thus there was a little world of varying doctrine within the Count's own family.

Late in the summer an old family custom was revived, for which there had been neither time nor interest earlier. A literary letter-box was set up, into which a person might put every week a contribution in prose or verse, which ultimately appeared in a little journal issued at irregular intervals, called "The Yasnaya Polyana Broadside."

On August 28, shortly before I was to leave, I attended the Count's birthday party, which included only the narrower family circle. Tolstoy's second son, Ilia Lvovich, a sturdy, rather stocky young man twenty-one years old, had come down to Yasnaya Polyana from Moscow for the occasion. He was in army uniform; he had just finished his first year of military service. I think he was a chip of the old Tolstoy in his youth; he led a carefree cavalier life, refused to let his father's social doctrines worry him, and incidentally cost his mother, who was strong on living up to the family standing, a pretty sum of money.

It was glorious weather, and a birthday dinner was served to some twenty of us present in the open air. The centenarian cook had taken charge of the kitchen again for this single day, and he provided us with many delicious dishes and many a pleasant drink. Even Lev Nikolaevich was prevailed upon to relax his total abstinence for the occasion, as he had to respond to numerous toasts and birthday wishes. All in the way of eating and drinking that is ever provided in Russia on such occasions was here in abundance.

After dinner our party scattered through the park. As we were walking along we approached the pond in the park, and the idea of taking a refreshing bath suddenly occurred to my young companion. Before I could prevent it, or even make a protest, he was out on the little wharf undressing hastily, and sprang with a great splash into the water. This prank disturbed me greatly. Didn't the lad know how dangerous it was to jump into a cold pond after a full meal, when he was warm and perspiring? When he did not appear immediately after his dive, I feared that he might have had heart failure. But he popped up a moment later, floundered around with a great splashing, swam about for a short time, and came out greatly refreshed. Nevertheless, I felt it incumbent on me to read him a lesson upon his recklessness; and as Lev Nikolaevich himself came along just then I turned to the father and described how startled and frightened I had been at his son's recklessness.

The Count merely smiled and asked his son, who by this time had complete dressing: "Well now, how do you feel after your swim?"

"Magnificent! Like another man!" was the answer.

Thereupon the Count turned to me and said: "My dear Fedor Fedorovich, you see we cannot always generalize. The doctors may have proved that it is dangerous for the heart to take cold bath right after eating. But that does not disprove the old familiar fact that what may harm a weak physique, may not injure a sound one. My son Iliusha has a strong, vigorous body, and instinctively knows it. His swim did him a lot of good. He feels like another man. Do you think I ought to forbid him such a pleasure? A weak man is apt to call reckless what a strong man thinks commonplace."

So I got the lecture instead of his son Iliusha.

The porch that ran along the front of the house had no railing and was sadly weather-worn and dilapidated. Directly in front of it was a gravel path, and beyond that a broad, square, closely mown English lawn, where the young people, especially the young ladies, often played games, including lawn tennis. Along the border were several flowerbeds, some of which were still in bloom.

The evening following the Count's birthday was as beautiful as the day itself. After supper our guests took their departure and the birthday party itself was over; but some of the younger people still lingered to enjoy the calm evening and the glory of the starry heavens that arched over the black park. The young men lay stretched outside, the glow of their lighted cigarettes punctuating the darkness. We studied the stars and constellations and pointed out to each other Orion, the Big Bear, the Little Bear, Cassiopeia, and all the countless worlds that twinkled and glimmered above. The moon was already approaching its setting over the black forest line and was half obscured by light fleecy clouds.

On the left end of the porch Countess Tatiana, the eldest daughter of the Count, sat with her guitar. Her sister Vera and the two other Veras — the inseparable "Clover Leaf of Three Creeds"— were sitting at her feet. They sang melancholy folk-songs that seemed to accord perfectly with the solemn stillness of the evening. Countess Tatiana led the singing in a low voice, and the young girls at her feet joined in a chorus subdued to the accompaniment of her guitar.

Count Lev Nikolaevich had brought out a chair to the other side of the porch, where he sat a little apart in the shadow, his cigarette alternately glowing and dimming like a distant star. The magnificent evening and the melancholy notes of the songs that the, girls were singing had obviously evoked a flood of thoughts within him that he must struggle with alone; and I fancied that I could divine what the old man above there, on the porch, was thinking. Did not his anniversary make him to review his whole past life? Was he not asking himself what all his labor, his teaching, and his writing were really doing to better the world? Were his hands not empty and his heart filled with inexpressible grief? He had delivered many noble messages, but had performed no noble deeds to correspond. Would his words not therefore prove sterile? His doctrines, like all doctrines, craved incarnation in living realities — but he saw no signs of that on any side. The crude materialism of his age, the faults and prejudices of society, opposed him at every step. At one time he had cherished the hope that he might be able at least to bring up his sons and daughters in the spirit of his own teaching. But had he any disciples in his own family — outside the Clover Leaf of Three Creeds? Surely he must not let his life end thus, in a resonance of empty words! The day must come when he would be forced to unburden his conscience before God and to cast from himself all his present shackles,— family, relatives, society,— when humanity would summon him to be its emancipator and pilot to salvation. And when that time came he must follow the call as if it were the voice of God Himself.

Thus I interpreted the thoughts and dreams of the lonely man on the verandah, whose soul, like his gaze, was lifted toward the starry heaven above us.

# 24

# A Day in Tolstoy's Life
## *by Stefan Zweig*

Stefan Zweig (1881–1942) was an Austrian writer and journalist who lived in the United States in the 1910s and 1940s; he published *Three Writers: Casanova, Stendahl, Tolstoy* in 1928.

Zweig, Stefan. "A Day in Tolstoy's Life." *The Living Age* (Boston), vol. 334 (1928): 56–62.

    Dawn. Sleep drifts slowly from the eyelids of the old man. He wakes and stares around him. Rosy morning light already tints the window. Day is arriving. Consciousness slowly emerges from the shadows. The first feeling is one of surprised happiness—"I am still alive." Last night, as every night, he had stretched himself upon his bed humbly resigned to be rising from it again. By a flickering lamp he had written in his diary, for the date of tomorrow, three letters standing for "If I am alive." It is a never-ending wonder. Once again the blessing of existence is bestowed upon him: he lives; he breathes; he draws a deep breath as if it were a special gift of God, and continues to look about him with gray, eager eyes.
    Gratefully the old man rises, disrobes completely. A douche of ice-cold water makes his well-preserved body glow. He performs some light athletic exercises, breathing deeply and supplely bending to and fro. Then he partly clothes himself, slips on a dressing gown, opens the window, and sweeps out his chamber, after tossing a few sticks of wood upon the crackling fire. For he is his own servant.

This done, he descends to the breakfast room. Sophia Andreevna, his daughters, his secretary, and a couple of friends are already at the table. The samovar is bubbling. His secretary brings in a motley heap of letters, periodicals, and books, their wrappings gay with bright-colored stamps from every quarter of the world.

Tolstoy glances half-resentfully at this mountain of mail. "Incense and trouble," he thinks silently to himself. "Confusion and distraction, to say the least. We should be left more alone with ourselves and God, and not try to be the axis of the universe. Better repel what disturbs and distracts us, what makes us vain, polite, ambitious, and insincere. Better, indeed, to throw stuff in the stove." However, his curiosity is stronger than aversion, and with nimble fingers he runs through the heap of begging complaints, petitions, business cards, requests for interviews, idle gossip. A Brahman writes to Tolstoy, a criminal sends the story of his life and asks young men to turn to him, paupers appeal to him humbly because "he is the only one."

"Whom can I help," he thinks. "I, who cannot even help myself? Every day I err and blunder and seek some source of consolation to make this puzzling life endurable, while all the time I talk pompously about truth simply to deceive myself. What wonder they come to me crying, 'Lev Nikolaevich, teach us to live!' My own life is a lie, mere affectation and pretense. In truth, I am an empty vessel, because I waste myself, because I spend myself vainly on thousands of others instead of retiring within myself, because I talk and talk and talk instead of keeping silent and listening for the word of God in my secret heart. But I cannot disappoint these people who trust in me. I must give them some answer."

He holds one letter longer than the others and reads it through two or three times. It is from a student who criticizes him violently because he "preaches water and yet drinks wine." It is high time for him to leave his comfortable home, to give his property to the peasants, to set forth as a pilgrim on the highways seeking God. "He is right," muses Tolstoy. "He speaks with the voice of my own conscience. But how can I explain to him what I cannot explain to myself? How can I defend myself when he accuses me in my name?" And he takes this single letter with him when he returns to his study, in order to answer it at once.

His secretary detains him a moment at the door to remind him that he has promised an interview that noon to a correspondent of the "Times," and to ask whether he will receive him. Tolstoy's face darkens. "What do they want of me — to pry into my soul? All I have to say is in my writings. Anybody who can read can find it there." But he controls himself and adds in a kindlier tone: "All right, so far as I am concerned; but only for a half-hour." Scarcely has he crossed the threshold of his study, however, before he mutters self-accusingly: "Why did I consent to that? Me, an old, gray-haired man on the verge of death, and not yet cured of vanity and love of publicity. I am ever a weakling. When shall I learn at length to hide myself and to keep silent? Help me, oh, help me, God!"

At length he is alone in his study. On the bare wall hang a scythe, a rake, and an axe. A rude, heavy settee stands in front of the bare table. The place is a cell, half monkish and half peasant. A partly finished article lies on the table—"Thoughts upon Life." He reads what he has written, erases, changes, starts again. His hasty, coarse, boyish handwriting is constantly interrupted. "I am in too much of a hurry—too impatient. How can I write about God when I have no clear idea of Him in my own mind, when I myself am not steadfast, and my thoughts change from day to day? How can I be explicit and lucid in describing God the Inexpressible and Life the Incomprehensible? What I presume to do is beyond my power. My God, how sure of myself I used to be when I wrote fiction, describing life to men as God unrolls it before us, and not as I, an old, bewildered seeker for truth, wish it to be! I am no saint—no, I am not, and I should not try to teach men. I am only a person to whom God has given clearer eyes and keener vision than to thousands of others, in order that I might see the world. Perhaps I was truer and better in the days when I served only the art which I now curse so irrationally."

The old man pauses and glances quickly around him, as if someone might be watching, and then takes out of a hidden drawer the novels upon which he is secretly working. For he has publicly denounced art as superfluous and sinful. There they are, the secretly written stories concealed from the world—"Haji Murad," "The Lost Coupon." He turns over the sheets and reads a few lines. His eyes light up. "Yes, that's good writing," he murmurs. "That's good. God designed me merely to portray his world, not to expound His thoughts. How beautiful is art, how pure is creation, how torturing is thinking! How happy I was when I wrote those pages! Tears wet my cheeks when I described that spring morning in the 'Wedding Day.' But I cannot do it. I must not disappoint the world. I must continue on the path I have now entered, because so many look to me for help in their distress of soul. I dare not stop. My days are numbered." And putting the treasured sheets back in their hiding place, he resumes his composition like a hack writer, silent and surly, with wrinkled brow and lowered chin, so that his white beard at times brushes across the paper.

Noon at last! Enough done for today! Away with the pen! He springs and with quick, light steps descends the staircase. A groom is already waiting with Delire, his favorite horse. He springs into the saddle, his desk-bent back straightens, he looks stronger, younger, more alive, lightly and easily as a Cossack, spurs the spirited animal toward forest. His white beard flutters in wind. He opens wide his lips to inhale in the fragrant, fresh air of the meadow to draw a draught of their ever-green life into his aging body. His blood stirred by the rapid motion, runs warm and vigorous through his veins; his finger tips tingle, his ears throb. At the edge of the forest he suddenly reins his horse in order to see at least once more how the waxen buds are opening in the spring sunshine, weaving a delicate tracery of nascent green soft and lacelike against the sky. Pressing his mount sharply with the knee, he turns to a birch tree, his sharp eyes sparkling with interest, to observe a column of ants busy bearing their burdens along its trunk. The gray old patriarch sits there motionless for several minutes, watching with tear-moistened eyes the tiny creatures at their labor. What a miracle! This nature, this wonderful mirror of God's thought, which has not changed for seventy years, and yet is never the same — always young, always wise, always the same and yet ever different!

But the horse whinnies impatiently. Tolstoy rouses himself from his reverie and dashes off with the speed of the wind, eager to share with Nature also her wildness and passion — as well as her microscopic care and tenderness. So he rides on, happy and thought free, for a full twenty versts, until white sweat dots the flank of his black tweed. Then he turns homeward at a quieter pace, his eyes afire, his spirit as happy and carefree as when he rode through the same woods earlier.

As he nears the village, however, the glow leaves his face. With an expert eye he surveys the fields. Here the very middle of his estate is an unkempt place, the fence rotting, and the ground untilled. He rides angrily to the cabin to make inquiries. A bare-footed woman with a tired look, and three little children clinging to her skirt, comes to the door. The old man asks, why is your land in such a neglected condition. The woman makes an apology: For six weeks her husband has been in jail for stealing wood. How can she look after things without him? He stole the wood because he was hungry. The master knows that: bad crops — high taxes — high rents. The children begin to bawl in sympathy with their mother's whining complaint. Tolstoy reaches hurriedly into his pocket, and without another word hands the woman a coin and rides away like a fugitive. His face is clouded, his joy has vanished.

"So such things are happening on my — no, on my wife's estate, the estate which I gave to her and my children. But why do I hide like a coward behind my womenfolk? Turning over that property was simply a lie to deceive the world, for my family are sucking the blood of the peasants just as I used to do. I know it perfectly well. Every brick used in the alterations on the house that shelters me is molded from their sweat and blood. What right had I to give my wife and children what did not belong to me — the peasants' land which they plough and sow. I should blush before God, in whose name I, Lev Tolstoy, am constantly preaching righteousness to men. Aye, a man into whose window the misery of others is staring every day."

The old man's face darkens with anger, which rises higher as he rides past the stone pillars of the manor house grounds. A liveried lackey and a groom rush out to help him from the horse. "My slaves," he mutters reproachfully to himself.

In the roomy dining-room the Countess, his daughters, his sons, his secretary, his family physician, the French governess, the English governess, a couple of neighbors, a revolutionary student who is serving as a tutor, and the English correspondent await him. The long dinner table is laid with blue and white china and silver. Tolstoy's entrance interrupts a lively conversation. He greets his guests with courteous seriousness, and then seats himself silently at the table. Liveried servants place his vegetarian meal before him. It includes imported asparagus beautifully prepared. But his mind is running on the ragged peasant woman to whom he has just given ten kopecks, and he stares gloomily at the table with a self-searching expression on his face.

"If they could only understand that I cannot and I will not continue to live this way, surrounded by lackeys, with four courses at dinner, and silver, and all these superfluities, while my neighbors lack the simplest necessities. They all know that the only sacrifice I ask of them is to give up their luxuries, which are an offense in the eyes of God. But she there, my wife, who ought to share my beliefs as she has shared my life, bitterly opposes it. She is a millstone around my neck, a weight upon my conscience that drags me down into false and vicious conduct. I should have cut the ties that bind us long ago. What have we in common? These people are ruining my life, and I am ruining theirs. I am superfluous here, a burden to myself and to all of them."

With an involuntary flush of anger, he glances up and looks at his wife. "My heavens, how old and gray she has become! How wrinkled her forehead has grown! What hints of secret suffering her quivering lips betray!" A wave of tenderness sweeps over the old man. "Can it be true," he thinks, "that this is the same woman whom I asked as a young, laughing, innocent maiden to share my life? We've been living together a generation, forty — no, forty-five years. She came to me a young girl when I was already a hardened, vice-callous, middle-aged man. She is the mother of my thirteen children. She has helped me do my work, and I — what have I done for her? Made her a despairing, overwrought, almost insane old woman, whom we can't trust with sedatives lest she take her life in her despair. And my sons there — I know they do not love me. And my daughters — I am robbing them of all the pleasures of youth. And there are my secretaries, who take down every word I say like sparrows picking up crumbs in the streets. They already have gathered balsam and incense to preserve my mummy when I die. And that English chap is waiting with his notebook to take down how I elucidate God Almighty — the God to whom this table, this house, this whole gathering is an offense. And I sit here in this inferno and am warm, and comfortable, and well fed. It would be far better if I were dead. I have lived too long, and I have not lived true to my faith."

A servant offers him another course, consisting of preserved fruits and whipped cream chilled on ice. With an angry gesture he lays his silver spoon to one side.

"Is it all right?" Sophia Andreevna asks solicitously. "Is it too rich for you?"

Tolstoy answers bitterly: "Yes, that's the trouble — it's too rich, it's good for me."

An expression of irritation flits across the faces of the sons, and the wife looks worried. But the reporter is alert — an aphorism for his article!

Finally the meal is over and all rise from the table and go to the reception room. Tolstoy debates with the young revolutionist, who ventures to mis-interpret his views in spite of the deep respect he feels for him. Tolstoy's eyes flash; he talks vehemently, almost shouting. An argument excites him as violently to-day as hunting or tennis used to in his youth. He makes a sudden effort to control himself.

When dusk approaches Tolstoy descends again to the family circle. His work is done. Goldenweiser asks if he would like him to play. "Yes, indeed." The old man leans upon the piano, his eyes shaded with his hands, so that people cannot see how deeply the magic of the melody affects him. He listens with closed lids, breathing heavily. Ah, this miracle of music, that flows through him like a cleansing stream, washing away all his bitter and burdensome thoughts. "How dare I despise art?" he thinks to himself. "What other consolation is so great. Where do we feel

God's presence so vividly as in the artist's touch? Beethoven, Chopin, you are my brothers. I can feel your eyes resting upon me. I can hear your heartbeats. Forgive me, brothers, for abusing you."

The piece ends with a few resounding chords. The company applaud, Tolstoy joining them after a moment's hesitation. His cares seem to have departed, as he joins the conversation with a pleasant smile. The day of many moods promises to end cheerfully after all.

But once more before going to bed the old man paces up and down his bare study. He will not sleep until he has passed final judgment on himself, until he has exacted a stern reckoning for every hour of the past twenty-four. His diary lies open on the table, its white page staring at him like the eye of conscience. He re-views every moment of the day and judges it. He thinks of the poverty-stricken peasant woman whom he left with no other help than a miserable little coin. He recalls that he was impatient with the beggars. He remembers harsh thoughts toward his wife. And all these failures to live up to his ideals he records unsparingly in the book, closing the day's entry thus: "Again found wanting, again soul-crippled, not enough good done. Once more I have proved that I have not learned to do what is difficult, to love the people around me, instead of humanity at large. Help me, God, help me!" Then once more he enters the date of the following day, and the three mystical initials indicating "If I am alive."

Now his job is done. Another day has been lived to the end. With bowed shoulders, he goes into his bedchamber, pulls off his heavy boots, disrobes, and lies down in bed, his thoughts again on death. Those winged thoughts. They still flit through his brain, little by little lose themselves like butterflies in darkening woods.

"What's that?" he suddenly asks himself. "Wasn't that a step?" A step in the next room, soft and stealing. He jumps lightly and noiselessly out of bed and presses his burning eye to the keyhole. Yes, a light. Sophia has come in with a lamp and is sacking his desk, fingering the leaves of his diary, peeking intimate secrets of his soul. It is Sophia Andreevna, his wife. Insatiable curiosity. He is beset by her desire to spy into the profundities of the deepest sanctities of his life.

His hands tremble with anger. He seizes the latch with an involuntary impulse to open the door and suddenly seize his wife. But at the last instant, he controls himself. "Perhaps this has been laid upon me." He creeps silently back to bed, not to sleep. Lev Nikolaevich Tolstoy, the greatest, the most gifted man of his time, lies there, betrayed in his own house, tortured by doubt, submerged in loneliness unutterable.

# 25

# How Tolstoy Died
*by General Lvov*

General Lvov was the Chief of Police of the Moscow District who wrote in 1910 a "strictly confidential" police report upon Leo Tolstoy's death. It was kept in the Moscow Police archives, and then was published in New York in 1924.

Lvov, General. "How Tolstoy Died." *The Living Age* (New York), vol. 321 (1924): 979–986.

On the evening of October 31 of this year (1910), a few moments before train No. 12 left the station of Astapovo on the Riazan-Ural line, a lady passenger got out of a second-class car to ask the station-master to provide her with a room for a sick man, Count Tolstoy, whose condition was so serious that the doctor said he could not continue the trip. This young lady, who was later discovered to be Alexandra Lvovna Tolstoy, the writer's daughter, was given permission by the station-master to place her father and his traveling companions in his own room, since there was no other suitable room at the station, and the nearest village is some distance away. The room reserved for injured people had to be kept free for emergencies in case there should be an accident on the line. Tolstoy's traveling companions were Vladimir Chertkov, Doctor Makovitski, and a young lady, Varvara Mikhailovna. Later, at the instance of the Assistant Department Director of Police, the Chief of Section, Captain Savitsky, ascertained that this Varvara Mikhailovna was named Teokritov, that she was born at Saratov, and was Count Tolstoy's stenographer and also the companion of his daughter Alexandra.

## 25. How Tolstoy Died (Lvov)

At first, the people accompanying Count Tolstoy seemed disinclined to give information regarding their movements. Alexandra Tolstoy stated that they had tickets as far as Novocherkask, but it was later shown that the tickets were really for Rostov-on-the-Don.

When the tickets were shown to the train conductor, Alexandra Tolstoy requested that her father's destination should not be made public, but it was too late, for it was generally known at all the preceding stations, and even at Astapovo, that Count Tolstoy was one of the passengers on train No. 12, and that he was accompanied by the people just mentioned. Doctor Makovitski and the surgeon of the railway company, Stakhovsky, immediately gave medical attention to the sick man. Doctor Semionovsky, of the local Zemstvo Hospital, was also summoned, but did not arrive until a few days later. All the people who attended the patient remained constantly in the stationmaster's apartment, and did not appear in public until they left on the seventh and eighth of November.

No stranger was admitted to Tolstoy, and several efforts made to see him proved futile. An old man living in the vicinity tried to do so, but was not admitted. Although it was generally known that Tolstoy was at the station, it did not create an excitement. The residents of the neighborhood and the passengers on the trains showed no special interest in the fact.

Beginning with November 2, Tolstoy's friends began to arrive, among them Doctor Berkenheim and the pianist Goldenweiser. On November 3 there was a consultation with Nikitin, a Moscow physician who had just come. The diagnosis was that Tolstoy was suffering from an inflammation affecting the tips of both lungs, but that heart weakness rather than this inflammation was the principal danger. On account of the latter, the patient occasionally lost consciousness.

On the night of November 3, Tolstoy's family came by special train — his wife, Sofia Andreevna, his daughter Tatiana, Madame Sukhotin, his sons Andrei and Mikhail, and a nurse, Madame Skorobogatov. Their car was sidetracked near the station-master's apartment. Not one of the members of the family was permitted to see the patient.

When the special train arrived, some of the employees were attracted by curiosity to the platform, but, learning that they could not see any of the new arrivals, they soon left and the station resumed its ordinary aspect. On the fourth of November, Prince Obolensky, the Governor of Riazan Region, arrived. He asked Captain Savitsky of the gendarmes what the situation was, and directed that officer to keep him exactly informed as to Tolstoy's condition, as to the persons who came to the station, and as to the general state of public sentiment. The Governor was assured that there had been no excitement, that eight noncommissioned officers had been added to the four regularly detailed to the station in order to assure perfect control of the situation, and that up to the present it had not been necessary to take any special measures to maintain order in view of the small number of visitors.

At the direction of the general superintendent of the railway, a few less reliable people — that is, newspaper correspondents — were lodged in a railway building which no one was permitted to enter except with a special permit issued by the authorities.

The superintendent of buildings and the gendarme officers had been ordered to admit no person either to the building where the journalists were or to the railway station without this special permit. Consequently, no meeting of any kind could be held in the building assigned the journalists, and no unauthorized person could enter the station. Furthermore, the newspaper correspondents had given no grounds for uneasiness since they had arrived.

Thanks to the fact that one of the telegraph operators and the Captain of Gendarmes, Savitsky, were close friends, it was possible to read the telegrams received and dispatched. In that way the authorities were kept constantly conversant with all the correspondence relating to Tolstoy's detention at Astapovo. This correspondence revealed to some extent the attitude of the press and of Tolstoy's admirers toward what was occurring at Astapovo, and gave no reason to suppose that the incident would be utilized in a way detrimental to internal order, although only three of the journalists were Russians. All the others were either Jews or of Jewish descent.

The first day that the correspondents were at the station they demanded that the building and the buffet be kept open all day long for their convenience. Upon learning that the regulations specified that both should be open only at certain hours, they telegraphed a complaint to me and likewise to their newspapers, charging the Government and the gendarmes with trying to keep visitors away from the station. But as accommodations were being provided for them at that time, and they were installed in comfortable lodgings on the evening of November 4, several felt that the situation demanded that they retract their hasty complaint against the Government in their newspapers.

On November 5, nearly everyone who had any legitimate reason to come to Astapovo in connection with Tolstoy's illness had arrived. Indeed, only a few came the next day. Including members of the family and correspondents, there were altogether thirty-two people. Among the later arrivals were J.I. Gorbunov, representing the Posrednik publishing house (sponsored by Tolstoy — ed.); Princess Obolensky, Tolstoy's niece; A. Prokhorov, a Moscow merchant; Vladimir Filosofov, whose daughter married one of Tolstoy's sons; and the wife of Andrei Tolstoy.

Tolstoy's family, except his daughter Alexandra, took dinner and supper in the station dining-room, where they often conversed with their relatives and friends, and with the correspondents.

Countess Sofia Andreevna was always accompanied and assisted when she walked by the nurse, Madame Skorobogatov. She gave the impression of an old lady in very feeble health, who moved with difficulty. When she was in the station restaurant, she was almost always seated and silent, taking no part in the conversation. At rare intervals she was heard to complain because she was not permitted to see her husband. She mentioned Chertkov several times in connection with this. From certain phrases it was easy to conclude that Tolstoy's family was not permitted to see him for reasons having nothing to do with his state of health. Later Andrei Tolstoy, in talking with Captain Savitsky, expressed the opinion that his father was kept separated from his family, and particularly from his wife, by Chertkov's influence over the physicians and by his sister Alexandra. Countess Sofia Andreevna Tolstoy expressed surprise, because formerly, when Lev Niltolaevich was ill, she and her children could see him without disturbing him or threatening his health, while now they were sedulously kept away from him.

As all intercourse between Count Tolstoy and his relatives and friends — either personal or by writing — was controlled by his daughter Alexandra and by Chertkov, who never left Tolstoy's room, the Count did not learn that a telegram had come addressed to him from Metropolitan Anthony, appealing to him to reconcile himself with the Church. This telegram was not answered. A little later a telegram was received from Monk Joseph of Optina Pustyn Monastery, where Tolstoy had taken refuge on several occasions during his religious crises, asking if he could see Tolstoy on the evening of November 5, and talk with him. I handed this telegram to Alexandra Tolstoy. She replied that the condition of her father's health did not permit him to see anybody, and that a telegram should be sent to Monk Joseph to this effect.

Astapovo station is nominally very quiet, except during the arrival of trains in the morning and evening, that is, about meal hours, when the travelers and others fill the station and the dining room.

The number of local residents who came to the station was not larger than usual when trains arrived. Local interest regarding Tolstoy's presence speedily subsided. Captain Savitsky is personally convinced that not one of the peasants whom business brought to the station, and with most of whom he talked, knew who Tolstoy was. When he asked them: "Who is at the station now?" some would answer: "Count Tolstoy." Others did not even know his name. Not a single one could say anything definite regarding him, and when asked: "For what is he celebrated?" the usual answer was "God knows!"

The station-master's apartment opens upon the station courtyard, and during the whole time that Tolstoy occupied it, there was a going and coming train time, because just at this season military trains were constantly passing, bringing home reservists and taking away new recruits, whose relatives and friends accompanied them to the station. Only rarely, however, did anyone approach Tolstoy's apartment. The people went directly from their villages to the station, and from there back home.

On the evening of November 4, the Governor left for Urusovo, leaving instructions that he should be notified immediately by telegraph in case his personal instructions were required. General Globa, Commander of Gendarmes at Riazan, who had come with the Governor, returned to Riazan, considering it unnecessary to detail secret agents. He asked Captain Savitsky to notify him if he discovered any agitators or suspicious characters in the vicinity or considered it advisable to take special precautions regarding strangers. Nothing of that kind occurred, and he was merely notified on November 7 of Tolstoy's death.

The general manager of the Riazan-Ural line reached Astapovo on November 5 and took immediate measures to improve telegraphic communication between that point and Moscow, besides assisting in every way possible the members of the family and others who arrived at the station — securing lodgings for them and looking after their comfort. Beds were put in the building assigned the newspaper correspondents, and the station-master's own office was placed at their service for writing, since the Captain of Gendarmes requested that they should not be admitted to the telegraph office, where they would be in immediate vicinity of the instruments and might accidentally or intentionally learn the contents of official dispatches.

At first there was little change in Tolstoy's condition, though the first evening he seemed so much better that rumors of his possible recovery got abroad. He was perfectly conscious and showed interest in all those who surrounded him. Having learned from certain articles brought from Yasnaya Poliana that his daughter Tatiana and his son Sergei had arrived, he had them called in. However, his wife and his other children were not permitted to see him, and their presence at Astapovo was kept a secret from him.

The same day the Departmental Sub-Director of Police arrived, accompanied by Captain Dolgov, Sub. Director of the Okhrana (or secret police). These gentlemen were lodged in a first-class compartment car, which had been detached at the station in case high officials should arrive. The Governor of Riazan likewise occupied this car on his return from Urusovo. Sub-Director Kharlamov instructed Captain Savitsky to keep his presence an absolute secret, but Captain Savitsky informed him that just as the train was arriving one of the train conductors, having seen his personal permit, asked who he was. The Captain answered that Kharlamov was connected with the Department of Public Works, which satisfied the conductor. Consequently no one living at the station knew that the Sub-Director was there, and his arrival caused no comment.

Having learned from the report of the station-master that a telegram had arrived from Metropolitan Anthony, addressed to Tolstoy, the Sub-Director expressed a desire to know its contents, and Captain Savitsky showed him the original dispatch. He also submitted a report of all that had happened at the station, including the arrival of the Superior of the Optina Pustyn Monastery, Father Varsonofii, and the priest, Panteleimon.

The Sub-Director instructed Captain Savitsky to learn why they had come to Astapovo — that is, whether they had plans of their own accord or at somebody's orders. Father Varsonofii, when questioned by the Captain regarding this, answered evasively. He told the correspondent of Nome Vremia that he had come of his own accord to see Tolstoy, who wanted to see him the last time he visited Optina Pustyn, but had not had an opportunity. Captain Savitsky learned in the course of a private conversation with Father Varsonofii, confidentially, that he had come to Astapovo on an errand for the Holy Synod, that he was commissioned to prepare the ground for a reconciliation between Tolstoy and the Orthodox Church.

As is known, that object was not attained. The monk was refused an interview with Tolstoy in spite of the personal intervention in his behalf of Countess Sofia Andreevna and his son Andrei who, although eager to arrange an interview with Tolstoy, were not able to overcome the opposition of Alexandra Lvovna and Chertkov. Father Varsonofii wrote a letter to Alexandra Tolstoy in which he promised her that he would not enter into any religious argument with her father likely to excite him, that all he wished was "to see Tolstoy and give him his blessing." Varsonofii said confidentially that he had brought the Eucharist with him, and that if

Tolstoy merely uttered these words, "I repent," he would consider, in virtue of his authority, that the latter had abjured his false doctrines and would administer the last sacrament to him as a member of the Orthodox Church. This letter was handed to Andrei, who transmitted it to Alexandra Tolstoy through a third person; but she did not answer it.

In speaking of Tolstoy's sojourn at Optina Pustyn, Varsonofii said that on two occasions the Count went to the door of the cell of Monk Joseph, with whom he had been very friendly previously, but did not go in; and that he had said in the cell of his sister that he had decided not to enter, thinking that he would not be received because he had been "excommunicated." Father Varsonofii was present at this conversation of Tolstoy with his sister, the widow of Prince Obolenskii. All this information was transmitted by Captain Savitsky to the Sub-Director of Police.

The bulletins regarding Tolstoy's condition, issued on the night of November 6 and signed by all the physicians, including Shchurovsky and Usov, who had arrived from Moscow, expressed great concern because of the patient's heart weakness, which had resulted during the last few days in several cardiac crises. The patient's condition grew constantly worse from that day on, and caused serious concern; most of the time he was unconscious, recovering consciousness only for brief intervals. On such occasions he called to him his daughter Tatiana and his son Sergei, who were undoubtedly under the constant surveillance of Alexandra Tolstoy and Chertkov. During his periods of consciousness Tolstoy also asked to have certain passages of his "The Circle of Reading" read to him, or talked with those surrounding him, showing interest in the people whom he had not seen with him before, as for instance Doctor Shchurovsky and Doctor Usov. About one o'clock in the afternoon, when he was fully conscious, Tolstoy took the hand of his daughter Tatiana, raised at the bedside, and said: "Well, this is the end."

The same day and during the night of the seventh, the physicians had recourse to camphor and morphine injections.

Life ran on as usual at the railway station and in the village. There were not many newcomers at this time, and the concern felt for Tolstoy's condition expressed itself only in the activity of the correspondents, and frequent consultations between the members of the family and the physicians. The residents of the neighborhood and the employees of the railway, with a very few exceptions, seemed to take little interest in the bulletins from the station-master's apartment. Father Varsonofii, at his own request, was taken to the car occupied by the Countess Tolstoy about six o'clock in the evening. The Countess was asleep and the monk was not received. He did not see her later. On the night of November 7 the patient's condition grew worse, and at two o'clock in the morning all the members of the family were summoned to his bedside. After a morphine injection the patient became calm and fell asleep. Thereupon Countess Tolstoy and some of the children retired to their private car. Tolstoy did not recover consciousness again up to his death. About five o'clock in the morning all the family assembled once more, but he recognized no one and did not speak. At five minutes past six he expired.

During the night no one was in the vicinity of the room he occupied except the members of the family and the correspondents. Now and then the local railway officials were on the platform. No stranger was admitted to the death chamber until ten o'clock the next morning. Then visitors began to come, having learned of Tolstoy's death.

Train No. 8 on November 7 brought Father Parfeny, the Archbishop of Tula, to Astapovo. Through the monk who accompanied him, he requested Captain Savitsky to come to his compartment. As soon as they were alone and the door closed, the Archbishop said: "The Holy Synod has sent me, at the personal wish of the Tsar, to learn if there was no indication while Tolstoy was at Astapovo that the Count wished to repent of his errors; or possibly some allusion indicating that he would not object to an Orthodox funeral. I should like to be clearly informed regarding all this by some member of his family. Tell me whom I should consult."

As Andrei had shown the friendliest attitude toward the representatives of the Government, he was invited to visit the Archbishop in his compartment. Their conversation lasted nearly ten minutes. After Andrei Tolstoy left, the Archbishop summoned Captain Savitsky again and related to him the substance of the conversation with Andrei Tolstoy, at the same time requesting him to write a telegram informing the Holy Synod that his mission had been unsuccessful. According to the statement of the Archbishop, Andrei Tolstoy, when asked the opinion of his father and of other members of the family regarding the possibility of an Orthodox funeral, said that he did not now that his father had expressed any definite wish upon that subject. But in view of the fact that during his last days the deceased had shown a kindlier attitude toward the institutions and the officials of the Orthodox Church, Andrei Tolstoy thought that he might have welcomed an opportunity, if not to reconcile himself completely with the Church, at least to avoid any misunderstanding regarding his funeral.

To this Andrei Tolstoy added that his relatives and intimates said the deceased had written some instructions for his funeral, but no one knew if he expressed there any desire to be buried according to the Orthodox rites. Andrei indicated that his sister, Tatiana Sukhotin, probably knew of the existence of this note among his other papers at Yasnaya Yoliana. The latter, who left Astapovo in the same coach with Archbishop Parfenii, knew of her brother's conversation with the Archbishop, but refused to speak to him. Andrei Tolstoy told the Archbishop — lowering his voice — that if the deceased was buried according to the Orthodox rites the other members of the family would protest for fear of violating the wishes of their father, who had not expressed a definite wish to be buried according to the rites of the Orthodox Church. As to the memorandum, the existence of which they did not deny, they did not know if Tolstoy expressed in it opposition to an Orthodox funeral.

These conversations convinced Archbishop Parfeny that there was no reason to believe that Tolstoy wished to reconcile himself with the Church, or desired to be buried with Orthodox rites. That is why the Archbishop said, when he took leave of Captain Savitsky: "I can go now and report to the Holy Synod that it is impossible to give Tolstoy Christian burial."

On November 7, several hours after Tolstoy's death, Alexandra Tolstoy, Chertkov, and Mme. Teokritov left for Yasnaya Poliana. Doctors left the following day with the other members of the Tolstoy family.

After ten o'clock in the morning, at the desire of the family and with the authorization of the Government, strangers were permitted to enter the death chamber. The deceased was dressed in a gray blouse, and was left on the bed until the following morning. There was nothing that the Orthodox are accustomed to place around the dead — that is to say, no candles, no cross, no little icon between his hands. It happened that Ozolin, the station-master, was a Protestant, and did not have an icon in his room. The bed was decorated with pine boughs. There were only a few visitors — railway employees and villagers. One could see that they came to gratify their curiosity, and to say they had seen something they had read about in the newspapers. On the day of Tolstoy's death, someone suggested that wreaths be brought, one in the name of the railway employees of the Riazan-Ural line, the other in the name of the employees of Astapovo station. The superintendent of the road ordered the former, the assistant station-master the latter. At eight o'clock that next morning the two wreaths arrived from Moscow. On the ribbon of the first was the inscription: "The employees of the Riazan-Ural railway to Lev Nikolaevich Tolstoy." On the second: "The employees of Astapovo railway station to the great Lev Tolstoy."

On the evening of November 7, Captain Bondar of the Eighteenth

Regiment of Hussars and W. Kishkin arrived at Astapovo from Elets, to express their sympathy to the family. The same evening Kharlamov, the Departmental Sub-Director of Police, left for Tula. Father Varsonofii had an audience with the Governor and left for Optina Pustyn.

Visitors were allowed to see Tolstoy's body until very late in the evening. There was no disorder. At eight the following morning the body was placed in a simple oak coffin without the inscriptions used by the Orthodox, and covered with a drapery of white muslin. The same day an artist arrived from Moscow, who took two death masks and made sketches of the deceased.

About eleven o'clock in the morning people who wished to visit the death chamber were again admitted. Their number was considerably augmented after the arrival of the morning train from Moscow. Some students and working men kissed the hands of the deceased. No visitors were admitted later than one o'clock in the afternoon. After the members of the family and intimate friends had paid their last respects to the corpse, the uncovered coffin was carried out and placed in a railway coach.

Just then a number of people, including students and young girls, began to sing "Eternal Glory," but the song was immediately stopped by the orders of the police. A special train was made up with one coach for the body and the family and another for the manager of the railway and the correspondents. Three coaches were then added for those who wished to accompany the corpse. The number of persons who participated in this ceremony was about three hundred and fifty. The train left Astapovo station at 1:15. As it drew out of the station a few people in the crowd cheered.

# 26

# What Tolstoy Means to America
*by V. Wentz*

Wentz, Virginia. "What Tolstoy Means to America." *Current Literature* (New York), vol. 98 (1908): 403–404.

  The comment elicited in this country by Tolstoy's eightieth birthday illustrates anew the difficulty of properly estimating a man of genius during his lifetime. By general consensus of opinion, *Tolstoy is the greatest living writer.* Some go so far as to say that he will rank with Shakespeare, Goethe and Victor Hugo. But when it comes to an analysis of the elements that have contributed to give him his commanding position, the most contrary views are voiced. On the one side are the literary partisans who declare that the author of "War and Peace" and "Anna Karenina" is sure of deathless fame, but that the "pamphleteer" has perished already. On the other side are those who believe, as Tolstoy himself does, that his novels are unimportant when compared with his moral message.

  Perhaps because of an excess of "Tolstoy literature" in past years, perhaps because Tolstoy has discouraged the celebration of the anniversary, the American birthday tributes are scattered and somewhat fragmentary. Yet this very fact gives added significance to their contents. The merely perfunctory is thereby eliminated, and those who speak speak with conviction. Religious papers of the more conservative type have little to say, but the monthly organ of Benjamin Fay's independent congregation in Los Angeles devotes a whole number to the praise of Tolstoy. "The celebration of Tolstoy's eightieth birthday," it says, "by artists and literary men, by reformers and statesmen, and by men of the world, has a greater significance and holds a greater promise for the future progress of humanity, than the sailing of any fleet, the outcome of any local election, or the triumph or decline of any church, because it is the race's tribute to a man of principle; and men of principle are the world's ultimate redeemers." The conservative *New York Sun* joins with the Socialist daily, *The Call,* in eulogizing Tolstoy; and *The Book Monthly* for September is a Tolstoy number.

The most brilliant of the newly-published tributes is that of Benjamin de Casseres in the *New York Times Saturday Review*. His emphasis is all on Tolstoy the artist. He says:

"The world will remember two Tolstoys. One was a great artist; he died many years ago. The other is a neo–Schopenhauerian, a stranded Platonist, a sick soul: he still lives. The latter Tolstoy sticks his tongue in his cheek and pronounces the former Tolstoy a fraud. He tossed the bayleaf into the mud and donned a hair shirt. He forsook the slopes of Olympus to wail on the dunghills of penitence. Then he sent for a photographer. For Tolstoy has no sense of humor.

"But Tolstoy still remains a wonderful man whether we consider him as artist or prophet. He is as significant and as perplexing as life itself. Nature hewed him out of her own bowels. She made him the slave of every vice and put into him the aspiration for every virtue. He is Goethe's 'Faust' come to life. In that wonderful book, 'My Confession,' Tolstoy has laid before us the record of a soul's adventures in hell, the minutiae of spiritual torture. He has been gambler, murderer, lecher and drunkard. He has been lashed, like Orestes, by the giant whips of the Furies of retribution, and in his hair, if one look closely, there can be seen twisted serpents. He is the most august personality in the world today.

"Into his novels and plays he has distilled himself. All great art aspires to philosophy, consciously or unconsciously — that is, all great art tends to explain life; all great art is a searchlight flung upon the naked soul of man, that soul that cringes and cowers and hides under the rags of conformity. Tolstoy has found out our most secret springs; he has peered into the vats of the unconscious; he has put on paper a few facts, and they will last as long as anything in contemporaneous literature. In 'Anna Karenina,' 'The Dominion of Darkness,' 'Ivan Illych,' he demonstrates like a man in a clinic; he slits like a surgeon, he scrapes to the bone.

"His collective works might be entitled 'Views of the Nude Human Soul.' In 'Anna Karenina' we see the soul in the coils of passion; in 'War and Peace' we see the soul in battle and intrigue; in 'A Night's Lodging' we see the soul where vodka and worse gnaw it. 'The Dominion of Darkness' takes us into the catacombs of the hideous. 'Ivan Ilyitch' is the greatest study of death ever made. His philosophical doctrines will go into the wind; his art will remain. He is already, before his death, in the Pantheon of immortals."

Mr. Casseres, however, is not representative of the Americans who have done the most to spread Tolstoy's message, both as a novelist and as a moral teacher, in this country. His attitude is primarily intellectual, while theirs proceeds from the heart and emotions. Among these Tolstoyan pioneers the late Ernest Howard Crosby is pre-eminent. He was, in a very real sense, the friend and disciple of the great Russian, and he wrote a number of books interpreting Tolstoy to America.

Clarence Darrow, the Chicago lawyer, whose successful championship of Moyer and Haywood is fresh in the public mind, is another ardent disciple of Tolstoy. He lectures on Tolstoy, writes on Tolstoy, and in some of his most famous legal defense of labor agitators and striking workmen has turned to Tolstoy for his vindication.

Tolstoy is "one of the greatest masters of fiction that the world has known," he says in an article in *The Rubric*. But, he adds:

"Leo Tolstoy will live in history for his philosophy of life. Brilliant his novels be, these are but the gold and tinsel which flutter at the theater to beguile the crowd. The world is full of entertainers. They paint pictures — write books — make music — sing songs — blacken their faces and contort their bodies — all to amuse an idle class of parasites, a class of men and women who have managed to separate themselves from work, and their fellow men, and who must therefore be amused. These authors and painters and actors and contortionists call themselves artists, and they dance and parade before the idle public to buy a portion of the ill-gotten wealth that is extorted from the labor of the poor.

"Tolstoy's fame will not rest upon these early creations of a master's art. It will rest upon his life, upon the message that he speaks to man, upon what he tells us of the duty that each owes to his kind, of the true solution of that endless awful, ever present mystery, the purpose and the meaning and the end of life."

In even more memorable language the dean of American novelists, William D. Howells, has given us, at the close of his book, "My Literary Passions," the following confession of faith:

"Tolstoy has not influenced me in esthetics only, but in ethics, too, so that I can never again see life in the way I saw it before. He awakens in the reader the will to be a man; not effectively, not spectacularly, but simply, really. He leads you back to the only true ideal, away from that false standard of the gentleman, to the Man who sought not to be distinguished from other men, but identified with them, to that Presence in which the finest gentleman shows his alloy of vanity, and the greatest genius shrinks to the measure of his miserable egotism. I learned from Tolstoy to try character and motive by no other test, and tho I am perpetually false to that sublime ideal myself, still the ideal remains with me, to make me ashamed that I am not true to it. Tolstoy gave me heart to hope that the world may yet be made over in the image of Him who died for it, when Caesar's things shall be finally rendered unto Caesar, and men shall come into their own, into the right to labor and the right to enjoy the fruits of their labor, each one master of himself and servant to every other.

"I believe if I had not turned the corner of my fiftieth year when I first knew Tolstoy, I should not have been able to know him as fully as I did. He has been to me that final consciousness which he speaks of so wisely in his essay on Life. I came in it to the knowledge of myself in ways I had not dreamt of before, and began at last to discern my relations to the race, without which we are each nothing.

"The supreme art in literature had its highest effect in making me set art forever below humanity, and it is with the wish to offer the greatest homage to his heart and mind which any man can pay another, that I close this record with the name of Leo Tolstoy."

# *Bibliography*

Bentzon, Th. "A Recent Interview with Tolstoy." *The Critic* (New York), vol. 41 (1902): 570–574.
Bonsul, Stephen. "Tolstoy Prophesies the Fall of America." *New York Times*, 7 July, 1907.
Creelman, James. "A Visit to Tolstoy." *Harper's Weekly*. vol. 36 (1892): 380.
Crosby, Ernest. "Conversations with Ernest Crosby Embodying Personal Impressions of Count Leo Tolstoy." *Arena* (New York), vol. 25 (1901): 429–439.
\_\_\_\_. "Count Leo Tolstoy at Home." *Leslie's Weekly* (New York), vol. 87 (1898): 374.
\_\_\_\_. "Tolstoy's Plan of Redemption." *The Living Age* (Boston), vol. 219 (1898): 386–388.
\_\_\_\_. "Two Days with Count Leo Tolstoy." *The Progressive Review* (London), vol. 2 (1897): 407–422.
Durland, Kellogg. "Tolstoy at Home." *The Independent* (New York), vol. 69 (1910): 1191–1195.
Everling, N. "Three Evenings with Count Leo Tolstoy." *The Nineteenth Century and After* (New York), vol. 93 (1923): 786–792.
George, Henry, Jr. "Tolstoy in the Twilight." *The World's Work* (New York), vol. 18 (1909): 12144–12154.
Hapgood, Isabel. "Count Tolstoy at Home." *The Atlantic Monthly* (Boston), 1891 (8) vol. 15: 71–76.
Holmes, John. "How Tolstoy and Tolstoy's Wife Wrote Novels." *Current Opinion* (New York), vol. 57 (1914): 49.
Howells, W.D. "Lyof Tolstoy." *Harper's Weekly*. 36 (1887): 299–300.
Johnston, Charles. "How Count Tolstoy Writes." *The Arena* (Boston), vol. 21 (1899): 269–272.
Kaun, Alexander. "The Last Days of Leo Tolstoy: With Translations from His Diary and Letters." *Atlantic Monthly* (Boston), vol. 129 (1922): 299–306.
Kennan, George. "Count Leo Tolstoy and the Russian Government." *The Outlook* (New York), vol. 96 (1910): 769–771.
\_\_\_\_. "A Visit to Count Tolstoy." *The Century* (New York), vol. 34 (new series, vol. 12) (1887): 252–265.

Kenworthy, John Coleman. "A Visit to Tolstoy." *The Humane Review*, vol. 1 (1900): 262–267.

Maude, Aymler. "My Last Visit to Tolstoy." *The Bookman* (New York), vol. 24 (1906): 108–114.

———. "Talks with Tolstoy." *The New Century Review* (London), vol. 7 (1900): 404–418.

Maude, Louise. "Tolstoy in 1906." *The Bookman* (New York), vol. 24 (1906): 104–107.

Nicchia, Alexandra. "My Last Memory of Tolstoy." *The Craftsman* (Syracuse, NY), vol. 4 (1903): 45–48.

Norman, Sir Henry. "Russia of Today (on Tolstoy)." *Scribner's Magazine* (New York), vol. 28 (1900): 387–406.

Rogers, James Frederick. "The Physical Tolstoy." *The Scientific Monthly* (New York), vol. 7 (1918): 555–562.

Steiner, Edward. "An Interview with Count Tolstoy." *The Outlook* (New York), vol. 66 (1900): 828–835.

———. "Tolstoy Today." *The Outlook* (New York), vol. 75 (1903): 35–42.

———. "Tolstoy's Marriage and Family Life." *The Outlook* (New York), vol. 75 (1903): 267–276.

Stevens, Thomas. "With Count Tolstoy." In his *Through Russia on a Mustang*. New York, 1891: 92–102.

Wentz, Virginia. "What Tolstoy Means to America." *Current Literature* (New York), vol. 98 (1908): 403–404.

White, Andrew Dickson. "Walks and Talks with Tolstoy." *McClure's Magazine* (New York), vol. 16 (1901): 507–518.

Zweig, Stefan. "A Day in Tolstoy's Life." *The Living Age* (Boston), vol. 334 (1928): 56–62.

# Index

Adler, Felix 89
Alaska 9
Alexander II 28, 84, 99
Alexander III 104, 114
America, Tolstoy's interest in 35, 43–45, 50, 60, 87–89, 136
American church organizations 90
American women, political rights 93
*Anna Karenina* 25, 37, 55–56, 61, 134, 144, 146, 211; Tolstoy's criticism of 120
Annenkov, K. 174
Archives in Russia, related to Tolstoy 152, 200
*Arena* (magazine) 75
Arnold, Matthew 68
Astapovo, railway station 200
*Atlantic Monthly* 151
Aurelius 162

Baikal 20
Ballou, Adin 89, 98
Balzac, Honoré de 88
Bashkirs 38
Beethoven, Ludwig van 99, 104, 110
Bellow, John 86
Bentzon, Thomas 100
Bishop of Moscow 155
Bishop of Petrograd 155
Bishop Parfenii 207–208
Bobrinsky 64
Bonsul 133
*The Bookman* (magazine) 126
Boston 34
Brahms, Johannes 110
Buckle 95
Bulgakov 152

Cadet Corps 42
California 28
Cart driver 35, 65, 145
*Casanova, Stendahl, Tolstoy* (S. Zweig) 193
Cassares, B. 211–212
Catherine II 44
Caucasus 103, 123, 170
*Century Magazine* 61
Chaucer 88
Chertkov, Tolstoy's assistant 80, 111, 155, 200; conflict with Tolstoy's family 156
Chicago 138
Chopin, Frédéric 110, 164
Christ, Tolstoy views of 16, 23, 45, 170
*A Circle of Reading* 130, 162
*Confession* 10, 26, 150
Cornell, Mr. 84
Cornell University 94
*Cossacks* 15
Creelman, James 51
Crimea 37, 141
Crimean War 45, 88, 189
Crosby, Ernest 75
*Current Literature* (magazine) 61, 210
Czar 111, 120

*Daily Telegraph* 65
Danilevsky 30
Dante 99
Darwinism 29
Daudet, Alphonse 88
*Diary* (Tolstoy) 152
Díaz, President of Mexico 51
Dickens, Charles 15, 102
Don River 65
Dostoevsky, Fyodor 164, 165

Doukhobors in Canada 80–81
Dragomirov, General 102
Dreyfus Case 74
Duma 127
Dunaev 124

Elliot, John 93
Emerson, Ralph Waldo 60, 89
England 43, 86
English-speakers in Russia 90
Everling, N. 174

Famine in Russia, Tolstoy's support of its victims 54, 65, 70, 65
*Florida Citizen* 139
*For Every Day* 154
Freedom of press in Russia 127
French Literature 88
French-Russian War of 1812 96

Gallery of Russian Art 84
Garnett, Constance 121
Garrison, William Lloyd 27, 89
George, Henry 44, 131, 127, 139, 142
Ginzburg (sculptor) 118
Gladstone, William Ewart 38, 68
Gloucester 86
Gluck, Christoph Willibald 110
Goethe, Johann Wolfgang von, compared with Tolstoy 163, 165, 167, 210
Goldenweiser, A. 157, 163, 164, 165, 168, 170
Gospel parables, explained by Tolstoy 120, 122
Griboedov 118
Gurko 98

Hafferberg, Theodore 179
Handel, G.F. 110
Hapgood, Isabel 34
Hawthorne, Nathaniel 89
Haydn, Franz Josef 99
Hertzen, Alexander 118
Holmes, John 61
Holy Synod of Russian Church 152
Howells, William Dean 89, 212–213
Hugo, Victor 77, 166, 210

Imperial Academy of Sciences 117
India 55
Irish 55
Irkutsk 11
*Ivan the Fool* 26

Jewish journalists at the Tolstoy funeral 201
Johnstone, Charles 55
"Journal of St. Petersburg" 187

Kant, Immanuel 94, 162
Kaun, Alexander 151
Kazan 16
Kellog, Durand 145
Kenna, George 9, 18
Kenworthy, John 64
Kharlamov 209
Kiev 41
Kingdom of Heaven 46, 119–120, 138
Kishkin, W., police officer present at the Tolstoy funeral 209
Koumiss (drink) 38
Kremlin 72, 84
"The Kreutzer Sonata" (Beethoven) 110
"The Kreutzer Sonata" (Tolstoy) 39, 50, 67, 184
Kursk 11, 12
Kutuzov, Field Marshal Mikhail 99
Kuzminskaya 187–190
Kuzminskii, Senator, Tolstoy's brother-in-law 179

Liubatovich, Olga 17
*Living Age* 179, 200
London 6, 101
Longfellow, Henry Wadsworth 60, 89
*Looking Back* (Bellamy) 40–41
Lowell, James Russell 60, 89
Lvov, general of Russian police 200

Makovitsky, Tolstoy's friend and assistant 155, 156, 200
Mallory, Lucy 138
Manchuria 147
Marks, Tolstoy publisher 123
Maupassant, Guy de 88
Mecca 41
Medina 41
Mennonites 69
Mexico 135
Michelangelo 99
Mikado, Japanese General 169
Mont Blanc 83
Mormons 92
Moscow 11, 13, 17, 26, 31, 37, 41, 72, 74, 90, 101, 170
Moscow-Kiev highway 133
Moscow-Kursk railway 115
Moscow River 88
Mozart, Wolfgang Amadeus 99
Muslims 41
*My Religion* 16, 144

Napoleon 96, 99
New England, resemblance with middle Russia 72
New York 26, 37, 75, 87

New York Society of Ethical Culture 89
*New York Sun*, praise of Tolstoy 211
*New York Times*, praise of Tolstoy 211
Nicchia, Alexandra 112
Nikitin, Tolstoy's friend 156
*Nineteenth Century and After* (magazine) 174
Norman, Henry 71
*North American Review* 139
Novgorod 48

Obolensky, Prince, the Governor of Ryazan 101, 201
Obolensky, Princess Maria Lvovna, Tolstoy's daughter 101, 107–8, 116, 117
"Old Believer" 94
Optina Pustyn Monastery 154, 203, 205, 209
Orel 12
*The Outlook* (magazine) 106

Pacific 9
Parker, Theodore 28, 89
Pascal, Blaise 162
Petersburg 26, 31, 37, 42, 74, 80, 90
Petrovka 64
Philistines 61
Pobedonostsev 26, 28, 94, 114
Portland, Oregon 138
*Power of Darkness* 56, 211
Pushkin, Aleksandr 68

Quakers in America 86

*The Red Reign* 145
Repin 51, 104
*Resurrection* 103, 146
Revolution of 1917 152
*Revue Blanche* (magazine) 102
Rome, the fall of 137
Roosevelt, Theodore 139
Rossinskaya 20
Rossolimo, Professor, Tolstoy's friend 158
Rousseau, Jean-Jacques 99
Russian Church 46; and excommunication of Tolstoy in 1901 152
Russian government 10, 21, 31; parliament 127
Russian-Greek Church (orthodox) 95
Russian history 95
Russian-Japanese War 1905, 169
*Russian Messenger* 63
Russian peasants 69
Ryazan 64
Ryazan-Ural railway 200, 208

Saadi, Hafiz 163–164
Salt Lake City 92
Samara 38, 66–67

Savitsky, Captain 200
Schiller, Friedrich von 165
Schopenhauer, Arthur 15, 162
Schumann, Robert 110
*Scribner's Magazine* 71
Sergeenko, Tolstoy's friend 155
Shakers 86
Shakespeare 66, 99, 165; as compared with Tolstoy 210
Shamordino village 159
Shurovsky, Doctor 205
Siberia 9, 17, 139; and Lake Baikal 10; rivers 135
Skobelev, Russian general 98
Spinoza 81
Stakhovich, local nobility leader 118
Stasov, V.V., literary and music critic 117
Stead, William 49
Steiner, Edward 59, 104
Stevens, Thomas 36
Sukhotin, Tatiana Lvovna, Tolstoy's daughter 101, 156, 158, 204
Surtaev 48
Suvorov, Field Marshal Alexander 98

Talmud 119
Thoreau, Henry David 60
Tikhon, Father, Tolstoy's parish priest 34, 156
Toledo, Ohio 60
Tolstoy, Aleksandra Lvovna, Tolstoy's daughter 116, 117, 159, 200, 201, 203
Tolstoy, Alexey, poet 100
Tolstoy, Ilya Lvovich, Tolstoy's son 61, 211
Tolstoy, Leo: Americans visiting Tolstoy 48, 116, 135; birthday party of 190; Church's excommunication of 139; conversations with 38; as critic 120, 165; on education 38–41; escape from Yasnaya Polyana 160–161; estate 20, 36–37; explains Gospel parables 120, 122; family 149, 180; favorite writers (Pushkin, Lermontov, Gogol, Dostoevsky) 164; friends (Annenkov, Sergeenko, Biriukov, Dunaev, Gorbunov-Posadov, Maklakova) 124, 175 176; grandfather 44; home 78; house and furniture 52; interest in America 35, 43–45, 50, 87–89, 136; knowledge of languages (Greek, Russian, French, German, English, Latin, Hebrew, Italian) 122; last days of 152; last rites refused by Tolstoy 207–208; letters on religion 153; love for children 130–131; and manual labor 76; museum in Moscow 172; and music 99, 110, 183–185; non-resistance to violence 46–48, 69, 103; portrait of 51; praises American writers (Channing, Thoreau,

Emerson) 148–149; talks to peasants 35; views on Christ 16, 23, 45, 170; views on love 47; views on religion 82; at work as a writer 57, 62
Tolstoy, Maria, Tolstoy's sister, nun at the monastery 117, 155
Tolstoy, Sergei Lvovich, Tolstoy's son 158, 200, 204
Tolstoy, Countess Sofia 37, 47, 49, 55, 65, 67, 68, 101, 107–109; preserved Tolstoy's papers and manuscripts 172–3
Tolstoy, Tatiana Lvovna, Tolstoy's daughter 101, 156, 158, 204
Tolstoy Museum (Moscow) 170–171
Trans-Siberian Express 140
Trinity Monastery 12
Troitsky, the Rev. Dimitry, Bishop of Tula 153
Trubetskoy, Prince 177–178
Tula 15, 36, 40, 59, 114, 126
Turgenev, Ivan 34, 164
Twain, Mark 88
*Twenty-Three Tales* 130

United States 43, 55

Varsonofii, Father, at the Tolstoy funeral 205–208
Vegetarianism 46
Vorontsov 11

Wagner, Richard 104, 120
*War and Peace* 25, 37, 113, 113, 134, 144
Washington, DC 9
Wentz, Virginia 210
*What Is Art?* 121, 166
White, Andrew 84
Whittier, John Greenleaf 60, 89
Witte 73
*World's Work* (magazine) 139

Yasnaya Polyana, Tolstoy country estate 11, 12, 23, 31, 35, 36, 59, 80, 109, 117, 129, 140, 141, 145–146, 152

Zola, Émile 88
Zweig, Stefan 193

www.ingramcontent.com/pod-product-compliance
Lightning Source LLC
Chambersburg PA
CBHW032052300426
44116CB00007B/708